SAP™ R/3™
Business
Blueprint

Understanding Enterprise Supply Chain Management

second edition

Thomas A. Curran
Andrew Ladd

Prentice Hall PTR, Upper Saddle River, NJ 07458
http://www.phptr.com

Library of Congress Cataloging-in-Publication Data

Curran, Thomas (Thomas Aidan)
    SAP R/3 business blueprint : understanding enterprise supply chain
management / Thomas A. Curran, Andrew Ladd. -- 2nd ed.
        p.   cm.
    Includes index.
    ISBN 0-13-085340-2
    1. SAP R/3.   2. Business--Computer programs.   3. Client server
computing.   4. Reengineering (Management)   I. Ladd, Andrew.   II. Title
    HF5548.4.R2 c87 1999
    650'.0285'53769--dc21   99-15767
                                                         CIP

Editorial/Production Supervision: Patti Guerrieri
Acquisitions Editor: Tim Moore
Editorial Assistant: Bart Blanken
Marketing Manager: Bryan Gambrel
Buyer: Alexis R. Heydt
Cover Design: Anthony Gemmellaro
Cover Design Direction: Jerry Votta
Art Director: Gail Cocker-Bogusz
Interior Series Design: Meg VanArsdale

Prentice Hall books are widely used by corporations and government agencies
for training, marketing, and resale.

The publisher offers discounts on this book when ordered in bulk quantities.
For more information, contact
Corporate Sales Department
Phone: 800-382-3419; FAX: 201-236-7141
E-mail (Internet): corpsales@prenhall.com
or write:
Prentice Hall PTR
One Lake Street
Upper Saddle River, NJ 07458

SAP is a registered trademark of SAP Aktiengesellschaft, Systems, Applications and Products
in Data Processing, Neurottstrasse 16, 69190 Walldorf, Germany. The publisher gratefully
acknowledges SAP's kind permission to use its trademark in this publication. SAP AG is not the
publisher of this book and is not responsible for it under any aspect of press law.

Printed in the United States of America

10 9 8 7 6 5 4 3 2

ISBN 0-13-085340-2

Prentice-Hall International (UK) Limited, London
Prentice-Hall of Australia Pty. Limited, Sydney
Prentice-Hall Canada Inc., Toronto
Prentice-Hall Hispanoamericana, S.A., Mexico
Prentice-Hall of India Private Limited, New Delhi
Prentice-Hall of Japan, Inc., Tokyo
Prentice-Hall (Singapore) Pte. Ltd., Singapore
Editora Prentice-Hall do Brasil, Ltda., Rio de Janeiro

Contents

Chapter 13

Customer Service 249

Part 3   *Architecture, Framework, and Tools* 265

Chapter 14

Architecture of the R/3™ *System* 267

Foreword

Today's global business environments are characterized by unprecedented competitive pressures and sophisticated customers that demand speedy solutions. Understanding and optimizing business processes is a cornerstone of success in these fast-changing environments.

This book provides a basis for managers who desire an in-depth, hands-on understanding of business processes, explaining how to use them for the benefit of a corporation. SAP ™ R/3 ™ Business Blueprint goes far beyond the well-known R/3 ™ system; it is a comprehensive reference for standard business-processes and has broad application for business, consulting, and academia.

Let me start with the value the book offers to business in general. There is a body of business knowledge and procedures embodied in business processes that every manager should know and comprehend in order to communicate problems, make judgments about efficiency and optimization, and assess the company's competitive advantage.

Moreover, in the '90s, with the emergence of powerful personal computers at home and the fabulous success of the Internet and electronic commerce, consumers are no longer waiting for business to lock them into any particular technology. They have turned the tables and now force business to rethink and adapt to their world. Consumers use the Internet to book flights, conduct banking transactions, purchase computer hardware, buy and trade financial instruments, and configure their own automobiles. Corporations cannot afford to sit and wait. They are forced to react to the technology demands, rethink their system infrastructures, and create better solutions. Software, systems, and business processes can certainly help in this respect, especially if they are based on a thorough understanding of what they are supposed to achieve.

Yet, business still deals with people. At the end of nearly every business transaction, people tend to be the primary decision makers in most situations. Thus, understanding how people function in an organization is also an important aspect of business-process knowledge. The business-process blueprint presented in this book not only describes how transactions take place but delivers a wealth of information about how parts of an organization and its people are involved.

In my work with companies around the globe, I constantly run across difficulties because of a lack of understanding of how a business works in another country. The cultural nuances of doing business with peers in another culture consume much of the time managers need to make their businesses successful. Having a common understanding will increase the speed and inspire new confidence.

This book also offers specific benefits to consultants. Consultants are sometimes seen as the "high priests" of business-process management and business design. They develop process descriptions for corporations and benefit from a repetitive application of analysis principles. The faster they can present the basic business-process blueprint, the more time they will have to spend on the real issues that drive business success. Their focus will change from broad business descriptions to point processes that really matter to a company's livelihood.

Finally, in business education, one of the hardest—yet most essential—concepts that I need to communicate to my students is the idea of cross-functional integration. Our business education is structured around functional areas. Asked to describe how a procurement process takes place in a multinational firm, many students are at a loss due to the dearth of educational material available. This book will fill this gap by familiarizing tomorrow's managers with the practice of integrated business processes.

Equipped with the body of knowledge offered in this book, business decision makers, consultants, and students will be able to concentrate their work and study more effectively on areas that are strategic to running a company. When a firm understanding of business processes is in place, the real issues of business—those that provide value to customers, such as developing new products and brands and taking them to new markets—can be tackled more effectively.

Bernd Schmitt
Associate Professor of Business
Columbia Business School
Columbia University, New York

Preface

T his book is intended for the wide range of business professionals who are interested in knowing more about process orientation in business and the implementation of these concepts in R/3™, SAP™'s client/server business application suite. It provides an inside look into the conceptual framework and strategy behind SAP™'s business engineering initiative. Most of all, the book explains the fundamentally different approaches to business change between the use of process model templates and the consulting method known as business-process reengineering, which promotes a zero-based business analysis and modeling.

Based upon our research and experiences, we have found that business professionals too often maintain an "at war" mentality toward their data processing departments and systems. Fed up with the jargon garden of technospeech and sick of the endless meetings needed to get everyone reading from the same page, business professionals, line managers, and system users crave a consolidated knowledge-based system that describes business processes in their own terms. This need was the spark that ignited the ideas in this book. Companies are paying millions to professional consultants to "implement" standard business processes, yet there is no common language on which to base their discussions or their process descriptions.

A guide to the business blueprint or reference model of the R/3™ system, this book is written for business executives, senior decision makers, business engineers, and members of R/3™ evaluation and/or implementation teams, along with students and academicians devoted to understanding business and information technology. We have attempted to make the book specific enough to satisfy the expert but general enough to provide a good overview for the capable newcomer. Our main objectives are to:

- Help senior decision makers understand the business benefits of the SAP™ R/3™ system
- Explain the methodology behind the Business Blueprint and its implications
- Examine the human and organizational requirements for change
- Provide detailed descriptions of key business process scenarios in the R/3™ system and their meaningfullness in e-commerce and supply chain management
- Describe the features and tools available for the evaluation and implementation of R/3™
- Document for the first time the deep process knowledge contained in the R/3™ system and use it as a benchmark for explaining business in general

For business leaders either currently or about to be involved in new business design, this book will explain SAP™'s Business Blueprint. To that end, we have labored to explain the R/3™ Reference Model clearly, keeping the big picture in mind, especially for those who do not want to get too bogged down in technical detail. Part 1, Business Engineering, examines the business theories behind the R/3™ Reference Model and its implications for optimizing business. Where possible, we draw on real business examples and interviews with some of the most successful R/3™ implementers around the world.

Part 2, Process Design, will be of special interest to business users working in the fields of sales, production, procurement, controlling, finance, human resources, and asset management. This section works through a number of organizational and functional scenarios and explains how the R/3™ system aids in the streamlining and structuring of key processes of different business areas. We cover primary value activities such as sales and distribution, production planning, procurement, and external accounting. We then move on to the supporting value activities, human resources management, business planning, finance, and controlling. Here and throughout, we draw from many real-life examples of how various companies have put R/3™ to use.

For the information technology staff member, programmer, or developer engaged in business design, Part 3, Architecture, Framework, and Tools, describes where R/3™ fits in the overall scheme of information technology and enterprise application systems. We first explore middleware transaction management and application distribution in R/3™. We then discuss the framework and infrastructure, focusing especially on the R/3™ Repository and Business Framework. Finally, we examine the R/3™ Business Engineer, SAP™'s latest platform for planning and configuring applications.

The last chapter documents the momentous change in application landscape that is being driven by business blueprints and the plethora of new technology alternatives ushered in with the advent of the Internet. We call this the Next Generation Enterprise, a future vision for how SAP™ and other ERP vendors will need to adapt their products in this new era. In the Next Generation, many common business practices and theories will change, but the most prominent will involve business-process thinking and the assembly and delivery of applications. This challenge will be a significant one for SAP™ and its counterparts in the enterprise software industry.

On the one hand, this book provides a comprehensive overview for those who are currently considering SAP™ as a solution for their business reengineering problems. On the other, for those who are already familiar with R/3™ and would like to know more, we offer a holistic approach to explaining how key parts of the R/3™ system are integrated. Ultimately, we hope to satisfy in part the growing need in the current business community to know more about business engineering with R/3™.

The customer quotations in this book stem from a comprehensive market research survey conducted by TCM, a management consulting company which is owned by Thomas Curran, lead author of this book. This work was the basis for SAP™'s positioning and product development in business engineering.

We gratefully acknowledge the kind assistance of SAP™ AG.

The authors would like to thank Peter Zencke for his understanding of Business Engineering and the concepts behind it; Hasso Plattner for his vision of Enterprise Software; Paul Wahl for his insights into market drivers and customer needs; all SAP™ development managers, especially Dennis Ladd, Stefan Meinhardt, Wolfgang Zuck, Carsten Dirks, and Kenichiro Shimizu, who provided guidance on technical issues and future R/3™ development; industry analysts Barry Wilderman (Meta Group) and Erik Keller (formerly Gartner Group) for their insights into the future; Leslie Constans for her research, writing, and customer interviews; Hendrik Mager, Håkan Källberg, and Frank Wittmann for examples of technology architecture and framework discussions; Jill Wagner, Thomas Teufel, and Max Bezahler for their understanding of how the Business Blueprint is used in consulting and software sales; Peter Mullen (Visio Corp.), Piet Christiansen (IntelliCorp Inc.), and August Wilhelm Scheer (IDS Inc.) for their insights into third-party products development; and Heike Matz for all the graphics contained in this book. Special thanks go to Andrew Ladd for his patient support and professional writing. Without him this book would have never appeared. Lastly we thank the staff of our publisher, Prentice Hall, for their guidance and support along the way.

Copyright and Trademark Acknowledgments

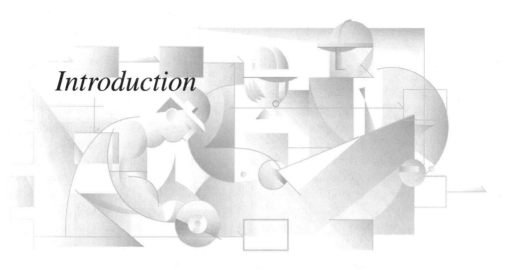

Introduction

- "Business engineering is the rethinking of business processes to improve and accelerate the output of processes, materials or services." (Philip Morris, Lausanne, Switzerland)
- "It's the search for an optimal flow in a company." (Messerli AF, Switzerland)
- "It's the streamlining of business processes to have maximum effect with minimum resources in supporting company goals." (Ernst & Young, South Africa)
- "Generally, it's a customer focus. It's also the designing of new processes using new information technology to create an efficient business network that involves creative staff in the process redesign." (Fahrzeugausrustung Berlin GmbH, Germany)

Companies from around the world are taking advantage of information technology (IT) to radically alter how they conduct business. In the past, IT was used simply to automate existing business functions, but now IT can improve or completely change how businesses operate. This approach is called Business Engineering, which has been the logical next step in the business-process reengineering revolution.

Unlike business-process reengineering (BPR), which used IT mainly to automate certain functions performed in individual organizations—such as manufacturing, finance, or production—Business Engineering (BE) utilizes IT for designing or redesigning processes, the set of connected steps or "chains" performed in a business. In this way, BE takes advantage of information technology to support the redesign of organizations. By using BE to engineer entire process chains that span functional or organizational boundaries, companies can integrate all their critical business activities. Moreover, they can do so much earlier in an IT implementation than if using the older, function-centric approach of early BPR strategies. Completing process chains rapidly and efficiently is of great added value to both the company and its customers. It makes such core processes as production and finance more efficient and can bring competitive advantages through reduced costs, faster time-to-market, and improved responsiveness to customers.

Business engineering arose out of the need created by BPR for software systems that could adequately support changing business processes. Although companies have gained a great deal from improving their business processes, many also have encountered problems with their business-process reengineering. After examining existing business processes, many companies completely dispensed with them, creating new process designs instead. Too often they miscalculated the risks and costs not only of reinventing new processes but of finding a software solution to match the new process design. After various trials and tribulations with poor software tools and systems, many companies have had to do away with their process design work simply because their information system software could not support the new design.

In Business Engineering, IT is used both to create and support new process designs. Software can describe, simulate, or model organizations. It can also show how changes made to the organizations will affect processes. BE is not limited to describing processes, however. A model or business-process diagram illustrates not only a company's tasks and organizational structure but also how the company gets things done. A company's information model usually includes descriptions of aspects such as data, function, organization, information, and communication flow. A well-integrated information system not only improves overall business operation but makes it easier for the company to identify areas for further improvement. With prefabricated models of business applications, companies can reduce their risks while taking advantage of best-business procedures for business process engineering.

As is the case in all engineering efforts, a good blueprint will map out the best strategies for implementing new designs. This book centers on a specific blueprint designed by the international software vendor SAP™, a company that has successfully integrated IT with business engineering. In support of its R/3™ system, SAP™ provides sample business objects and business processes that reflect the best-business practices in successful companies and that can either be used either "as is" or extended and customized by a company to suit its needs. These predefined processes are supplied in a comprehensive business blueprint called the R/3™ Reference Model, which is actively linked with the R/3™ running system.

SAP ™ R/3™ Business Blueprint: Understanding Enterprise Supply Chain Management is designed to function as a map of this system. Our aim is to guide the reader through the most important aspects of SAP™'s Reference Model. All business professionals who are considering implementing or are currently using SAP™ software may benefit from this book. From the theory behind the applications to real-life business examples, this book guides the reader through the key areas of the R/3™ system. In order to help the reader better navigate through this book, the remainder of this Introduction will answer general questions about the book's subject matter as well as direct readers to places where more in-depth treatments of key terms and issues may be found.

I.1 WHAT IS SAP™?

Founded in 1972 in Walldorf, Germany, SAP™ (Systems, Applications and Products in Data Processing) commands a significant share of the worldwide client/server enterprise application software market. SAP™ is the number one vendor of standard business application software and is the fourth largest independent software supplier in the world. More than 10,000 companies in over 90 countries use SAP™ software. Current SAP™ company facts include:

- Leading client/server business software company
- Leading vendor of standard business application software
- Worldwide market share of 33%
- Fourth-largest independent software supplier in the world
- Availability in 14 languages
- 34% of customer base under $200 million
- 10 out of the top 10 U.S. companies with highest market value
- 8 of the top 10 largest U.S. corporations
- 8 of the top 10 highest profit U.S. companies
- More than 10,000 customers in over 90 countries

For a more detailed examination of SAP™ and its history, see Chapter 1, SAP™ and Client/Server Technology.

I.2 WHAT IS R/3™?

Initially, SAP™ made the move from mainframes to open systems in the late 1980s with R/2™, a monolithic, mainframe legacy solution. As early as 1988, however, SAP™ chose to move toward client/server technology and began developing R/3™. In 1992, SAP™ unveiled R/3™ just as client/server and its potential were beginning to be fully realized in the business world. R/3™'s success is largely due to its ability to provide a highly integrated environment that can fully exploit the potential of client/server computing.

A full description of R/3™'s product architecture can be found in Part 3, Architecture, Framework, and Tools, but here we define R/3™ simply as SAP™'s enterprise application for open-system platforms. More specifically, R/3™ is an integrated enterprise software system that runs in open-system environments. The R/3™ architecture is essentially a three-tier client/server consisting of a database server, application server, and presentation server (see Chapter 1). These dedicated, task-oriented servers are linked in communication networks, which allow them to integrate data and processes within the system. The applications are developed using SAP™'s fourth-generation language ABAP/4 and the ABAP/4 Development Workbench[a] (see Chapter 15).

R/3™'s advantages lie in its flexibility, scalability, and expandability. R/3™ can be used in client/server architectures with 30 seats as in installations with 3,000 end users. This scalability ensures that R/3™ can provide support for current business operations and allows flexible adaptation to change and progress. Designed as a total system, but also suitable for modular use, R/3™ is expandable in stages, making it adaptable to the specific requirements of individual businesses. R/3™ can run on hardware platforms of leading international manufacturers and can integrate with customers' in-house applications. It is also open to allow interoperability with third-party solutions and services; it can be installed quickly and efficiently. R/3™ is so designed that such experts in scalable software as Microsoft, IBM, and Apple have all deployed SAP™ as their enterprise solution.

In the age of Internet computing, SAP™ R/3™ has emerged as a platform for electronic commerce, supply chain management, and data warehouse applications.

I.3   *WHAT IS THE R/3™ REFERENCE MODEL?*

SAP™ has packaged 25 years of best-business practices in many different industries in the form of a "blueprint" called the R/3™ Reference Model. The Reference Model, also known as SAP™'s Business Blueprint, guides companies from the beginning phases of engineering, including evaluation and analysis, to the final stages of implementation. It is the definitive description of R/3™, providing a comprehensive view of all the processes and business solutions available in the system. Technical details, however, are "hidden" so that the business user can focus solely on business-process issues. Thus, the Business Blueprint is written in the language of the business user.

The Business Blueprint can be the starting point for business engineering efforts. Documenting processes in R/3™ is a critical part of the "understanding equation" at customer sites. To date, few companies have been able to provide a comprehensive, process-oriented description of a business that fits into almost any industry. The Business Blueprint is a means of streamlining processes and implementing R/3™ without a business having to start from scratch.

The Business Blueprint concentrates on four key areas necessary for understanding business: events, tasks or functions, organization, and communication. These areas define who must do what, when, and how. Events are the driving force behind a business process, prompting one or more activities to take place. This model is the essence of SAP™'s Event-Driven Process Chain (EPC) Methodology, which is discussed in Chapter 2.

In Releases 4.0, SAP™ offered more than 1,000 predefined business processes, with variants, that generally correspond to different industries and corporations—a milestone in the evolution of process management and enterprise software. These business processes are illustrated with the EPC graphical method. By connecting events and tasks, the method models and analyzes even very complex business processes. An EPC model can show where breaks in the chain of tasks and responsibilities hurt the ability of a company to optimize its processes. Graphical models help users select and understand the software, visualizing how data flow through business areas and showing how various functions interact with each other. The EPC model is the central, process-oriented view. Other models show function, process, information flow, and organization views.

The Business Blueprint can be viewed and analyzed with the help of the R/3™ Business Engineer, which is discussed in full in Chapter 16. A set of integrated tools for configuring R/3™, the Business Engineer has graphical browsing facilities for displaying the Business Blueprint directly from the R/3™ Repository, which contains all the data definitions and structures required by ABAP/4 programs. The Business Engineer also includes customizing components that allow a user to adapt or modify the system to meet the user's own specific needs.

Benefits of the R/3™ Reference Model during R/3™ implementation include quick overviews, business engineering support, and better communication among different departments (see Chapter 3 for implementation issues). A majority of R/3™ Reference Model customers use the blueprint for business-process modeling. Some organizations, however, use modeling tools and methods in different ways to suit their specific needs. In many organizations, process modeling is used for documentation, visualization of processes, better comprehension, training, and process optimization.

I.4 WHO USES R/3™?

R/3™ is the accepted standard in key industries such as software, oil, chemicals, consumer packaged goods, and high-tech electronics. Other industries include automotive, building and heavy construction, communication services, consulting (software), financial services, furniture, healthcare and hospitals, pharmaceuticals, public sector, raw materials, retail, services, steel, tourism, transportation, and utilities.

Table I-1 is a partial list of R/3™ users.

Table I-1   R/3™ Users

Industry	Company
Automotive	ITT Automotive Europe
	Yamaha
	Audi
	General Motors
	Chrysler
	BMW
	Subaru
	Toyota
	Volkswagen
Building and Heavy Construction	ABB Industrietechnik AG
	Gebauer
	Kawasaki Heavy Industries
	ADtranz ABB Daimler-Benz
	Babcock Prozess Automation GmbH
	CEGELEC AEG Anlagen und
	GESOBAU GAG
	Dover Elevator International, Inc.
	Dürkopp Adler AG
	E. Heitkamp GmbH
	Eldim B.V.
	Frequentis
Chemicals	Bayer
	Procter & Gamble
	CCPL
	Degussa
	Henkel
	Kemira
	Lever Europe
	Pirelli Pneumatici S.P.A
	Reichhold
	Sasol Alpha Olefins
	Schülke & Mayr

Table I-1 R/3™ Users (Continued)

Industry	Company
	Wintershall, Wingas, Kali und Salz
	Zeneca
Communication Services, Media	Random House
	Simon & Schuster, Inc.
	IPSOA Editore S.R.L.
	Optus Vision
	Ringier AG
	Seattle Times
	SFR
	Telecom PTT
Computer Software	Apple
	3com Corporation
	Autodesk Inc.
	Fujitsu Microelectronics
	Fujitsu Network Communications, Inc.
	Hewlett-Packard
	IBM
	Samsung
	Wang
	Intersolv
	Legend QDI Ltd.
	Logistix
	Micrografx
	Microsoft
	Micro Software Group
	Visio
Consumer Products: Food	Alfred Ritter GmbH & Co. KG
	Anheuser-Busch Companies
	Boston Beer
	Cameo, S.P.A.
	Guinness
	Heinecken Italia S.P.A.
	Imperial Tobacco
	Nestlé
	Keebler Company
Consumer Products: Non-Food	Braun AG
	Colgate-Palmolive
	Hans Schwarzkopf GmbH
	Heissner
	Unilever Italia S.P.A.-Divisione Lever
Financial Services, Banks, Insurance	ABB Holding Ltd. (CN)
	Allied Irish Banks plc (IE)
	BMW Bank GmbH (DE)

Table I-1 R/3 ™ Users (Continued)

Industry	Company
	BMW Finance Ltd (GB)
	Banca D'Italia (IT)
	Banco De Portugal Det Dep. Emissão E Tesouraria (PT)
	Banco Itau S.A. (BR)
	Bank of Canada (CA)
	Bank of Slovenia (SI)
	Bayerische Landesbank (DE)
	Bayerische Vereinsbank (DE)
	Commerzbank AG (DE)
	Countrywide Banking Corporation Limited (NZ)
	Credit Suisse (CH)
	Deutsche Bank AG (DE)
	First Chicago NBD Corporation (US)
	First National Building Society (IE)
	Jyske Bank A/S (DK)
	LGT Bank in Liechtenstein (LI)
	Lloyds TSB Group plc (GB)
	Mercedes Benz Finance Ltd (GB)
	National Westminster Bank plc (GB)
	PARIBAS BANQUE France PT Bank Bali (ID)
	PT Bank Bali (ID)
	Putnam Company (US)
	The Bank of N.T. Butterfield & Son Ltd. (BM)
	The Government Savings Bank (TH)
	The Nomura Securities Company (JP)
	Toyota Finance (AU)
	UBS Schweiz. Bankgesellschaft (CH)
	Volkswagen Financial Services (DE)
	Volkswagen Leasing Polska SP. Z (PL)
	WestLB Westdeutsche Landesbank (DE)
	Zürcher Kantonalbank (CH) Bruderhilfe
	LBS Bayerische Landesbausparkasse
	Mercedes-Benz Lease Finanz
	Sega
	Victoria
Industrial and Commercial Machinery	Fiat Avio
	Gurtec GmbH
	Kapp
	Mann & Hummel
	Metabo
	Sulzer Electronics
Oil and Gas	British Gas
	Chevron

Table I-1   R/3 ™ Users (Continued)

Industry	Company
	Conoco
	Shell
	Exxon
	Mobil
	Petromidia
Pharmaceuticals	Boehringer Mannheim Italia S.P.A.
	Ciba-Geigy
	Degussa AG
	FRESENIUS AG
	Warner Lambert
	Merck
	Weimer Pharma
	Zeneca Plc.
Primary Metal, Metal Products, Steel	Carnaud Metalbox
	Degussa AG
	EBG/Thyssen
Retail	Diethelm Holdings
	Grofa GmbH
	Prisma-Aspri
	STANDA S.P.A.
	CompUSA
	Fleming
	Florsheim
	Home Depot
	Kerr Drugs
	Maxim Group
	Office Max
	PetsMart
	Reebok
	Shoe Show
	Woolworth
Transportation Services, Tourism	Condor Flugdienst GmbH
	Copenhagen Airport A/S
Utilities	British Gas
	GEA AG
	Industrielle Betriebe Aarau
	New York Power Authority
	Pacific Gas and Electric
	STEWEAG Energie
	Westcoast Energy
Wood and Paper	Gizen GmbH
	Papierfabrik August K
	SCP

I.5 *HOW DO CUSTOMERS VIEW R/3™?*

In a 1995 survey, TCM contacted over 500 SAP™ customers in an extensive effort to evaluate the technical and customer requirements of SAP™'s R/3™, and R/3™ Reference Model, as well as associated methodologies and software products related to R/3™ implementation. The goal of the study was to ascertain how R/3™ customers, consultants, prospects, and complementary software vendors deal with models and model-driven software configuration and implementation. This study revealed a number of novel approaches for using R/3™, the Reference Model, and other SAP™ tools.

Reasons for Using R/3™

Integration, price, SAP™'s reputation, standard software, client/server technology, business engineering, and migration from R/2™ were some of the reasons companies chose R/3™.

- "The key factors were demand of the company's strategy (PDM integration) and the methodology for implementation."
  (ABB Turbo Systems Ltd., Baden, Switzerland)
- "Standard techniques support C&L R/3™ implementation methodology."
  (Coopers & Lybrand, Brussels, Belgium)
- "We were in the process of a R/2™ implementation and felt R/3™ had a longer future. Our company chose SAP™ because of its integration."
  (Rapistan Demag Corp., Grand Rapids, Michigan, USA)
- "R/3™ was decided upon to replace the self-created software, which is in use up to now, and to improve economic performance. At the same time, it's seen as a chance to reengineer processes."
  (Rheinbraun AG, Cologne, Germany)

Approaches to Using the R/3™ Reference Model

The Reference Model can be a good starting point for customer BE projects. Customers who begin engineering projects with other modeling tools often switch to the Reference Model in later phases, finding the models and analysis techniques more helpful during R/3™ implementation.

- "In a high abstraction level, we modeled the overall business. In manufacturing and sales, the Reference Model was very helpful."
  (ABB Turbo Systems Ltd., Baden, Switzerland)

- "We began with the R/3™ Reference Model and proceeded to create a specific model from there; we always tried to stay to the standard processes wherever possible."
  (Hewlett-Packard Austria)
- "We used the Reference Model as a starting point for business engineering projects. It has been extremely successful."
  (Fahrzeugausrüstung Berlin GmbH, Berlin, Germany)

Perceived Benefits of the R/3™ Reference Model

Stabilization, easier implementation, and better communication were some of the benefits customers found when using the Reference Model during R/3™ implementation. The following statements characterize how each customer uses the Reference Model during implementation.

- "Implementation of R/3™ gains stabilization. Also it provides helpful support in identifying which process elements in R/3™ will be useful."
  (ABB Turbo Systems, Baden, Switzerland)
- "We don't have to start from scratch when we are modeling."
  (Ascom Hagier AG, Solothum, Switzerland)
- "It provides a quick overview and very good introduction to application architecture."
  (Berufsakademie Mannheim, Mannheim, Germany)
- "The benefits lie in the visualization of processes, resulting in improvement of communication and higher transparency."
  (LUHNS GmbH, Germany)
- "It offers a better view of what SAP™ is able to cover and examples of 'best practices.'"
  (ICS International Consulting Solutions GmbH, Bottmingen, Switzerland)
- "It will allow us to arrive at a proposed solution faster and more completely than otherwise."
  (Pilkington, St. Helens, Great Britain)

Business Engineering with R/3™

Most R/3™ Reference Model customers are engaged in BE, although uses and methods often vary significantly from customer to customer.

- "We use the R/3™ Reference Model as visual help to discuss our processes, and we modify models of the Reference Model according to

our needs; furthermore, we create new models to describe interfaces
between the SAP™ system and other non-SAP™ applications, using
terminology and symbols of the Reference Model."
(Miele & Cie GmbH & Co., Gatersloh, Germany)

- "We have essentially modeled our entire enterprise to help determine
  'fits' and 'gaps' between our desired state and what R/3™ can provide."
  (Mentor Graphics, USA)

- "The function and process diagrams are used to identify business
  activities that are deemed applicable. These are then reviewed and
  adapted for our company's business practices. Process modeling
  insures a standard methodology and allows the activity to be identified
  and refined based on process data flow."
  (Rapistan Demag Corp., Grand Rapids, Michigan, USA)

Documentation of Business Processes

Documenting processes in R/3™ improves an overall understanding of the system. The Reference Model not only provides a good overview of the R/3™ system, it also can be used to define current business processes.

- "It plays a major role as a documenting tool, as well as feedback to
  clients to show understanding and point out conflicts and omissions."
  (Ernst & Young CSI, Johannesburg, South Africa)

- "The R/3™ Reference Model has been the basic model. Our teams have
  designed in the first project phase of R/3™ the new business processes.
  All new processes are stored, including documentation, in a user
  model (company model)."
  (Fahrzeugausrusting Berlin GmbH, Berlin, Germany)

- "We used the Reference Model as a starting point—detailed processes
  were described using the EPC methodology."
  (Philip Morris, Switzerland)

Approaches to Business Modeling

As standard software, R/3™ offers standard business solutions. R/3™ is also flexible enough, however, to be customized or extended to meet special customer demands. Some companies create customized models for sales and distribution, procurement, financing, and project management. Using the EPC methodology, these customers created the models listed in Table I-2.

I.6   CONCLUSION

As we have seen, R/3™ and the R/3™ Reference Model are highly flexible means of assisting BE. Throughout *SAP™ R/3™ Business Blueprint*, we will continue to draw from real business experiences and practices to illustrate basic principles of the R/3™ system. Furthermore, we have attempted to provide examples from a wide variety of industries so that the reader can intuit the many possibilities inherent in the R/3™ system.

Table I–2   Modeling Strategies of R/3™ Customers

Model	Customer
Order processing inside and outside of R/3™	Ascom AG, Switzerland
Order fulfillment; sales and quotations	B hler AG, Switzerland
Package distribution	Ernst & Young CSI, South Africa
Branch-oriented models for the chemical industry	ICM Unternehmensberatung GmbH, Germany
Entire enterprise model to determine "fits" and "gaps" between the company's desired state and R/3™	Mentor Graphics, USA
Order processing model with customized scenarios for invoicing, order, and distribution	Miele & Cie GmbH & Co., Germany
Manufacturing process and organizational responsibility; material process flow for factory; generic process control systems	Nestl , Great Britain
Concurrent engineering; global logistics	Nokia Mobile Phones, Finland
Flow charts showing process flows divided into system steps, information used, manual steps, and external steps	Pilkington P/C, Great Britain
Handling of new contracts; installation of equipment at customer site; scheduling workers for reading meters at customer site	Raab Karcher Energieservice, Germany
Project-related order processing; manufacturing order and requirement processing	Rapistan Demag Corp., USA
Process of acquisition of land for mining purposes	Rheinbraun AG, Germany

Table I–2 Modeling Strategies of R/3™ Customers (Continued)

Model	Customer
Process of creation of a sales order for export; goods receipt and recycling of equipment	STG-Coopers & Lybrand, Switzerland
Presales process; consulting process	Systime AG, Switzerland
Operating funds administration; freight data management	ZF Friedrichshafen AG, Germany

While our main focus is BE with R/3™, we have tried to explain as much of the R/3™ system and its variants as possible. We understand that different parts of this book will interest different readers, and for that reason we have tried to steer the reader toward his or her areas of interest in this Introduction. Generally speaking, the best strategy for readers with specific areas of interest is to follow these option paths:

- Readers who are most interested in business engineering and implementing R/3™ with the Reference Model should begin with Part 1, Business Engineering.
- Readers who would like to examine specific business-process scenarios and business objects available in R/3™ should begin with Part 2, Process Design.
- Readers interested in learning about the sophisticated platform for supporting business-process design and configuration for enterprise application software systems should examine Part 3, Architecture, Framework, and Tools.

PART 1

Business Engineering

1

Business Engineering and Enterprise Optimization

- "Business Engineering revolves around information technology and continuous change. It is the constant refinement of an organization's changing needs."
  (Esso, Austria)

- "Business Engineering is the re-thinking of business processes to improve the speed, quality, and output of materials or services."
  (Philip Morris European Union Region, Switzerland)

Business Engineering (BE) is a method for changing the way a company works. The BE approach has its roots in information technology, where it was necessary to develop models or blueprints, similar to an architect's blueprints. The models are based on best practices, which have proven to be both reliable and adaptable. In BE, these models represent the standard business processes and objects that are applicable to a variety of businesses and are able to be configured to meet the needs of individual companies.

A close relative to BE is Business Process Reengineering (BPR). BPR is the methodology by which a company examines and redesigns all aspects of its business processes in accordance with the company's goals and organizational structure. BPR was hailed as a necessary transition for companies to make in order to keep pace with today's ever-changing global markets. According to Michael Hammer and James Champy, authors of *Reengineering the Corporation* (Harper Business, 1994), "[i]n the post industrial age...corporations will be founded and built around the ideas of reunifying...tasks into coherent business processes."

Information technology (IT) was used as a tool to automate the processes dictated by the BPR-redesigned model. Thus, although IT was an integral part of the success of BPR, it was only used as a tool to effectuate BPR goals.

Business Engineering has extended the use of IT by creating process models based on IT structures and applying those models to BPR's vision of better business processes. The most important aspect of BE is the way in which business practices are captured in models that are used to guide the IT system development and implementation.

The results of this merger of ideas are process-oriented business solutions, intertwined with the IT of client/server computing. Thus, BE represents the true intersection between information technology and BPR. More specifically, BE strives for the efficient redesign of a company's value-added chains. Value-added chains are the set of connected steps running through a business area which, when quickly and efficiently completed, add value to both company and customer. Information technology, instead of merely streamlining existing value-added processes, now serves as a model assisting in the redesign of those processes. SAP™'s R/3™ system, a business solution, BE blueprint, and an advanced integration solution, is the foremost example of business process methodology reaching its full potential due to its implementation on information technology.

This chapter will explain fully the BE movement, the profound importance of IT, and the impact of cross-function integration on business processes. This chapter also examines the future of BE, in particular its potential, not only to change business process methodology, but to make the solution accessible to end users.

1.1   *SIGNIFICANCE OF BUSINESS ENGINEERING*

The BE movement is a product of our shift into the "Age of Information." Society has shifted from an era where productivity is driven not by labor and machinery, but by knowledge and information. BE creates solutions for the profound social, technological, and economic changes implicit in the shift to the information era.

The rise of technology created a movement toward business efficiency in corporate America, which in the early nineties exhibited itself in a movement to "downsize." Downsizing focused on obliterating existing organizations and using technology as a surrogate for human capital. Practical, real-world constraints (such as a deficit of human capital) often prevent even the best business process from affecting a company's performance due to the implementation risks.

Even though BE may have some of the same effects as downsizing, its main objective is to *optimize* business processes. Thus, the focus shifted from honing and cutting existing business processes to *restructuring* and building a leaner, more efficient company. Instead of cutting existing organizations and ideas, the focus shifted to implementing new ideas modeled on the new information technology. Hence, BE created a new company infrastructure based on a combination of process-oriented business solutions and IT. This new infrastructure was particularly designed to meet the challenge of creating a business environment that would optimize performance and remain flexible enough to accommodate change.

This new approach has gained wide acceptance by companies seeking to maximize their business performance. Throughout the world, companies have turned to BE to solve the problems created by the Age of Information. In fact, companies such as Aetna Life and Casualty, Eastman Kodak, and Cigna, have created special groups, often led by senior executives, that focus solely on BE.

1.2   *PRINCIPLES OF BUSINESS ENGINEERING*

Business Engineering represents a shift in business strategy necessitated by the demands of a changing economy. In the past, companies benefited from economies of scale—that is, the increasing of output in order to reduce production costs. Economies of scale allowed companies to offer standard products and services to large, relatively stable consumer markets and to concentrate on optimizing tasks in well-defined areas.

More recently, competition and increased customer power have decreased the importance of economies of scale. The relationship between a company and its customers is no longer limited to the mere buying and selling of a product. It now encompasses the whole gamut of business activities, from customer service, consulting, and pricing, to production and shipping. With more goods available to them than ever before, consumers can now be more selective. In response to these developments, executives have reexamined their business processes and reimagined the organizational structures, job definitions, and workflows created to manage the growth era of the 1950s.

Business engineering makes companies more customer-focused and responsive to changes in the market. It achieves these results by reshaping corporate structures around business processes. BE implements change not by the complete automation of a business but rather by the redefinition of company tasks in holistic or process-oriented terms.

Only companies with innovative staff, products, and services, as well as short development cycles, will be able to retain their share of the market or hope to get a bigger slice of the pie. By maximizing individual and team creativity and emphasizing a process-oriented approach, BE enables a company to realize company goals.

1.3   ELEMENTS OF BUSINESS ENGINEERING

The main objective of BE is to *optimize* business processes. BE ensures that the key steps in business processes—say, from the time a customer places an order to the time the company delivers it—are as efficient, responsive, and service-oriented as possible.

In order to achieve this goal, an organization must reexamine long-held beliefs. As noted before, undergoing BE is much more than automating existing processes or cutting existing organizations. BE is a complete rethinking and reshaping of business processes based on structures native to IT. Furthermore, the impact of BE extends not only to business processes, but to management methods, job definitions, and organizational structures as well.

When successfully done, BE enables a company to simplify, integrate, and reorganize all areas of the business *before* automating them. Business processes do not recognize the barriers that separate departments, such as purchasing, production, sales, accounting, and human resource management. When commencing BE, companies must break down the walls—real or imaginary—that separate different departments within a company. BE makes individuals responsible for a wide range of activities and decisions. Companies become less hierarchical, and their organizational boundaries no longer impede information flow. Companies, suppliers, and customers communicate and work together more effectively. Technology is used to automate the business processes according to the new model after the reorganization is complete, thereby avoiding the practice of automating obsolete processes. The end result? A leaner, more-efficient organization that reacts quickly to consumer demands and changes in the marketplace. To realize such holistic concepts, effective communication within a company is essential. Everyone from software vendors, to department users, to reengineering planners must all speak the same language. Because misunderstandings in the planning phase of BE cause delay, increased costs, and decreased productivity, it becomes especially important for top management to take a leading role in communicating the business process redesign to the rest of the company.

Because BE often involves a drastic reorganization of a company, it can be a painful event. In fact, before BE emerged as a technique for implementing ERP products such as R/3™, the cost of installing new solutions was about 1:10. Many companies postpone BE initiatives in order to avoid the disruption, but to the detriment of their long-term financial goals. In BE, companies must have patience and flexibility. Not only must a company endure the initial upheaval, they must also constantly improve business processes as they evolve and respond to changes in consumer demand.

Table–1-1   Summary of the Elements of Business Engineering

REEXAMINATION	Rethink existing business processes
SIMPLIFICATION	Distill business functions into efficient models
REORGANIZATION	Search for new ways to organize work
INTEGRATION	Integrate all critical business processes
AUTOMATION	Use technology to automate redesigned business processes
COMMUNICATION	Increase communication to assist new holistic business processes
ADAPTATION	Constantly reconsider and improve business processes

1.4   *REQUIREMENTS FOR SUCCESSFUL IMPLEMENTATION OF BUSINESS ENGINEERING*

In a recent survey, companies that had completed or were currently undergoing BE were asked to rate their success in meeting goals. About 32 percent considered their projects very successful, 45 percent felt the project was somewhat successful, and 23 percent said BE was not very successful or unsuccessful.

All types of organizations benefited from BE, including multinational corporations, small businesses, government agencies, nonprofit organizations, individual departments, divisions. Typical results were increased sales, reduced time-to-market, and lower operating costs at a corporate or departmental level.

The companies involved in reengineering generally targeted about 15 to 20 broad business processes, with customer service, product quality, and product development being the most common. In these areas especially, reengineering created process-oriented possibilities for cutting costs, boosting quality, enhancing flexibility, minimizing time-to-market, and generating new sales opportunities.

As the survey suggests, a reengineering project does not automatically guarantee benefits. However, companies that have enjoyed the most success from their BE initiatives have common characteristics. Similarly, companies who have found their BE initiatives the least successful also share a set of common characteristics. The following chart summarizes those traits:

Table–1-2   Comparison of Business Engineering Initiatives

Successful BE initiatives	Unsuccessful BE initiatives
• The company focuses on compelling reasons for changing its business processes.	• A company lacks knowledge of its business processes and how those processes are interrelated. As a result, the company tries to reengineer parts of processes or relatively unimportant processes.
• The project is led by the most qualified and experienced people available, including consultants with a proven BE track record.	
• Management communicates often with employees to allay fears about change.	• The information technology department recognizes the benefits of reengineering but does not have the clout to lead the BE effort.
• The company uses technology in new and innovative ways.	• A company attempts to fix a process rather than radically reengineering it.

1.5   IT IMPLEMENTATION ISSUES

Even though BE is virtually unthinkable without IT, this does not mean that IT can be used thoughtlessly or recklessly in the BE process. Just as there are recognizable characteristics of successful and unsuccessful engineering efforts, there are also acknowledged guidelines for deciding how, when, or whether to apply IT.

No matter how efficient the technology, it will never help a company achieve its business goals unless the actual business processes have been scrutinized carefully. The BE team must maximize and streamline business processes—determining whether they should be changed or even thrown out—*before* they apply technology to them.

Another important consideration is cost. Startup costs, training costs, and networking costs all vary with the size and scope of the IT project. Hans Visser, managing director of Ernst & Young in Johannesburg, South Africa, emphasizes the importance of implementation costs. To fuel business change, Visser states, IT must help "streamline business processes to have a maximum effect with minimum resources in supporting company goals."

Along with implementation costs, companies must consider the longer term financial benefits of implementing BE and information technology. The following financials are possible when IT is coupled with BE:

- Increased revenues per sales call
- Decreased inventory, hardware, administrative, and operating costs
- Recaptured market share
- Reduced or eliminated overtime

In assessing these financial benefits, one must remember that many of them are due more to BE than IT. Companies take best advantage of IT if they already have an underlying business model and extensive process engineering in place. Only when IT and careful business engineering work together can companies enjoy increased revenues and decreased costs.

Finally, companies must consider more than mere pecuniary benefits when making the decision to apply IT to BE. For example, Bernina of America, Inc., a textile machine manufacturer, found that the combination of IT and BE helped it reach its goal of improved customer service. "We're able to take care of our customers with one phone call and one person without having to put them on hold, go through the files, research the files and return the call," explains Michael Perich, vice president of finance and administration. Companies also refer to product development, sales, and marketing as areas improved by BE and IT initiatives.

1.6　*EFFECTS OF INTEGRATION OF INFORMATION TECHNOLOGY*

If a company has carefully and conscientiously planned and implemented a new IT system, the effects on that system are usually revolutionary. Even though the radical restructuring caused by new IT systems upsets the status quo, it offers companies a prime opportunity to reconsider existing business processes and replace them with more efficient ones.

The effective integration of processes and their expansion into new areas become decisive factors in maintaining a company's competitiveness. The implementation of process-based software aims to achieve the full benefits of integration early on through the immediate realization of full-process chains. In this way, the deployment of standard software becomes an evolving learning experience. Companies also become focused more on permanent, goal-oriented change and less on individual success stories within the company.

As in the case of Nokia Mobile Phones, Finland, successes of reengineering efforts often depend on integration of processes. According to Markku Rajaniemi, vice president of information systems, "In the realization phase of information systems, more integration than engineering takes place." Systems not coordinated or integrated may cancel each other out and negate any gains in productivity generated by IT.

Companies might be tempted to tailor their processes individually to suit a particular market segment, customer group, or product line. Meeting this objective could, however, make an individual process uniquely and indelibly programmed into the system. If that process should ever need to be changed, companies would find themselves straitjacketed by their own routines. Thus, the details of many varied processes must be easily modified en masse in response to changing market requirements.

New technology, then, must never serve as a one-time vehicle in BE. Standard software must support the ability to adapt and change within a live system as well as to support rapid implementation. Therefore, a company should always consider whether the underlying architecture of a new software system will support an organization's ongoing change.

It is far easier for a company to adapt technology to suit the structure of the company than vice versa. Continuous responsiveness must be a central attribute of a restructured business process. As Michael Schulz-Ley, a DP manager at LUHNS GmbH, notes, "We see business engineering as the development of business processes according to changing requirements."

1.7   *EVOLUTION OF INFORMATION TECHNOLOGY*

Changed perceptions toward information technology produced major breakthroughs in applying IT to BE. Instead of viewing IT as simply a means of improving productivity and lowering costs, companies began to regard it as a strategic business weapon that could restructure critical processes, such as customer service, product development, delivery, and accounting-related activities (e.g., invoicing, processing of payments, and dunning procedures).

Prior to this breakthrough, mainframe computing handled vast amounts of information and processed it at high speeds. However, mainframes are complex, multilevel machines that are expensive to maintain and slow to adapt to change. Mainframes are also inadequate to meet changing business demands, such as 24-hour bank services or frequent advances in telecommunications.

Similarly, software was designed as separate applications, within a narrow, single-business-area perspective. Generally, it was used in isolation or in specific areas—first, financial accounting and materials management, and then sales, production, and management. The software integrated only after the separate applications were implemented. This approach caused the full value-added potential of new software to be realized only after the last application was implemented.

Developments in business processes required more effective IT solutions than conventional mainframes and piecemeal software could support. For example, as employees undertook more complex jobs, they needed access to information previously available to managers only. Because company departments required information from each other, data needed to flow across organizational boundaries. Toward the end of the 1980s, proprietary software products designed for use only with certain hardware vendors began to give way to internationally accepted standards. Operating systems became open, allowing for the exchange of data between computers from different vendors. Systems users experienced new freedoms in choosing hardware, operating systems, programming languages, database technologies, and software architecture. In addition, the rapid pace of technical progress in chips and microprocessors, based on RISC technology, increasingly packed more performance into less space. Data processing became faster than ever. Graphical User Interfaces (GUIs), the user-friendly pictures and tools on a computer screen, have also improved. In all these areas, quality increased and prices fell.

In the 1990s, two technological trends have coincided to enable the full integration of critical business processes: 1) new, more productive, and cost-effective platforms for client/server computing and 2) innovative process-integrated business solutions. These trends have increased companies' flexibility by enabling them to be more responsive to customers, market changes, and global competitions. They have also eliminated wasteful and unnecessary layers of decision making by giving more power and responsibility to individuals.

Another result is the increasing importance of IT staff in business. A 1995 TCM survey (see Introduction) of 62 companies from different industries around the world found that IT staffs play important roles in BE projects. Although many companies believe that management usually initiates BE efforts, TCM found that about one third of BE products today are driven by IT staff. In fact, BE teams almost always include IT people from the outset of implementation.

Now, use of client/server systems in business processes is a prevalent and accepted business strategy. At a conservative estimate, about two thirds of large American companies have invested in client/server solutions to deal with a variety of modern business situations. Companies in every industry are using client/server technology to reduce employee-training periods, cut product development time, improve customer service, and integrate data such as monthly statements or reports.

In 1996, nearly half of every dollar spent in the multibillion dollar financial services market was earmarked for client/server accounting systems, giving companies immediate access to information that once took days or even months to obtain.

1.8   CLIENT/SERVER TECHNOLOGY

Because the term "client/server" is used in two ways, it is important to distinguish between hardware-oriented and software-oriented approaches. The hardware-based definition refers to the PC network operating systems of the 1980s, including Microsoft® MS-Net, Novell® NetWare®, Microsoft® LAN Manager.

Desktop systems (usually PCs) at the workplace of end users are connected via local area networks (LANs) to dedicated background systems that are employed as file servers, print servers, and so forth. In the context of this hardware-driven definition, one usually refers to desktop systems as *clients* and to background systems as *servers*.

Using a more generalized, software-based definition, one characterizes all software either as a client (software that can request a service) or a server (software that can provide a service). With client/server technology, software can either be centralized on one computer or expanded onto many. The client/server system is also free of hardware constraints. In other words, a client or a server can run on a PC, workstation, mainframe, or any combination of the three, regardless of the brand of hardware. Also, client/server software is flexible enough to be linked via telephone lines, on the same computer, through local area networks, or by using any combination of these.

Client/server software is frequently based on a three-tier design, which enables the system to be distributed among PCs, workstations, and midrange computers. This design allows a functional split to be made between front-end presentation servers and back-end database servers, with application servers operating in between.

Table 1-3   Three-tier Design of client/server software

Presentation Server	The presentation tier of the client/server system that allows human-to-computer interaction by means of the keyboard, mouse, and monitor. System users deal directly with this first level only. The software includes a user-friendly GUI that takes requests from the user and passes them on to the application server.
Application Server	The intermediary or the second tier of the client/server system. Using UNIX® or Windows NT®, they can run on one or more computers. Application servers prepare, format, and process incoming data. Sometimes, application servers connect with databases and on-line services to provide information that users request or to make changes to the database. Typically, the application server is dedicated to a large group of users, such as a department.
Database Server	The third tier stores information that servers can use. The software on the database server, or central computer, controls database management and batch processing. The software retrieves the data from the database and contains all the programs downloaded to the appropriate application servers.

The three-tier approach to the design of client/server systems takes advantage of both the strengths of local workplace computers and the computing power of central systems. The result is an integrated processing of all business routines and transactions.

1.9   *BENEFITS OF CLIENT/SERVER TECHNOLOGY*

The three-tiered approach used in the new client/server technology creates a simple and flexible environment that provides many benefits to companies and individual users.

The software architecture of client/server technology offers such benefits as increased power and control over all aspects of the software architecture. More traditional two-level client/server software requires the user's workstation to act as both a presentation and application server. In both the two-tier and three-tier architectures, GUIs allow users to process information with considerable flexibility and control. However, three-tiered applications software makes more power available on the application server or workstation.

In addition, client/server applications can hide the complexity of a sophisticated business system from its users. Employees can easily focus on getting the information that customers need—everything from delivery dates to a customer's payment history—without having to know the system's technical structure or having to deal with difficult programming commands. Users can work faster and more productively with less training. Networked client/server software also allows many different people in many different locations to see and edit the same information in real time. Someone in New York, for example, can easily share ideas and files with others around the world, including customers, salespeople, or suppliers. This free exchange facilitates, for instance, the design of a product, which can be discussed and decided on long before mock-ups are built or expensive mistakes are made.

The flexibility of client/server software architecture enables companies to protect their hardware and software investments. Client/server software should address every significant business function and run on all major hardware platforms. If this goal is achieved, companies can choose the hardware best suited to the needs and preferences of individual departments and divisions. This flexibility enables the productivity of each personal computer, workstation, and mainframe-class machine to be maximized.

Moreover, the flexibility of client/server technology extends into other areas. Flexible databases allow a broad array of people to access important information, such as sales or customer feedback data, which was formerly locked away in mainframe data hierarchies. Salespeople in the field can use portable computers to carry data with them or tap into corporate networks. They no longer have to rely on others in the company office to dig out information or numbers for them. Also, client/server technology translates into more employees being given the ability to tap into financial data, to measure and plan activities, or to make business decisions. These technological innovations enable financial managers to quickly consolidate financial results from many different locations, bringing processes and data closer to line management.

As a consequence of such flexibility, companies can take advantage of the globalization of business practices. Internationally, IT can alleviate problems such as physical distance, the safety of employees abroad, and the high costs of overseas investment. Client/server technology also makes it possible for companies to move quickly into new markets at home or abroad.

1.10   *SAP™ AND CLIENT/SERVER TECHNOLOGY*

One of the premier client/server vendors today is SAP™ AG. SAP™ is one of the largest software vendors in the world and the largest headquartered in Germany. In 1998, SAP™ posted sales of more than $5.05 billion, a 41% increase over the previous year. As of year-end 1998, SAP™ had more than 19,308 employees, a 50% increase from year-end 1997. 68% of SAP™'s employees are part of Research and Development staffing. SAP™ America is the largest of the company's 28 global subsidiaries and affiliates and includes corporate headquarters in Philadelphia, a technology center in Foster City, California, and sales and support offices throughout North America.

SAP™'s entry into the client/server arena took place against the backdrop of rapidly changing data processing technology. Although the company's traditional strengths were based on its mainframe business, users began to look for new computing solutions to overcome mainframe drawbacks such as competition between applications and users for the same central computer resources, little or no graphics support, and sluggish response times. Mainframes were focused more on scarce resources than on user needs.

On the advice of customers who sought more-open systems, flexible databases, fourth-generation programming languages, computing solutions for medium-sized companies, and new hardware technology, SAP™ took the bold and industry-leading step toward client/server technology with the introduction of its revolutionary R/3™ system.

Peter Zencke, member of the SAP™ board of directors, explained the rationale for this step, noting that "the computer industry has just gone though a revolution with the switch from mainframe to client/server architecture. In the next few years, most companies will first have to digest or make efficient use of the dramatic changes which that revolution involves. The age of the virtual corporation will be marked by customers linking very different technologies together in a network. Justifiably, customers expect SAP™ to integrate new technologies with maturity and to take on a pioneering role in offering open integration tools. The R/3™ system is still at the beginning of its development, and in the future it will realize its full potential on the basis of its open architecture and best-business practices."

SAP™'s R/3™ system was the software industry's first client/server software designed to integrate all business functions of an enterprise. Like the company's mainframe-based R/2™ system, R/3™ was designed to help companies solve business problems. As a client/server system, however, R/3™ enables companies to take advantage of new technologies, such as relational databases, GUIs, and open systems.

"When we started in 1988," says Hasso Plattner, SAP™'s founder and Chief Executive Officer, "the data processing environment was completely different from that of today. The mainframe computer still dominated the scene in the vast majority of companies, and workstations were already very sophisticated but not nearly as superior as they are today. No one could have predicted that the concept of open systems for use with products from a broad range of manufacturers would catch on quite to the extent it has."·

The architecture of SAP™'s R/3™ system conforms to the three-tier design of presentation, application, and database servers. R/3™ architecture ensures that the system is sufficiently flexible to expand with a company's needs and enables individual computers to reach their maximum performance capability. It also helps companies optimize business processes by integrating data and making it available online and in real time to every user and workplace.

In addition, the R/3™ architecture includes Business Application Programming Interfaces (BAPIs), which comprise an essential architectural layer for hosting a client/server system. For example, Microsoft® Excel is used as an interactive presentation-level BAPI for balance sheet consolidation. Without ever leaving Excel, the user triggers consolidation between it and other servers running on the R/3™ system.

Besides the benefits offered by relational databases and the availability of open BAPIs for incorporating third-party products, R/3™ is also oriented toward central "business objects." Before client/server technology, software architecture was designed in an ad hoc fashion. It performed individual business functions, such as purchasing, inventory management, or financial accounting, in response to functional requirements. In many companies, such functionally oriented applications gave rise to an unmanageably complex maze of system components. Interfaces had to be programmed to link the applications together. The problem was compounded by the fact that once instituted, function-oriented structures could not be transformed into process-oriented structures. Companies sacrificed flexibility and the ability to introduce change.

Rather than being function oriented, R/3™ is a process-based system geared toward business objects. Business objects are sets of business data, transactions, and events within R/3™. Business objects, such as "order," "goods receipt document," or "financial accounting document" can assume different guises and attributes within R/3™ architecture. An order, for example, can take many forms depending on its context: standard order, delivery schedule, or outline agreement. It can also refer to a purchase requisition or be assigned to an account.

The flexibility of R/3™ allows the parameterization of such business objects and makes it possible to use the same system to model quite different processes. R/3™ architecture is such that the most important business objects are encapsulated along with the required methods. Business objects can also be freely invoked, permitting context-sensitive integration at any point along a company's business-process chain.

Since its market launch in 1992, R/3™ has already been through nine releases, each time reducing the technical problems associated with upgrading. Now, R/3™ is very close to including a fully automated upgrade that adapts to new model changes, which will allow a customer's R/3™ system to be reconfigured without affecting any existing customer processes. In accordance with the principle of continuous engineering, R/3™ offers the ability to incorporate into the customer's particular R/3™ system new configuration data based on continuous feedback from users. Users thus can serve as members of a learning community and help to identify the best business practices for the company.

1.11   BEYOND BUSINESS ENGINEERING

The next stage of the Enterprise Resource Planning (ERP) software revolution is upon us. Now that companies have successfully implemented ERP software, the next challenge is to leverage the improved business processes to create a business model for companies that supports continuous improvement across the organization.

Continuous Engineering

The R/3™ system, with its integrated Reference Model, makes it possible for continuous BE. Business processes are described in the integrated R/3™ Reference Model, and these processes are, in turn, linked to the R/3™ System by referencing its underlying object-oriented modules. Parameters can be set within each module to adapt and fine-tune a multitude of different business processes to suit the individual needs of the enterprise. The inherent object orientation of the R/3™ system makes it possible to wield one standard system to implement different business processes. Because of the integration of R/3™ modules with the Reference Model, the system is continuously adaptive and provides rapid response to the ever-changing needs of the business.

The Business Engineer, a suite of tools incorporated into the R/3™ system, further supports the goal of continuous engineering. The Business Engineer helps users work their way through R/3™ with clear business language, rather than with technical jargon. It also employs online graphics to map the processes, configurations, and variations in R/3™. Its versatility provides a key ingredient in customizing R/3™ into a powerful information technology system. By selecting and adjusting the model data, a user can determine the scope and content of the actions to be performed within a chosen process. The ability to navigate through the variety of model types and collect information about the process design are essential for understanding the business information behind R/3™.

Supply Chain Management

The R/3™ information management system enables the integration of all business processes and areas into coherent and well-structured supply chain management. Supply chain management involves the planning and control of all tasks along the business value chain—from production planning to capital asset management. The goal of supply chain management is to reduce inventory levels, lower costs, hasten time to market, and ultimately to provide better customer service and satisfaction. In the past, companies tended to isolate each of their operations and analyze them without consideration of the causes that impacted them or the effects that would result from changing them. By introducing the supply chain, companies have a more comprehensive understanding of everything that affects the delivery of goods and materials from the original supplier to the customer.

The R/3™ system stores invaluable information that pertains to every aspect of the enterprise. From sales and distribution to production planning, R/3™ incorporates logistical and operational areas into an integrated workflow of business events. The R/3™ system automatically links together logistically and operationally related areas, eliminating the need to repeat time and resource-intensive procedures. By integrating such important value activity areas as finance or human resources, businesses make themselves more effective and efficient.

Desktop ERP

Desktop ERP represents the next wave of BE. Desktop ERP improves the delivery of information of R/3™ to end users and makes ERP software easier to understand. This new technology suggests that the individual user is now being seen as a key success factor for ERP systems. It further promises to extend the benefits of streamlined organizations to support a business model that enables continuous business engineering, supply chain management, and improved decision support.

SAP™ and its growing list of third-party software suppliers have made great strides in making R/3™ software more manageable for the end user. From SAP™'s new Business Information Warehouse solution to the promising desktop ERP solutions provided by third-party software vendors, SAP™ R/3™ will soon become the kind of software that everyone in the organization will be able to understand and use.

1.12   *CONCLUSION*

Changing market dynamics compel many enterprises to rethink both their organizational structure and use of technology. In the past, "economies of scale" produced benefits by offering standardized products to stable and large consumer markets. Technology was used to optimize well-defined, discretely functioning areas within the enterprise. Information specialists created and maintained application software to automate certain business functions. The systems were designed to take snapshots of the business. Each snapshot provided data for hierarchical control, local decision making, and financial accounting. The downsides to these systems were cost overruns, slow response times, a painfully awkward user interface, and an inability to cope with change.

Today, by contrast, companies must produce their products better, faster, and cheaper. To compete better in this environment, companies must adopt a business-process orientation and a global, supply chain perspective in order to allow "business optimization" to shape their business processes into adaptable business structures that respond to customer demands.

The essential prerequisite for business optimization is an integrated information system. This system allows the business engineer to explore every pathway where value is added within a company and to design business processes that maximize value while minimizing costs. The transformed role of transaction-based systems is to help actualize these goals so that management can continuously realign business operations with company objectives.

The R/3™ system, with its integrated Reference Model, supports continuous business optimization. Business processes are described in the integrated R/3™ Reference Model, using the "event-driven process chains" (EPC) process description language, which is discussed in detail in the next chapter. Through the integration of customers' creative ideas and industry experience with R/3™, the IT and business infrastructures adapt and respond to ever-changing business needs.

2
The Business Blueprint

- "We started to do BPR with R/3™. Modeling tools help transfer know-how from persons to systems, and they help to establish a common language between users and IT."
  (Ascom Hasler AG, Solothurn, Switzerland)

- "The R/3™ Reference Model is a 'fast track' approach for systems implementation."
  (Coopers & Lybrand, Belgium)

For centuries, disciplines such as chemistry or mathematics have used formulas, pictures, and models to visually portray interactions between chemical agents or numeric systems. Now the same idea is taking hold in the business world, where computer-based, graphic modeling methods help guide business people through the maze of business processes.

As the above comments attest, new business modeling methods are helping bring processes and information technology closer together. Computer-based graphic modeling methods in general and process-oriented modeling approaches in particular have made great strides in making both technology and business processes clearer and more comprehensible.

The blending of business knowledge of processes and technology is largely a current phenomenon. Until only recently, most engineering efforts have used simple drawing and process modeling methods that make processes clearer to business people but leave out necessary technical details. Likewise, application development tools often have included object modeling or Computer-Aided

Software Engineering (CASE) tools that create code unreadable to anyone who isn't an expert. In terms of process and data modeling, it has been difficult to coordinate the two because IS staff and business users aren't always on the same wavelength. In order to eliminate this discrepancy, vendors such as SAP™ offer more integrated development and modeling methodologies and tools that can be used by a variety of different users, from business people to programmers. By integrating data and process modeling techniques, these tools work to the advantage of business users and IS people alike.

From a technological standpoint, modeling can be an extremely complex endeavor. Add the implementation of a new software system to the equation, and the task becomes onerous indeed. Even though highly integrated applications tend to be used throughout an organization, the lack of understanding of how these applications execute a process often prohibits the adaptation of the software by the business. Prefabricated models of the applications, however, allow companies to reduce their risks while benefiting from a recognized benchmark for business-process redesign.

In a business context, a model or business-process diagram illustrates processes, tasks, and the organizational structure of a company. A company's information model can also include the description of other aspects of a company, including data, function, organization, information flow, and communication flow. Or it can be used to emphasize a company's individual requirements, creating a model of a company's ideal or goal situation based on its present situation (see Chapter 3).

The most effective business blueprints successfully integrate BE with IT. Whereas business blueprints have not always successfully aided the business engineering effort in the past, a superior blueprint based on sounder business theory, better logical models, and well-defined business processes has emerged in the form of SAP™'s Business Blueprint. To understand how this technology works, we will explore the general trend toward business models and then examine the specific ideas behind SAP™'s Business Blueprint.

2.1   PROS AND CONS OF BUSINESS BLUEPRINTS

Six sound arguments can be made for using a blueprint in BE efforts:

- Processes are not easy to model.
- A blueprint made by leading business professionals inherits all their experience, knowledge, creativity, and depth.
- Few businesses can afford a zero-based approach.
- Optimization of business processes is critical to reaction time.

- Businesses reduce the risk of not finding a software product that fits the process model.
- Blueprints serve as a common starting point and language for teams engaged in process design.

Historically, the road to blueprints has given many a company a bumpy ride. In the late '70s and early '80s, data modeling became a primary task for data processing departments. "Enterprise modeling," as it was later called, was an attempt to create a complete blueprint of data and process structures within a company, primarily with the aim of creating applications. Due to the lack of sophisticated modeling techniques, however, creating a database blueprint from scratch often led to disaster. The costs were simply too high.

In fact, many of these projects failed to deliver any added value to reengineering or even to application development—a bitter lesson IT management learned. For example, with the help of IBM and McKinsey, the Deutsche Bank, Germany's premier banking institution, spent well over 30 years on building a comprehensive enterprise data model before canning the project in the early '90s as soon as a standard reference model became available.

Fortunately, blueprint technology has evolved. Several factors have improved the conditions for better process modeling: 1) the increase in productivity of software development projects; 2) the general trend toward quality, total quality management, BPR, and lean management movements; and 3) a shift in management philosophy from managing all parts of particular business transactions to actually optimizing the transaction itself. Once companies began to have a better understanding of their processes, they then looked to a reference model that could indeed deliver added value to reengineering and application development.

Blueprints illustrate complex processes in a way that business users can understand. In fact, according to most companies involved in BPR projects, understanding processes is one of the most important reasons to use a blueprint. As a business engineering method, a business blueprint is important for business users who want to know more about processes but not about technical details. The goal of a business blueprint is not to prototype, generate code and screens, or design specifications, but to streamline complex business processes. In this way, the technical details are taken care of behind the scenes, while the business processes themselves take center stage.

Companies around the world find business blueprints a relevant and critical part of business-process engineering. Senior computer analyst Marin Giacoro, who is a methodology expert at Phillip Morris European Union Region in Switzerland, sees a multipurpose role for modeling methods. "Modeling tools are important," he states, "to standardize the way business is carried out among Phillip Morris' different development communities." At Systime, a small Swiss business engineering consulting firm specializing in SAP™, business blueprints are used not only to document processes for basic understanding but also for training employees for newly designed roles. Furthermore, the CIO of a leading European-based retailing conglomerate, Metro Organization, revealed a similar situation. One of his first questions, after learning of the R/3™ blueprint, was if he could finally dismember his modeling team. The company had already spent 15 years developing a company-specific model.

2.2   GENERAL DESIGN OF THE R/3™ BLUEPRINT

In medieval times, cathedrals were usually built without any real blueprints. The master builder had a vague idea of what he wanted to do and then he began to build. As he went along, the patron might want some changes made, some structures might fail, or the builder himself might want to work in new styles from Italy or France. Rather than start anew, the builder would incorporate any modifications, and, using his experience, he'd keep working until something resembling a cathedral was completed. Usually the initial design looked nothing like the end product. Sometimes it worked out (those buildings still stand today); sometimes it didn't (the roof caved in on an unsuspecting congregation).

This Gothic mentality characterizes companies who don't have a well-conceived plan or blueprint when they begin business engineering. If they have a grand scheme, often it is only in a few master builders' heads. Often this same scheme changes so drastically that it barely resembles the original design. Sometimes the haphazard method works (BE becomes a great success story); most times it doesn't (the BE roof caves in).

In the past, good blueprints were hard to come by, causing most BE leaders to learn through trial and error. SAP™ has built on the experiences of both successful and unsuccessful BE projects and has created a "blueprint"—a BE reference model—that guides companies from the beginning phases of engineering, including evaluation and analysis, to final implementation.

The basis of SAP™'s model is the R/3™ system. The blueprint is the definitive description of R/3™, providing a comprehensive view of the main processes and business solutions available in the R/3™ system without clouding the user's understanding with technical detail. With its blueprint of the R/3™ system, SAP™ has devised a logical yet flexible method for shaping and optimizing business processes. The blueprint is like an atlas with overview and detail maps. These "maps" come in the form of a complete reference model of the R/3™ system. The blueprint can help companies define their own needs and develop solutions. Business solutions are already built into the blueprint, eliminating the need for companies to start from the beginning. Users can simply view the blueprint to look at what's possible in R/3™, print out relevant process models, and analyze the company's most critical areas. Later, the customizing features of R/3™ can aid in the smooth implementation of the system and the practical realization of the customer's specific business-process chains. The blueprint shows function, process, information flow, and organization views. It portrays business situations and supports navigation through all processes. With the blueprint, companies need only select the business processes relevant to their own specific needs (a task that typically takes 20 seconds and eliminates costly development of new coding). It's also user friendly, allowing even those with little technical background to understand the business object models representing their companies.

The Business Blueprint (also known as the R/3™ Reference Model) serves as the basis for BE. As a storage facility providing models and diagrams in two languages (German and English), its purpose is to clearly depict the structure, integration, and functions of R/3™. In other words, the Business Blueprint is designed to illustrate and describe the existing business processes in R/3™, help speed up implementation of R/3™ projects, support business-process engineering, and facilitate communication among customers, consultants, and SAP™.

The Blueprint helps users understand business processes of SAP™ applications—such as finance and accounting, logistics, and human resources—with the help of graphic models. Using easy-to-understand symbols and icons, models portray business processes as Event-Driven Process Chains (EPCs), clarifying exactly what processes are important for supporting business activities and how they are linked. Hence, with the R/3™ Reference Model, companies can map their business needs into a logical business-process framework.

2.3   FOCUS OF THE R/3™ BLUEPRINT

The initial intent of the Business Blueprint was to create an easy-to-understand description of the business processes contained in R/3™ and to supplement the existing descriptions of R/3™ information objects (entities) in the SAP™ data models. SAP™ started out with data models from individual areas plus a knowledge of the structural relationships among the organizational units in R/3™. This initial description was aimed at the IT engineer.

Later on, the description of the Business Blueprint came to focus on business users. To achieve greater accessibility for these users, two main goals of the Blueprint were developed:

1. Model orientation: Models portray real-world happenings in an abstract way. However, a balance must be struck between information content and comprehensibility. Considering how complex most

corporate structures are, especially those of internationally active companies, a straightforward, but naive, approach to modeling will not work. The numerous possible business scenarios would soon bog down in a morass of applications and models. This consideration also applies to modeling computerized information systems. Modeling all the possible combinations that can be configured in R/3™ would offer a complete picture but would also overwhelm users with more information than they could handle. Because of this, the R/3™ Reference Model describes the business processes that are most commonly practiced, along with their variants. Such descriptions ensure that the most frequently selected business processes can be implemented efficiently with R/3™. Modeling other alternatives can be done on a case-by-case basis with customization tools.

2. Customer orientation: As a basic principle, reference models must be created for different target groups. Whereas a software developer might want to see every detail, end users and planners may be hampered by an excess of detailed information during the first stages of BE. For clarity's sake, the SAP™ Reference Model selects a clear and simple method of description, with only a few different symbols organized in a set arrangement, which a lay person can immediately comprehend.

To facilitate both customer and model orientations, the SAP™ Blueprint concentrates on four key elements: events ("When should something be done?"); tasks or functions ("What should be done?"); organization ("Who should do what?"); and communication ("What information is required to do the right task?"). In other words, the model defines who must do what, when, and how. Events are the driving force behind a business process, prompting one or more activities to take place. For example, the event "goods arrived" triggers the task "check goods." In turn, "checked goods" moves on to the next steps in the chain, "goods released," "goods blocked," or "goods returned." All of this activity is based upon the EPC, the theoretical framework behind SAP™'s Reference Model.

2.4   *EVENT-DRIVEN PROCESS CHAIN METHODOLOGY*

Before the advent of EPC, other methods for describing business organizations and processes were too complicated. They did not offer links to parallel processes, nor did they provide key perspectives such as organizational or information-flow views. Other methods also were too IT-oriented or used complex symbology. The EPC method, on the other hand, portrays business information systems for the benefit of users, management, and consultants, while at the same time incorporating other important features, such as organizational structures, functions, and data and information flow. Using practical business experience and easy-to-understand symbols and language, the EPC method offers a look at the internal structure of SAP™'s Business Blueprint.

By connecting events and tasks, users can clearly model and analyze even very complex business processes. An EPC model can show where breaks in the chain of tasks and responsibilities hurt the ability of a company to optimize its processes. By matching the organizations with individual tasks, users can easily see which departments are involved in a given process.

When a company tries to identify the possibilities for optimizing its business processes, four basic design principles of the EPC—event, task/function, organization, and information—are usually involved, as shown in Table 2-1.

Table 2–1 EPC Methodology

Chain	Question	Answer
Event	When should something be done?	Customer order received
Task/function	What should be done?	Create material master
Organization	Who should do it?	Sales department, plant, secretary
Information	What information is needed to do it?	Material, order, etc.

These four areas are essential for understanding the EPC structure.

- *Event:* Asks "When should a task be done?" (depicted as a shaded *hexagon* in the EPC process flow charts). An event, be it an order, a purchase, or a delivery, triggers the chain of subsequent processes that flow through a company. For example, if a customer sends in an order for a product, the event "order has arrived" triggers the process chain to begin. The same goes for such events as a vendor delivering a production material ("production material is delivered") or a vendor sending an invoice ("invoice is sent"). Events trigger, or drive, the processes that follow.
- *Task or function:* Asks "What should be done?" (depicted as a *rectangle with rounded corners*). Within a company, a task or function describes what an employee actually does. In an information system, a task or function is a transaction. To be able to perform a task, a computer must have information about that task as data. That data, in turn, can serve as input for other related tasks down the line. Function trees, which show how different tasks are united, are stored in the Reference Model.

- *Organization:* Asks "Who should do a task?" (depicted as a shaded *ellipse*). An organization is a location, office, department, or person. One of the biggest challenges a business faces is to optimize its organizations. The most common practice is to distinguish between organizational structures and the organization of processes. Often, not enough emphasis is placed on understanding processes, whereas too much attention is paid to the actual structures. This lopsidedness usually creates fragmented process chains and unnecessary complexity, with too many different system interfaces and transactions being exchanged between departments, offices, and people.

- *Information:* Asks "What information is needed to do a task?" (depicted as a shaded *rectangle*). Information is needed to carry out a specific business task. Examples include information about customer orders or purchase requisitions. Information is either generated in an information system or fed into the system from the outside. The information serves as the input of a process or acts as the output of a process. In other words, the information is necessary for the process to take place and for the next process to begin.

Figure 2-1 illustrates the process description language elements in EPCs.

2.5   DESCRIBING COMPLEX BUSINESS PROCESSES

To keep the overall model manageable in scope while creating a complete and understandable picture of a company, SAP™ has created overlapping views of business processes. Built on a vast storehouse of knowledge and experience gained from thousands of customers in a broad range of industries, each view represents a different, detailed look at how a company is organized. These include process, functional, organizational, information-flow, data, and communication views. Each view answers a distinct question about what happens in business processes.

The EPC is the central view, which then incorporates the others into its structure. The EPC portrays the interconnections between tasks, data, and organizational units and the logical time sequence involved. An event always triggers a task. It is important for each EPC to begin with at least one event (the start event) and to end with at least one final event (the finish event). The organizational units (departments, people, etc.) responsible for doing the task are added to the chain to show a complete picture of how tasks are performed.

Designation	Icon	Definition	Example
Event		Events describe the occurrence of a status that in turn acts as a trigger.	Order is received
Function		Functions describe transformations from an initial status to a final status.	Verify order
Organization unit		Organization units describe the outline structure of an enterprise. The organization units in the R/3 system are system organization units.	Sales organization
Information, material or resource object		Information, material, or resource objects portray objects in the real world (e.g., business objects, entities).	Sales order Inspection result
Process path		Process paths show the connection from or to processes (Navigation aid).	Delivery processing
Logical operator		Logical operators describe the logical relationships between events and functions or processes.	"XOR", "AND", "OR"
Control flow		Control flows describe the chronological and logical interdependencies of events and functions or processes.	
Information/ material flow		Information/material flows define whether a function is read, changed, or written.	
Resource/organization unit assignment		Resource/organization unit assignments describe which unit (employee) or resource processes a function or process.	

▶ **Figure 2–1**   Elements of the EPC

Key to Figure 2-1:
- Geometric shape designates EPC function (see above).
- Arrows made up of dotted lines show the flow of business.
- "Connecting operators" (AND, exclusive/OR, OR) illustrate alternative or parallel flows of information through the chain.
- Arrows made up of solid lines indicate information is input into a task or generated by that task.
- Connecting lines show which task is assigned to which organizational unit.

The EPC can be depicted in a graphical model, using different symbols (see Figure 2-1) to represent the chain of events of even complex business processes.

Navigation between different process models is possible by way of start and finish events, as shown in Figure 2-2.

Direct connections between different processes are not visible on paper printouts. Consequently, "process pointers" have been added to show which processes come before or after others and how they are linked. For example, the process of checking incoming goods yields "goods released" as its finish event. After that, a pointer indicates that the next process is "production." For this pro-

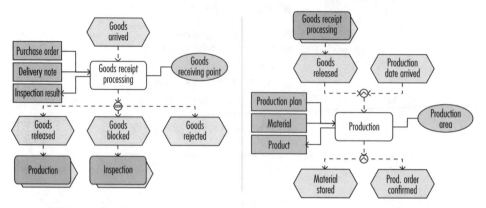

▶ Figure 2–2 Process diagrams link events, business objects, functions, and organizational units

cess, "goods released" is the start event. The pointer also shows where "goods released" came from. Each process pointer shows an event symbol in the background and a function or task symbol in the foreground.

Further illustration of how the blueprint portrays the processes and connections supported by R/3™ is provided in the following three examples.

Ordering Toner

Company A has two printers: one for monochrome printing, the other for color printing. The company's main purchasing office usually orders its color toner in bulk from three different companies, depending on the price or quality.

Once a month, the purchasing department collects the orders from different departments. Then, it calls the three companies that supply toner and asks for a quote for bulk supplies. When it has the quotations, it compares the offers and chooses the one with the best price and delivery time. Then the company sends in its order.

When the order is delivered, the goods receiving department first checks to make sure that the order is correct. At this point, the order is accepted or blocked (e.g., if it's wrong or damaged). At the same time, the toner company begins automatic billing, sending an invoice to the company after delivery of the toner.

When the invoice arrives, the purchasing department checks to see that it was charged for the correct amount of toner at the quoted price. If a discrepancy is found, the invoice is blocked. But if everything is all right, the company goes ahead and pays the invoice.

The EPC model based on the above sequence of events is shown in Figure 2-3.

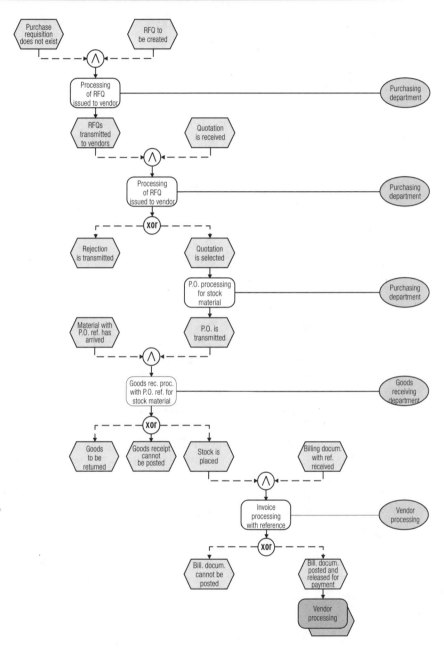

▶ **Figure 2–3**   Ordering Toner

Recruiting a New Employee

A position has opened up at Company B, and it's the responsibility of the personnel department to fill it.

The first task of the human resources manager is to create a job description for the open position. This task includes information such as writing down the main tasks, responsibilities, or skills of the job.

Once the job description has been created and entered into the system, three events can occur:

- Someone is found from within the company.
- Someone is employed based on an application on file.
- Someone must be found from outside the company.

If the position must be filled externally, the manager writes a "help wanted" ad and places it in the local newspaper as well as in some of the larger dailies in the region.

After a few weeks, more than 100 people apply for the job, and the manager begins the job of processing the applications. First, she inputs the necessary data about each applicant into the computer system and sends a letter to each applicant, saying that his or her application has arrived and the company will be notifying those selected for interviews at a later date.

After reviewing applicant data, the manager sends a letter of rejection to some of the applicants, a letter to others inviting them to an interview, and another letter to still others saying that they have been selected as alternates and their applications will be kept on file.

The human resources manager interviews 20 applicants and ultimately decides on one. The other 19 are notified by letter of rejection, while the manager calls the selected applicant with the good news. She then sends the new employee a contract and schedules his first day. He returns the contract and shows up to work a week later.

On his first work day, the new employee's application data, salary, vacation, insurance, social security number, tax information, and retirement plan are entered into the system. Now the position is filled. Figure 2-4 illustrates the EPC model for the process.

Planning a Seminar

Company C offers seminars and training courses every year, covering such topics as "Electronic Commerce," "Business Engineering," and "Quality Management in the '90s."

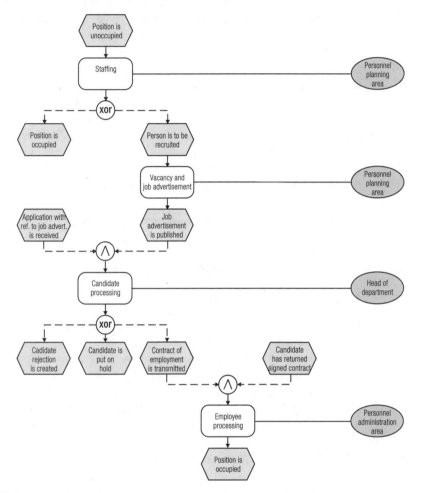

▶ **Figure 2–4**   Recruiting a new employee

The company's human resources department is in charge of planning the next seminar and begins with finding the right facility. They decide on a nearby hotel but first have to check to make sure that it has enough overhead projectors, space, chairs, and catering services.

Next, the company plans what kind of seminar to sponsor, including such details as the topic, the length of the seminar, speakers, whether it's a speech or a workshop, target audience, etc. When all details have been decided on and planned, the company then has a room for the event, a date and time, and a written brochure.

Before the seminar actually takes place, the department is busy taking reservations and entering confirmations received. Participants could either be internal, meaning they also work at Company C and will attend the workshop, or external, that is, from outside the company. In any case, all attendees must pay a fee, which includes a commission for the speakers. For example, perhaps employees of the company pay 3 percent, whereas others pay 5 percent.

The individual departments of the company sending people to the workshop pay their own cost accounts directly to Company C. External participants are sent a bill after the seminar takes place. The price of the seminar can vary, however, depending on if external participants 1) registered by a certain deadline (maybe a 10 percent discount), 2) didn't show up or canceled, or 3) could only attend for one of the two days.

Figure 2-5 illustrates the seminar-planning model.

2.6   *EPC METHODOLOGY AND VIEWPOINTS IN THE R/3*™ *REFERENCE MODEL*

In the preceding examples, the EPC method maps business processes and thereby promotes effective business engineering. The business-process view can be supplemented in the Reference Model by other views of R/3™. Because these additional viewpoints provide accessible, yet detailed, models of business processes and information system (e.g., client/server) capabilities, companies may wish to consult them when planning a BE effort. These viewpoints give answers to the following key engineering questions:

- Which tasks or functions must be performed, and what business functionality is offered by the application software in use?
- Which organizational units are entrusted with performing these tasks, and how can they be modeled within a computerized information system?
- What information is needed to make a company more efficient and, how can an information system support this information?
- What connections exist between task or function and application areas, and how can the exchange of information through different user applications be supported?

With the EPC method, it is possible to answer these questions by illustrating business processes and information system capabilities by means of several different viewpoints. These viewpoints, also known as models, correspond directly with the above questions. They are:

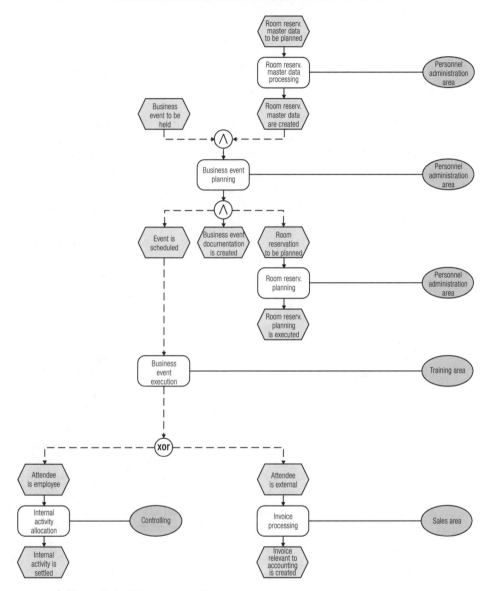

▶ **Figure 2–5**   Planning a seminar

- Component model—What is done?
- Organization model—Who does what and/or who is responsible?
- Data model—What is needed to do something?
- Interaction model—What information must be exchanged between different organizations or application components?

These EPC-based parts of the R/3™ Reference Model enable a company to dissect and understand business processes from different but consistent viewpoints. When a business process is modeled by the EPC method, connections are drawn between the different models or viewpoints contained within the Business Blueprint. The combination of these four distinct viewpoints constitutes the overall model of business processes. It is this overall perspective that forms the basis of business engineering.

These different viewpoints describe business processes, using EPC methodology and other parts of the Blueprint. In order to illustrate how this is done, let's look at the specific example of a car dealership, which we shall call "Carpark."

Reference Model Viewpoints—Car Dealership

Figure 2-6 illustrates our model for the discussion.

A potential customer arrives at the car dealership and asks for specific information about some of the various cars for sale. This customer inquiry generates a Request for Quotation (RFQ).

The salesperson makes a note of what the customer is looking for. He then checks the details of the customer's inquiry; for example, what type of engine and internal fittings she wants, whether she wants a sunroof or air conditioning. Assuming the dealership can provide all these specifications, the salesperson gives the customer a quotation, specifying the price, terms of payment, and when the car should be ready.

After a few days, the potential customer returns to the dealership and signs a legally binding sales agreement with the salesperson. This is the sales order; it contains all details concerning price, terms of payment, car specifications, and the scheduled delivery date.

One copy of the sales order is then given to the buyer, and another is sent to the car manufacturer. The manufacturer's distribution center determines the exact delivery date and triggers the production of the car. The distribution center calculates the basic delivery data and sends it to the dealership. The dealership's invoice department adds the transportation and registration costs to the price of the car and deducts any previously negotiated discount. Once the delivery period is up, the salesperson hands the car over to the customer and sends her the billing document or invoice. When the accounts department releases the invoice,

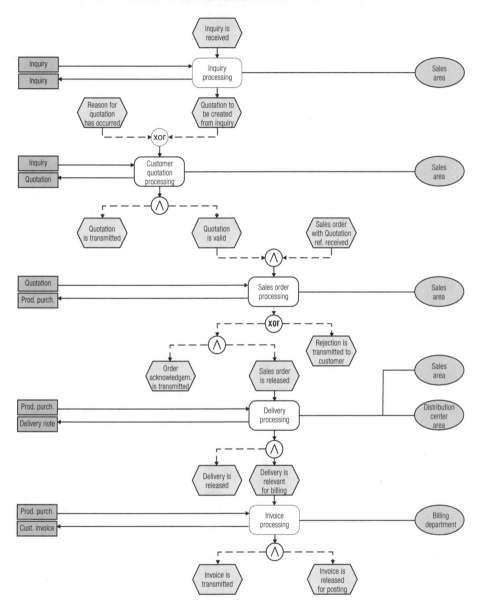

▶ **Figure 2–6**   Selling a car represented as an EPC

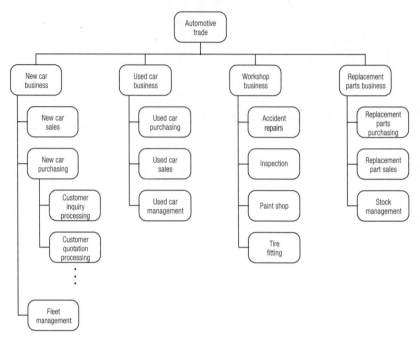

▶ **Figure 2–7**   Carpark represented as a component model

the invoice processing function begins automatically. This function checks whether the customer has made her payments on time. If she has not, the department can decide whether to write the customer an urging letter or a reminder.

The Business Blueprint models this entire transaction through the four viewpoints described above. SAP™ assures its customers that these individual viewpoints are designed as a whole and are consistent with one another.

The Component Model—What Happens?

The car dealership, "Carpark," deals in new and used cars. The activities of Carpark include buying and selling as well as managing stocks. Selling new cars involves processing customer inquiries, customer quotations, deliveries, sales orders, and billing, all of which are listed under new car sales. As well as selling cars, the company also has a repair shop (workshop business) where cars are repaired, inspected, sprayed, and fitted with tires. Carpark also deals in spare parts for the makes of car they sell (replacement parts business). Figure 2-7 above illustrates Carpark's business processes.

The component model shows what Carpark's main business processes are, but it doesn't describe the order of those processes or who carries them out. In the component model, a company's complex web of tasks is clearly modeled in the form of static and easily grasped diagrams (function trees). Relationships between tasks are also shown. When assessing these relationships, it's important to identify how and why different tasks relate to each other at higher and lower levels. SAP™ has developed a function tree to help in the breakdown of tasks:

- Level 0—Describes the application as a whole (automotive trade)
- Level 1—Contains the functional areas covered by the application (new car business, used car business, etc.)
- Level 2—Contains the main tasks of a given functional area (new car sales, new car purchasing, etc.)
- Level 3—Contains the individual tasks performed within the scope of a main function (customer inquiry processing, customer quotation processing, etc.)

The component model represents application functions and how they relate to each another. It shows how functions or tasks activate one another and which functions are subordinate to others. Functions can be broken down into more precise and detailed units. In a company, the highest functions relate to larger, general applications, such as materials management or product planning, and the lowest functions roughly correspond to a transaction in a company, such as the preparation of quotes.

The Organizational Model—Who Does What?

Carpark's organizational structure includes management—headed by two brothers—and four other departments. The sales area, which consists of sales management and salespersons, is responsible for buying and selling cars. The workshop has its own service desk, where it deals with customers. The repair shop has two areas, one for management and one for mechanics. The employees in the stock area, where spare parts and tires are kept, have to make sure that the parts the repair shop needs for spraying, inspection, and repairs are always available. They are also responsible for selling parts directly to customers. The personnel and billing department deals with the wages, manages personnel data (about vacation, training programs, employment contracts, and so on) and keeps the customer and vendor accounts. As well as issuing bills, the personnel and billing department also checks that payments are made on time and verifies and pays vendor invoices. Figure 2-8 illustrates Carpark's functional processes.

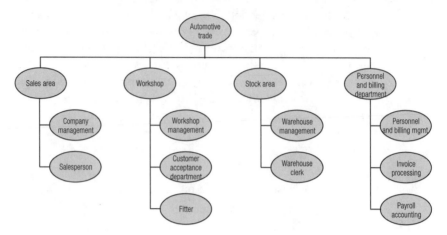

▶ **Figure 2–8**   Carpark represented as an organization diagram

The purpose of the organizational model is to allow R/3™ users to adjust and optimize the structure of organization units and even to store them in the system as "organization diagrams."

The organizational viewpoint shows the relationships among the organization units (plants, suppliers, subcontractors, clients, etc.). However, the huge variety of corporate structures in the real world sometimes presents cases that can't be completely mapped in organizational terms. To identify such cases at an early stage of BE, the organizational model presents a view of the R/3™ system that can be checked against a company's own structure. Because it is designed to accommodate the possibility of rapid changes in the web of organizational interaction, the organizational view offers adaptability to users.

The main questions that the organizational model answers are: "Which organization units should process which business processes in the future?" and "Which organization units perform which functions using which transactions?" The organizational model addresses these questions by depicting and analyzing organization unit, as well as structural relationships and the distribution of the information system among different users.

The Data Model—What Is Needed?

The Business Blueprint's data model deals with information objects. The Carpark data model includes the key information objects "workshop/garage," "customer," "product/material," and "vendor." The "workshop/garage" is a central object that accounts for much of the added value within the business process. The customer and vendor are the most important units with which the dealership has a business relationship. "Product/material" represents Carpark's main business area, that is, the cars, spare parts, etc., in which the company deals. Figure 2-9 illustrates Carpark's business information objects.

There are several types of customer: the orderer, the goods receiver, and the debtor. For example, a father taking out a loan at his bank to buy a car for his daughter would be considered the ordering party. The daughter would be the goods recipient, and the bank would be the bill-to party.

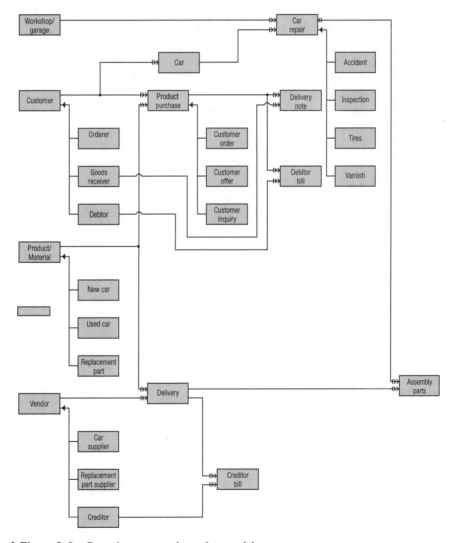

▶ **Figure 2–9**   Carpark represented as a data model

The product palette, represented by the "product/material" object, is divided into new cars, used cars, and spare parts. Customers can purchase items from any of these three categories, and any item from the product palette can be bought by several customers. All these possible transactional connections are represented by the links within the data model.

Before customers buy a car or a spare part, they might make a customer inquiry, which would result in the dealership presenting them with a customer quotation. The information object "customer inquiry" contains information about what products potential buyers are interested in, and it is used by the company for market segmentation and analysis. Because customer quotations are normally legally binding offers to potential customers, they have to be monitored with care, because vendors and product liability are involved at this stage. Sales orders are legally binding agreements that if broken by the dealership or customer may lead to contract penalties, such as customers' property being seized if they are unable to make the repayments, or the dealership being obliged to pay for a temporary car if unable to deliver the ordered car on time.

Customers can have one or more cars that they may need to take to the repair shop for various kinds of service: accident, damage repair, inspection, new tires, or spraying. Customers may require spare parts for their car, in which case they may make a transaction with spare parts suppliers. Vendors are either classified as car manufacturers or spare parts suppliers, but when the dealership begins making payments, a third type of information object is required: creditor. Suppliers of spare parts and used cars are classified as creditors following delivery. However, a new car vendor is classified as a creditor as soon as an agreement with the car manufacturer is signed, because it is obliged to pay as soon as a car is ordered.

Vendors can supply one or more products/materials, and the dealership purchases a range of products from various car manufacturers and spare parts suppliers. Once goods have been delivered, the dealership creates a "vendor invoice" information object (creditor bill) or, in the case of new cars, transfers the one created when the car was first ordered. Spare parts to be used by the dealership itself in repairs are classified as "assembly part" information objects. More than one type of repair part can be contained in any one delivery and/or be required for a repair. The difference between repair parts and spare parts is that repair parts are reserved for use by the dealership's repair shop and cannot be sold to customers.

The data model analyzes how information objects, that is, data, interact with preceding and following functions within the business-process model. The data model illustrates the information input needed to perform a given set of tasks. This data viewpoint depicts the most important information objects and describes them and their relationships with one another. To successfully perform a task, data input must first be received from preceding tasks. Once this is done, new information objects are generated or the state of existing information objects is changed. Such information objects and their operational relationships are stored in the data models of the R/3™ Enterprise Data Model (a subset of the Reference Model shown in Figure 2-11). This model contains the data structures that are directly or technically related to the question at hand at the user level.

Although a complete description of the data structures is needed for in-house engineering efforts, only those information objects required for defining processes are stored in the Business Blueprint.

The Interaction Model—How Do Company Models Interact?

The goal of every company is to increase the value of a product and exchange this value-added product with other parties. Some companies process raw materials to create a new product. Other companies provide information or a service so valuable that customers are prepared to pay for it. However, all companies, regardless of which products or services they offer, must generate business if they are to be successful.

In the course of this process, costs arise that have to be covered in the final price of the product or service. For some industries, such as mechanical engineering, fewer than one in ten requests for a quotation lead to a sale. A company should always keep track of quotation costs, including the costs of quotations that do not result in an order. It is important to analyze how company units interact so that the quotation processes can be carried out efficiently.

Information pertaining to the efficiency of the interaction of company units can be found in the EPCs. In our Carpark example, a great deal of interaction of information objects occurs between company units. The most important information objects are the customer, the salesperson from the sales area, possibly the sales manager (company management), and the car manufacturer. Significant interactions also occur with payroll accounting and administration management (personnel and billing).

The quotation process begins when the customer approaches one of the salespeople. The customer inquiry results in a customer quotation. The customer either asks for some time to consider the offer or tells the dealership immediately that she is prepared to pay the asking price. If any special technical features are required, a technical inquiry is sent to the sales managers and, where necessary, to the car manufacturer. If the customer intends to pay part of the amount with a bank loan, an inquiry about finance is sent to the administration department. Once everything has been sorted out, both parties sign the sales order, and the deal becomes legally binding. Incoming sales orders are collected together and are checked and approved by the sales managers. The orders are then sent to the car manufacturer, who bundles all the sales orders from all the car dealerships. The car manufacturer then schedules the production of the orders and two days later informs the sales manager of the exact delivery date. In addition to his basic salary, the salesperson receives 3 percent of the net profit made on the sale of the car. The salesperson advises invoice processing of the invoiced amount so they can monitor the payments made by the customer. Next, the salesperson informs the wages department of the invoiced amount. The wages department then takes this sum into account when calculating the salesperson's commission. These procedures are reviewed once a month by the administration managers. Figure 2-10 illustrates these interactions.

The business applications of an IT system and a company's organization units share one common characteristic: Both must exchange information with others in order to perform their intended tasks. The interaction model allows companies to analyze the way information flows between operational areas like sales and distribution, materials management and controlling, as well as between larger business areas like logistics, finance, and human resources management. Before a task can be performed, information input is needed. In turn, information generated by a task serves as input for other tasks. An information flow always accompanies the process flow depicted in the EPCs.

The interaction model allows companies to analyze how information flows between general applications. Interaction models reveal information flows from senders to receivers and vice versa. The interaction viewpoint describes these interactions at the applications and functional area levels without examining in great detail why or when they occur.

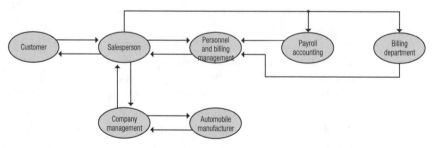

▶ **Figure 2–10**   Interaction model for selling a new car

2.7 SUMMARY

The various models or viewpoints contained in the Reference Model address specific aspects of a company's real situation. Once these have been used to create models of a company's present and target situations, the two scenarios can be compared and a plan of action decided on. In this respect, the integrated application of the Business Blueprint's viewpoints is the means by which a company can efficiently reengineer its business processes. Figure 2-11 illustrates the overall Reference Model.

The interaction model shows the main organization units involved in information exchange for business activities, for example, sales order processing, procurement, production, and human resources planning. The data model shows what information a company needs and what information processing capabilities R/3™ supports. The organization model shows how the company is structured and how the organization units interact. Finally, the component model gives users an overview of the main functions available in the R/3™ system. The R/3™ Reference Model shows how the various models or viewpoints interact. It also includes sample interaction scenarios taken from actual installations, which should help users understand how to analyze their own requirements.

Chapter 3 discusses the actual processes involved in implementing the Business Blueprint.

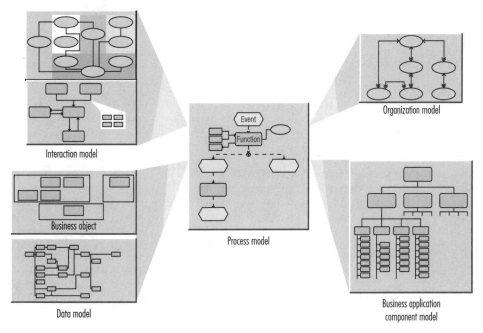

Interaction model

Business object

Data model

Process model

Organization model

Business application component model

▶ **Figure 2–11**   The parts of the R/3™ Reference Model

3

Configure to Order

- "The Reference Model allows you to see how changes in one area affect processes or data in another—even in other areas that are not part of the project. While implementing R/3™ applications, the Reference Model enables us to see what we'll get, to know what can be customized and to document what has been changed."
  (Miele & Cie GmbH & Co., Guetersloh, Germany)

- "The main benefit of the Reference Model is a consistent and complete picture of the processes and data used to run the company."
  (Mentor Graphics, Wilsonville, Oregon, USA)

When companies undergo business redesign, they typically look to business processes first and then search out a software solution to match the new design. Often, companies model the organization and its processes, creating new process designs as they go along. This modeling approach runs counter to the logic of "blueprinting," which begins with ready-made templates and then uses them as the basis for configuring company designs. Because companies tend to prefer one method over the other, the question is: Which strategy—modeling or blueprinting—is superior?

The argument for modeling approaches almost always revolves around issues of the uniqueness of a company's business conditions, goals, and procedures. Following this logic, a company's business engineers prefer to model their organization because they feel that the company has special needs that cannot be met in a template. Hence, the process of business design usually proceeds in the following manner. First the company redefines its business goals and then decides to create models of the company that coincide with these goals. Once the entire organization has been modeled, the company then either creates its own software solution or purchases a standard software that best matches the new models. The company then proceeds to implement the software across the organization.

Even though this modeling strategy has occasionally met with success, more often than not it has failed simply because of the large amounts of time, manpower, and resources such a process consumes. In creating new process designs from scratch, companies often miscalculate the cost not only of reinventing new processes but also of finding software solutions that match. Moreover, modeling runs the substantial risks of having the new designs supported by poor software tools and systems. Many companies have had to scrap their entire process design work simply because their information system software could not support the new design. Thus, acting on behalf of company uniqueness, the company discovers late in the process that its newly created models have failed simply because they are too unique, unable to be supported by current technology.

In its study of the importance of business modeling for SAP™ R/3™ implementations, TCM found that, contrary to the marketing and developmental strategy pursued by SAP™ at that time, customers felt that, because of the array of methodologies and tools available in the marketplace, modeling was difficult, cumbersome, and complicated, and it often resulted in slower, inefficient implementations. As Andreas Bienz of Ascom Hasler AG, explains: "We used an off-the-shelf model in the first phase and the R/3™ Reference Model in the second phase. Implementation was considerably faster and easier in the second phase."

The argument for blueprinting is that the best way to optimize a company's processes is to focus not on those areas that are generic or common to businesses in similar industries, but on those areas that are unique to individual companies. In the blueprint strategy, the company begins its business design with the blueprint and then matches its company structures accordingly. In the initial stages of this process, the company focuses solely on its own competitive advantage; it looks for areas in which it is special and then finds ways to optimize those processes. In blueprinting, these special areas, rather than those that are generic, are the focus. The generic areas can be found readily in the templates, which are based on ideal instances of particular business processes. By quickly mapping the generic parts of a business with the Business Blueprint, companies are better able to focus on the crucial areas of the business. For instance, a mail order business may feel that its two strategic advantages are speed of delivery and order risk management. Thus, it would want to focus on the "rush order" business process and functions such as the "credit limit check" process scenario in R/3™.

It makes little sense to reinvent the wheel over and over again, which is exactly what happens when companies invest their time and energy modeling generic processes. Rather than incur the risks of creating poor models, companies are better advised to make use of templates and then configure their software system to order. Configure-to-order is a visionary concept founded on the belief that blueprints can be built for major business-process areas and mapped to business software. It essentially entails reducing the R/3™ system at customer sites to suit individual functionality requirements. This philosophy has the advantages of consuming less time, costs, and manpower while utilizing the knowledge and experience contained in the templates.

Given the preferable results of blueprinting, we shall explore this strategy further by examining the actual process of implementing a blueprint, in this case, the SAP™ Business Blueprint. The primary activities of implementation are:

- Compiling a list of the processes that are important for a company's competitive advantage using the Business Blueprint as a template
- Redlining parts of the Business Blueprint so that specific needs are clearly defined
- Comparing what has been selected (redlined) with company objectives
- Identifying areas not sufficiently covered in the Business Blueprint and then developing customized models, using the Blueprint as a guide

The remainder of this chapter will explore the main implementation issues and strategies involved in using the Business Blueprint to configure a new business design.

3.1   STANDARD SOFTWARE IMPLEMENTATION ISSUES

In any business endeavor, the value of a project blueprint is felt most strongly during the initial stages of implementation. This is especially true of SAP™'s Business Blueprint, which not only provides a common starting point—and language—for all project team members but also enables quicker training and facilitates better understanding of the system.

Such capabilities help overcome problems commonly associated with standard software implementation. When companies select a standard software, the following problem areas typically develop:

- The business processes supported by the software are not documented.
- The company's existing business processes are inadequately known and/or documented.
- No procedure exists for designing business processes.
- The target concept is unknown or not documented.

The SAP™ Business Blueprint helps companies solve the above challenges in three ways.

First, during the first phase, when the main goal is to learn about the R/3™ system, the Blueprint helps convey a comprehensive picture of how R/3™ supports business processes. The Blueprint contains the set of processes that R/3™ supports, using the very clear process description language of EPCs (see Chapter 2).

Second, the Blueprint can be used as a tool for evaluating R/3™. In order to communicate how their organization works, a company must document their own processes. With the Blueprint, they do not have to start from scratch. The Blueprint builds on the best-business processes taken from SAP™'s extensive practical knowledge of numerous industries. Because projects often include team members who have no training or experience in using or modeling business processes, the Blueprint can also improve people's understanding through graphical models. With the aid of the Blueprint, it's possible to describe a company's current situation, identify weaknesses in how structures and processes are currently organized, analyze how many required functions are found in R/3™, and identify alternatives for optimizing business processes.

Finally, a main use of the Blueprint is to illustrate business, organizational, and technical concepts during R/3™ introduction. During the planning stage, a company's engineering project team draws up a rough picture of the company's current situation and uses that view to create a target situation for use with the R/3™ system. This stage lays the foundation for the rest of the implementation phase. Using the Blueprint to implement R/3™ offers a consistent, systematic approach.

In sum, the Business Blueprint meets the aforementioned BE challenges by:

- Documenting standard software processes
- Making it easier for companies to document existing business processes
- Developing procedures for designing business processes
- Designing and documenting a "final state" of desired business processes

3.2   MAPPING WITH THE BUSINESS BLUEPRINT

The Business Blueprint with its industry templates—an integrated compilation of common business functions performed in a variety of industries and supported in the R/3™ system—enables users to select new business processes, match theirs with those in the system, and configure company models. A company can also use the Business Blueprint to obtain a quick analysis of business processes contained in R/3™. Companies can simply print out the lists and matrices of processes found in R/3™ for each business area, select the processes they use and cross out the ones they don't, visualize value chains as EPCs, and generally determine the degree of system and process integration offered by R/3™.

One of the primary capabilities of the Blueprint is that it can help identify a company's organizational structure and how it can be optimized with R/3™, a process known as mapping. The two most important considerations for this phase of implementation are the people who actually make up the project team and the process of identifying business objects and processes.

The success of mapping largely depends on a good mix of people on the project team. The functional viewpoint of individual departments should not be allowed to dominate. Rather, the team should consist of work groups of people responsible for the processes in each business area: purchasing, sales, warehouse, accounting, and so forth. A good mix prevents the proliferation of unnecessary process variants by consolidating their use within individual areas. It's not uncommon to find a number of special solutions used in different departments to deal with the same problem (such as handling orders or purchase requisitions). By working in a team, the key people in each area or department can codevelop necessary process variants. Cooperation ensures that special solutions are created only when necessary.

The mapping process involves identifying the business objects and processes. Whereas business processes are well known, business objects require further elaboration. Business objects have two main objectives: They contain data structures that are linked to other business objects, and they are used to perform business methods. For example, some of the main business objects in a company would include purchase requisitions, orders, vendor quotations, and invoices. Business objects are important for integrating systems because they show how parts of an older "legacy" system can be integrated with a new one.

The Business Blueprint provides a starting point for understanding how the company may wish to develop new processes that align with key strategic areas. Here, the goal is to align the business processes identified in the Blueprint with the company's current situation.

The team may document the most important business processes and their links to one another, along with their control flows and organizational responsibilities. The deepest level of company-specific details—such as which fields should be used in a given screen—can only be defined and described by prototyping or studying the R/3™ documentation and customizing capabilities. A process diagram cannot illustrate all of the information needed to identify a solution for a given task, but the complete R/3™ documentation can be accessed from CD-ROM, providing additional information about details not visible in the graphic model.

Process changes that have the greatest impact on future handling and organizational responsibilities should be documented to show the removal of existing weaknesses (IT gaps, organizational fragmentation, data redundancies, inadequate system support, etc.) and provide the basis for managerial decisions. Documentation of changes in planned tasks, processes, and distribution of new responsibilities should also be used during user training to aid in the understanding of new business processes within R/3™.

In sum, the Blueprint is a good starting point for implementation because of its ability to identify and break down business processes into well-defined, manageable areas. It also has a number of other important benefits. First, those involved in the project share the same overview of the company's organization and specialized jargon. This shared view helps promote better understanding among team members of both the R/3™ system and the company's specific needs and makes it easier for the team to identify and choose those business processes that come closest to the company's target idea of BE. Second, the project team can spot problem areas or weak points within the Blueprint. They can, for example, identify company-specific or redundant tasks, discover missing but needed IT support, spot organizational breaks, or isolate points where information flows awkwardly. Third, decision makers can clearly see what changes must be made to reach business design goals. Such changes might include alterations in organizational structure, business processes, or the flow of information between functional areas. Finally, and perhaps most importantly, the Blueprint helps a company identify clearly what is strategic—that is, those areas that contribute directly to a company's competitive advantage—and what is generic—that is, those areas that can be found readily in the Blueprint's industry templates.

3.3   REDLINING THE BLUEPRINT

Redlining a business process with the Blueprint typically involves going through the directory of business processes and picking out the processes the company believes are most applicable and discarding those that are not. Redlining, as the term suggests, usually requires following through the process with a red pen and highlighting each important or required part. For correct process selection, certain important information should be gathered. First, the structure of the organization or company needs to be depicted in chart form, showing the responsibilities and tasks of various organizational units. Second, the processes, routines, and procedures currently in practice must be clearly represented. Finally, the way information flows through functional areas of the company should be depicted in chart form. The project team must ascertain which parts of a business process are needed and which can be discarded from the business process.

After a business-process chain has been designed with links to upstream and downstream processes, the next task is to completely describe the business processes. Here, the project team can study incoming and outgoing information objects to functions or tasks. Most importantly, the team identifies which organizational units in the system are involved. These will reveal which organizational arrangements are possible in R/3™. Finally, after the company's organizational units are aligned with the SAP™ organizational units of R/3™, the processes are selected from the Business Blueprint.

Business processes are made up of functions and events. Functions often have certain attributes that help with an understanding of the use, context, and necessity. Business processes should be grouped together according to their attributes. Attributes can be assigned such designations as the release identifier of functions, stipulation of "mandatory" functions, and stipulation of "optional" functions. If an optional function isn't needed, it can be turned off without affecting the overall business process. Target functions and events can also be assigned attributes to capture details about processes. For example, these attributes might include the following: quantity data; time and labor data (used for capturing throughput, delay, processing, and transmission times within a process); cost data; processing type (on-line, batch, automatic, manual, etc.); and an assessment of how well functional needs are met (good, so-so, poor).

The project team may also create a function tree from the available information and define how information is exchanged between applications. Business objects, data models, and interaction diagrams show the relationships among individual areas, including exchanged information objects (information flows) and communication flows among organizational units. The team may also check the information flow relationships of the Business Blueprint to ensure that all important information objects are transferred between functional areas. If any information objects are missing from the identified "current" business situation because they are not included as standard features of R/3™, they can be added (see Section 3.4). Ultimately, when business processes and information flows are matched up with the R/3™ system, they serve as a foundation for reorganizing procedures, routines, and processes.

Finally, the team may evaluate how well functional and organizational units match up and adjust them accordingly. Once all of the responsibilities of a given organizational unit have been examined, functions can be sensibly regrouped and assigned to the right organizational units.

3.4   EXTENDING THE BUSINESS-PROCESS DESIGN

If there are some special needs, strategic areas, or new functions needed, the company may choose to extend the business-process design. The organizational units of R/3™ are flexible enough to allow mapping of many different company structures. Sometimes, however, a company's organizational structure can't be mapped to SAP™'s units. To help users spot this problem during the early part of planning, a graphical model of the SAP™ organizational units and their relationships with another is provided in the Business Blueprint.

When ascertaining if any new business-process designs must be added, three crucial questions must be answered:

1. Does the selected Business Blueprint process include all of the functions of the company's corresponding business process? If any task cannot be mapped into a corresponding function in the Business Blueprint, it must be added.

2. Would adding any new tasks improve the business process? If so, these tasks should also be selected. For example, the standard order-processing routine in the Business Blueprint makes it possible for a company to:
   - Directly reference a quotation already stored in the system when entering a new one
   - Make distinctions between different business individuals—for example, goods recipients and invoice recipients
   - Immediately send instructions to the warehouse or plant to supply the materials needed to fill a standard order by a certain date
   - Immediately inform a customer by mail, telex, fax, or EDI of an order acknowledgment or rejection

3. Are any functions unnecessary? If so, they are simply deleted. If a company, for example, doesn't sell any batch-managed materials or does not need route finding, these functions can be eliminated from the Blueprint process "standard order processing."

These three questions help analyze identified problem areas, weak points, and proposed changes. Once they have been identified, the new design of a company is developed by selecting from, modifying, and adding to the Business Blueprint wherever necessary. The overriding aim of this project phase is to set up and document a system prototype in preparation for actual production use.

Configuration of business processes is extremely flexible. Many parameters with vast ranges of possible combinations are available, allowing fine-tuning of business processes when needed. The flexibility to make new or modified business processes quickly in R/3™ reduces the time and work involved in implementation projects.

When the detailed design and implementation phase is complete, the last phase before launching the system begins: preparing for production startup. The main activities in this phase are:

- Create user documentation
- Perform integration test
- Train users

Because user documentation is an active part of R/3™, users have access to its most up-to-date version. User documentation is based on the business-process models already documented and on the screen sequences recorded while building the R/3™ prototype. All that remains to be added are more detailed explanations of how to use the system.

Implementation Case Studies

A few case studies may make the above discussion clearer. We will first provide a hypothetical example of how a company might use the Business Blueprint to optimize its business processes. We then move on to cite actual examples of companies' experiences using the Blueprint.

Hypothetical Example

While mapping its processes with the Blueprint, Company B defines five organizational units involved in handling customer orders. The project team discovers, however, an organizational break between the tasks "accept order" and "analyze order." This break occurs, they find, because the department responsible for order entry enters customer orders without performing any checks beforehand. The department that deals with order processing decides whether an order should be accepted and, if so, under what terms. Only then can an order acknowledgment be sent to the customer.

The project team finds that the one or two days needed to send the order via in-house mail from the order-entry department to the order-processing department has a serious impact on the total time needed to handle an order. The existing setup doesn't meet the goal of optimum customer service because customers have to wait too long to receive an order acknowledgment.

The team also learns of another weakness involving IT support. The task "analyze order" is carried out with the support of the customer-order management system. But this system doesn't allow the order-processing department access to data on current or planned material stocks. Consequently, the order-processing department can't give customers a delivery date for the ordered item.

In Company B, the warehouse must keep a very large amount of stock on hand to ensure the ability to deliver, despite short-term changes in incoming customer orders. If it's impossible to service a particular customer order on time, the order-processing department doesn't learn about it until it's too late. When the shipping department attempts to put together the shipment, it may find that the needed materials aren't in the warehouse. To make matters worse, there's no way to notify a customer before such a bottleneck occurs. That, of course, hurts the goal of optimum customer service as well.

Aligning the business processes, business objects, and organizational units with R/3™ will pose no problem for the hypothetical company. Its organizational units and SAP™'s can be simply and directly lined up in R/3™. In our hypothetical Company B, for example, the R/3™ system eliminates all of the weak points identified in customer order handling. Organizational breaks in processing orders and invoices also disappear because R/3™'s integration reduces manual entry work to a minimum.

This organizational change also has a positive impact on the throughput time of the overall process because time is not lost waiting for the in-house mail service to deliver documents (which, as we saw, amounted to one to two days lost). Consequently, the company can acknowledge customer orders by mail, fax, or EDI immediately after the orders are received and accepted. Thus, R/3™ helps the company achieve optimum customer service.

In addition, the break in IT support during processing is also eliminated because of R/3™'s integration of sales, production planning, and warehouse management. Item availability and delivery dates can be checked during the processing of a standard order, offering immediate information about whether or not the customer order can be filled. Distribution requirements and material planning requirements—which result from the customer order—are also available at the same time, which is important for achieving the corporate goal of "reducing warehouse costs." Stock-on-hand can be reduced without sacrificing the ability to deliver quickly. If it is impossible to meet delivery deadlines (perhaps because of a problem in a production plant), the situation is quickly reflected in the updated overview of stocks and requirements. It's always possible to let customers know right away about a delay.

reflected in the updated overview of stocks and requirements. It's always possible to let customers know right away about a delay.

The break between the processing of a customer order and the preparation of an invoice is also a thing of the past. "Customer order" was automatically added to the delivery slip and invoice. Ultimately, the company can now complete customer invoices as soon as a delivery is processed instead of waiting one or two days for the various departments to process them.

Real-Life Example: Schwarzkopf

With integrated information about objects, processes, and organizations, the Blueprint significantly benefited Schwarzkopf, a leading healthcare products firm based in Hamburg, Germany and active in more than 100 countries world-wide. Schauma and Taft, two of the company's most successful and well-known haircare products, are made and sold in a number of European countries. As the company prepared to reengineer, Schwarzkopf used the Business Blueprint to test quickly whether the R/3™ sales logistics could replace the company's own homegrown software.

A main question facing the project team was whether the R/3™ sales and distri-bution application could handle the company's domestic invoicing system. Time was an important factor, too, as the company wanted to make a quick decision. Schwarzkopf wanted to replace its outdated mainframe system with a UNIX-based client/server solution and had already started to migrate from its existing operational systems—for the most part, SAP™ R/2™ programs—to R/3™ applications.

Utilizing a mainframe approach in the past, Schwarzkopf had developed its own system for domestic invoicing. But now the company wanted to tackle these tasks in a fundamentally different, more efficient manner. The alternatives were either to develop a new program from scratch or to implement the R/3™ sales and distribution application. The company needed to decide quickly, or it would have to maintain its outdated hardware environment for another year.

Because a variety of user departments took part in the decision-making process from the outset, the team required a model that explained the functionality of the R/3™ system in business terms, avoided technical jargon, and offered deci-sion support. The Business Blueprint fit the bill with clear, easy-to-understand business language and descriptions of business processes.

To begin the evaluation, a project team was set up, consisting of three Schwarz-kopf employees and two SAP™ consultants. This mix of skills and knowledge ideally suited the job at hand. From that point on, the Business Blueprint essen-tially guided the project activities.

As we saw earlier, for each application area, the Blueprint provides a complete directory of business processes, a function tree, and a process selection matrix covering all R/3™ business processes. At Schwarzkopf, these function trees were taken as the basis for selecting the processes that were most important for the company.

The process selection matrices indicated that the project should concentrate on the core process of standard order handling. All of the associated processes were examined by comparing them with EPCs contained in the Business Blueprint. Each process was redlined to determine the extent to which these pre-defined EPCs modeled it, with the ultimate aim of finding out whether the functionality of the R/3™ sales and distribution (SD) application met Schwarzkopf's needs. Customized solutions were sought only for processes that weren't adequately modeled, the goal being to offer users standard software that would be roughly equivalent to something the company might have developed itself.

Time-to-market is a competitive factor in today's business environment. Schwarzkopf's management and project team opted for moving quickly. They decided a Blueprint could result in faster implementation. Thus, the project team recommended implementing the SD application at Schwarzkopf.

Instead of having to start from scratch, the project team was able to build on an existing knowledge base, saving a lot of time in the process. The Blueprint's EPCs provided an objective basis for reconciling actual business practices at Schwarzkopf with the functionality of the R/3™ system. Drawing on the feasibility study, Schwarzkopf is now using the Business Blueprint to implement sales and distribution, focusing on the redlined blueprint and user documentation. The company also wants to take advantage of graphical depiction of business processes to pinpoint ways to reshape them for enhanced efficiency.

"If you use the Business Blueprint as a discussion basis, you always know what you're talking about. Communication with the user departments becomes more constructive and effective," says project manager Nicolay Ketelsen.

Real-Life Example: Conoco Ltd.

Conoco Ltd.'s Humber Refinery in Britain provides a prime example of how to implement a new business-process design using the Business Blueprint. Since the oil products refinery was commissioned in 1969–70, the plant has undergone continuous expansion and upgrading of its facilities. Today, the Humber Refinery is regarded as one of the most efficient and modern in the world and with R/3™ now in place, is completely integrated for the first time in company history.

As part of its R/3™ implementation project, Conoco decided to use the Business Blueprint to document the conceptual design of the future system. Before Conoco started the R/3™ project, the company had already completed an "as is" analysis of its organization and business processes with another modeling tool.

Margaret Buck, the Humber Refinery's change management team leader, says, "We wish we had the Business Blueprint earlier in the project. Looking at SAP™'s best-business practices would have saved us time and we would have had a consistent and especially an easy method of process capture from the beginning."

According to team leaders, Conoco's project team also found the Blueprint uncomplicated and requiring little training. "It was very easy to use," explains Derrick Hall, R/3™ project manager. "When we needed more detailed textual description, we triggered the R/3™ documentation directly from the Reference Model. The links between processes in the Business Blueprint and the R/3™ manuals on CD-ROM proved to be very helpful. This approach saved us a lot of resources because each project member could learn the system quite quickly."

In addition to mapping out the international company's target concept and process models, the Blueprint was employed in companywide R/3™ training. According to Buck, the idea behind R/3™ training was to make the information gained from the Blueprint available for many different uses. For example, when project team leaders used the Business Blueprint to connect the authorization levels needed to perform a routine in the system, they also documented that process chain in training materials. In fact, each stage of the project was appropriately documented for, and then later used to produce, employee training materials containing graphic models of different business-process chains and links to other business areas. Now, in addition to reading a manual about the R/3™ system, end users can look at a diagram of what they are supposed to do.

"We wanted them to have an appreciation of all the different processes and to be able to see how they affect someone else down the line," Buck explains.

Future training will also reflect the Humber Refinery's new integration. For example, the Finance and Materials Management departments will learn the system together. "Previously, we did the training by function," says Buck. "But we plan to do workshop training with mixed groups to build on the knowledge of what one group does and how it affects others so everyone will have an appreciation of the integration aspect."

3.5   CONCLUSION

When implementing standard software, companies are no longer faced with the choice of either giving up their individual requirements or investing time and money to write custom solutions. Instead, companies can draw on the wide range of standard business models contained in the R/3™ Business Blueprint to meet the specific needs of their business.

The Blueprint provides an extensive collection of business processes and their variants, integrated across functional areas. The variants provide enormous latitude for shaping business processes. The business practices supported in

R/3™ are described in the Blueprint, which enables customers to easily visualize and analyze different business solutions before deciding whether to use or purchase R/3™. As many SAP™ customers have already found, the logistical connections in R/3™ between areas such as sales and distribution, procurement, and production planning optimize the companywide integration of business processes. With the powerful integration of logistical operations in R/3™, corporate planners can now exploit the technology of open application systems to shape their business processes more efficiently. The large scope of logistical and business-processes scenarios that are contained in the Business Blueprint are the subject of Part 2.

PART 2

Process
Design

4

Value Chain Thinking

The best aspects of the R/3™ information management system lie in the ability to integrate all business processes and areas. This cross-functional integration allows R/3™ to avoid the pitfalls of traditional hierarchical and function-oriented structures, which too often obstruct the informational flows of businesses and severely inhibit a company's ability to seize on its competitive advantage. From sales and distribution to production planning, R/3™ incorporates logistical and operational areas into an integrated workflow of business events. Figure 4-1 illustrates the structural differences.

All tasks along the business value chain—from production planning to capital asset management—are planned, controlled, and coordinated across business areas. Designed to improve and speed up the flow of information, the R/3™ system automatically links together logistically and operationally related areas, eliminating the need to repeat time and resource-intensive procedures. By inte-

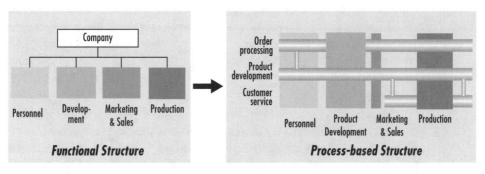

▶ **Figure 4–1**   Functional versus process-based structure

grating such important value activity areas as finance or human resources, businesses make themselves more effective and efficient.

This chapter introduces the main logistical and operational scenarios found in R/3 ™. In the following chapters, we will examine key scenarios in the value activity areas:

- Sales and distribution
- Production planning
- Procurement
- Financial accounting
- Business planning and controlling
- Organization and human resources management
- Capital asset management
- Finance management
- Customer service

In this and subsequent chapters, the discussion of these areas will be followed by examples of companies that have benefited significantly from the optimization of their business processes.

4.1   THE VALUE CHAIN PRINCIPLE

The concept of the value chain was popularized by Harvard Business School professor Michael E. Porter, who describes the value chain as a tool for ascertaining a company's competitive advantage. According to Porter, every firm can be understood as a collection of activities that range from the design, marketing, delivery, and support of a product. The value chain breaks these activities down to strategically relevant categories "in order to understand the behavior of cost and the existing and potential sources of differentiation".[1] By so considering each activity within a company in terms of the value chain, a firm can isolate potential sources of its competitive advantage.

Value activities fall under two generic categories, primary and support activities (see Figure 4-2). Primary activities constitute the physical production of the product, the sale and transfer to the buyer, and post-sales help, assistance, and so forth. Primary activities are grouped under five broad categories:

---

1.   .Michael E. Porter, Competitive Advantage (New York: The Free Press, 1985).

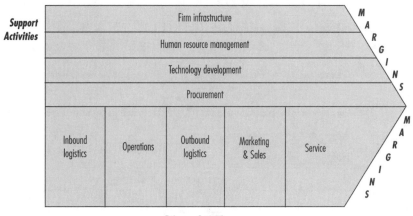

Figure 4–2 Porter's Generic Value Chain

- Inbound logistics (inventory control, vehicle scheduling, returns to supplier, etc.)
- Outbound logistics (collecting, order processing, delivery vehicle operation, scheduling, etc.)
- Operations (machining, packaging, assembly, etc.)
- Marketing and sales (advertising, promotion, quoting, etc.)
- Service (installation, repair, training, etc.)

Support activities bolster the primary activities and each other by providing purchased inputs, human resources, and some form of technology to perform a given function. Porter divides support activities into four areas: procurement, technology development, human resource management, and firm infrastructure. The first three can be associated with specific primary activities, or they can support the entire chain. Firm infrastructure obviously supports only the entire chain rather than a particular primary activity.

Everything that a company does can be categorized into primary and support activities. Starting with these generic value chain categories, a firm can then further subdivide each into discrete activities, categorizing those activities that contribute best to a firm's competitive advantage. In this way, a value chain (Figure 4-3) is defined, and a better organization structure can then be created around those value activities that can most improve a company's competitive advantage.

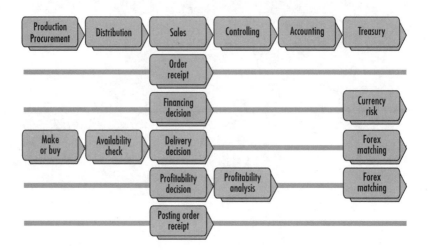

▶ **Figure 4–3**   Value Chains integrate primary and secondary business activities.

4.2   *R/3*™ *AND THE VALUE CHAIN*

The SAP™ strategy is to integrate all business operations in an overall system for planning, controlling, and monitoring a given business. This integration allows companies to restructure business activities along the value chain and hence help seize on their competitive advantage. To help facilitate the restructuring of company processes according to the value chain principle, SAP™ has included over 800 best business practices or scenarios in the Business Blueprint. These scenarios provide logical models for the optimization of specific business processes and can be modeled around primary and support value activities. For example, SAP™ provides detailed scenarios of such primary activities as materials management, sales and logistics, purchasing, and the like. Support activities include human resources management, business planning and controlling, capital asset management, and so on.

The process scenarios are based on best business practices that reflect the experiences, suggestions, and demands of leading companies from a wide range of industries. These industries include automotive, banking, chemical and pharmaceutical, high-tech and electronics, health care, consumer goods, oil and gas, telecommunications, utilities, and so on. (See the Introduction for a more complete list.)

With their integrated design, the R/3 ™ logistics applications are especially effective for the streamlining of value activities. Logistics encompasses most primary activities, ranging from sales and distribution, production planning, materials, and quality management to plant maintenance. All functions in the logistics chain between sales and distribution, procurement, production, warehousing, and the like, are planned, controlled, and coordinated across all business areas. Since the SAP ™ system automatically links logically related areas, it eliminates the need to repeat time- and resource-intensive procedures. In addition, R/3 ™ logistics applications can be integrated with other operational or support activities. Logistics, financials, and human resources merge to provide a tightly integrated structure, creating a streamlined value chain and a more effective organizational flow.

4.3 *OVERVIEW OF PART 2: VALUE CHAIN THINKING*

In Part 2 of this book, we will provide a single example of a streamlined value chain, as illustrated in Figure 4-4. Our value chain will cover events from the request of an order to the delivery of the product to the customer. Chapters 5–8 examine the primary value activities, and Chapters 9–11 explain the support activities.

Chapter 5 begins the process with a sales and logistics example, in which a customer requests an order and the request is checked on in the logistical area

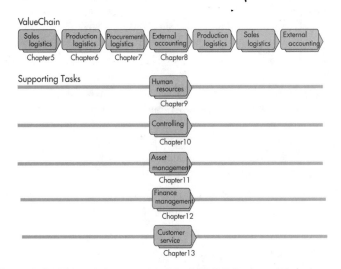

▶ **Figure 4–4**   Value chain example of the SAP R/3 Business Blueprint

for the feasibility of the request. In Chapter 6, we assume that the order is accepted and move on to produce the order. In our example, we need to buy certain components from a vendor to fulfill the customer request, which leads us to Chapter 7, procurement. Procurement involves choosing the vendor and having the vendor send us the required components, which then go into the production of the end product (or whatever is to be sent to the customer). Because we have to pay for this component, we then move on to Chapter 8, external accounting.

Obviously, the chain isn't perfectly linear but has links back to the previous scenarios, which will help get the product delivered to the customer. After external accounting takes care of our vendor, for example, we would then return to the production logistics scenario, where we would produce or assemble the different components according to the customer's specifications. We would then ship the end product to the customer, which involves the sales area again. Finally, we would return to external accounting once more to ensure customer payment.

This value chain is supported by other links, the aforementioned supporting activities. We will describe those that would likely impact the product during our process of delivering the product to the customer. Chapter 9 covers organization and human resources; Chapter 10 discusses business planning and controlling; and Chapter 11 examines capital asset management, including planning, new equipment, and/or technology. Finally, Chapters 12 and 13 take a look at finance management and customer service.

NOTE Before we move on, a word about reading the scenarios. After introducing the main scenarios in a given business process, this and each subsequent chapter then proceed with a detailed explanation of only the first scenario. Even here, given the vast number of tasks, events, and organizations involved, we can cover only so much ground. In Figure 4-5, for example, the left side describes links from a purchase requisition scenario found in procurement. In reality, a number of tasks, events, and so on, can occur "behind" each link. The shaded area of Figure 4-5 shows, for example, what the task purchase requisition assignment actually involves. Because of this complexity, at times we will refer to tasks, events, or functions that are not included in the detailed diagram of the first scenario. These diagrams, then, should be read only as general maps of the detailed scenario. We will direct the reader to the figure whenever applicable.

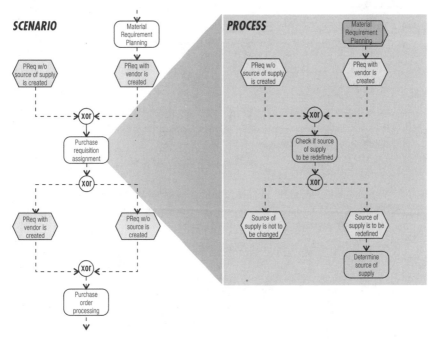

▶ **Figure 4–5**   Value Chain Scenario Process

Value Chain: Order-to-Delivery of Copy Machines

To better illustrate this value chain process at work, let's take a copy machine producer as an example. Let us suppose that a customer, responding from a product presentation, approaches a sales person and requests a quote for 50 custom-made copy machines. The sales person creates a quotation on the basis of this inquiry. With the customer's acceptance of the quotation, the salesperson creates a sales order document, in which he documents the customer's demand, prices the order, and checks both customer credit and material availability.

The salesperson then goes to the production logistics area, submits the customer's order and finds out when he can deliver it. Because each copy machine has various different components, such as toner cartridges, glass cases, plastic paper trays, and so on, the copy machine company must undergo a degree of production planning. In production planning, a decision is made on what part of the product needs to be produced internally and what needs to be purchased from third-party vendors. In this example, the company decides to purchase the glass cases and paper holder trays from vendors.

For these purchases, the company moves on to the procurement area, where a decision is made on which vendor or vendors will be used. In procurement, a Request for Quotation (RFQ) is created and issued to a number of vendors. After the bidding process takes place, a vendor is chosen. A date is then set for delivery of the glass and paper holder trays components from the vendor to the copy machine company. Paying the vendors involves external accounting. External accounting handles all invoices, payment schedules, and so on, needed to pay the vendors for their products.

Once the necessary components arrive, the copy machine company then assembles the product, which returns us to the production logistics area. Fifty copy machines are produced and sent to the customer. Finally, such activities as following up on payment for the product or making quality service checks are handled by external accounting.

Of course, during this whole manufacturing process, a number of support activities have been occurring "behind the scenes." Human resources management has obtained the required work force on the basis of quantity, quality, time, and location, as well as optimizing human performance. Corporate planning and controlling has taken care of all activities required for cost and revenue accounting. Finally, capital asset management has looked after all tasks relating to the project planning, provision, administration, and plant maintenance of operating facilities (assets).

Value Chain: Applied Micro Circuits Corporation (AMCC), San Diego, California

Applied Micro Circuits Corporation employs 350 people and has six regional sales offices as well as sales representatives worldwide. The company develops, manufactures, and markets application-specific standard products (ASSPs) and application-specific integrated circuits (ASICs) for the communications, computer, instrumentation, and military industries. AMCC products are highly technical and custom configured, requiring the company to maintain close contact with customers throughout the product development process.

Customer service and integrating processes in sales and distribution and production were the two main reasons behind AMCC's reengineering effort. Explains Buck Marty, vice president for business services at the high-tech firm: "Our customers don't get much lead time from their customers. They need rapid response times without carrying huge quantities of inventory. They want us to provide plenty of added value—from a technical and service standpoint—and at the same time deliver competitive pricing. We wanted to modify our processes to meet our customers' needs by, for example, reengineering the book-to-ship cycle for more responsiveness to the customer."

To meet the needs of its customers, the company has to manage a complex logistical chain—more than 100 customers, many different product types, and many different combinations of parts for those products. AMCC targeted information technology to help it reengineer its complex chain of processes.

"Our solution was to implement a corporate-wide approach to information, so that whether the information is engineering-, business-, or financial-related, people can access it easily and make the right decisions quickly. That meant introducing a common operating system, common data access, complete integration, and a very user-friendly interface," Marty says. AMCC chose SAP™'s business solution software for the R/3™ client/server environment and used the SAP™ blueprint during implementation to see how information could best flow through every aspect of the business, from financials to production planning to sales and distribution.

"With our original process, when an order came in, customer service would check with production control to see when it could commit to delivering the product," Marty explains. "Production control would then talk with manufacturing, work out a schedule and communicate it back to customer service, which would then contact the customer." R/3™ allowed AMCC to eliminate this time-consuming and convoluted process, and now the company can respond to customer inquiries immediately and online.

Marty continues, "We had already decided before we selected R/3™ that we wanted to reengineer our processes. R/3™ has facilitated that for us. Because of its integrated nature, it demands that you break down functional and organizational barriers within a company. It makes you think of doing things in the most efficient way, not the most functionally traditional. The key thing is that the system is so integrated. For example, sales and distribution are completely integrated with materials management and production planning. That's the number-one reason everything happens so effectively."

5

Sales Logistics

In the past, manufacturers controlled the marketplace by determining the price, quality, specifications, and delivery parameters of their products. Companies were organized as isolated departments, each dedicated to specific fulfillment functions along the value chain. Under a top-down, command-and-control philosophy, isolated departments optimized their own individual functions along the chain. This system rarely incorporated customer demands into the rigidly defined departmental structures. Rather, the system functioned by aligning customer expectations with the manufacturer's or distributor's structures and procedures. Today's customers demand that products be designed and built to their specifications and be delivered according to their terms. The isolated departmental approach simply will not work in the current environment of increased demands for product quality, massive product proliferation, and ever-shrinking lead times.

To meet these demands, companies are adopting the "customer-centric model," which unites the activities of the company around its customers' needs. They are engineering-efficient business processes to coordinate all activities that generate and satisfy customer demand. Optimal order management systems are also uniting customers with the company's internal operations (such as logistics, manufacturing, and accounting). The sales logistics business-process scenario in R/3™ allows users to so manage sales and distribution activities in an effective manner. The business processes include scenarios for sales, shipping, billing, sales support, and sales information. With real-time, online access to sales information, such tasks as order entry, delivery, and billing are all streamlined. In addition, sales and distribution can be integrated with procurement and production planning, improving turnaround time up and down the value chain.

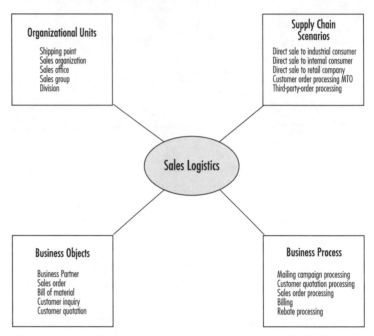

▶ Figure 5–1   Overview of scenario, process, organization, and business objects

The business-process scenarios in sales and distribution that we consider here are represented in the following activities: handling of standard orders, contracts and scheduling agreements, third-party orders, customer consignment stock, and others. This chapter offers a detailed overview of the standard order handling scenario, followed by a look at other main processes found in sales and distribution. Figure 5-1 illustrates the main sales logistics scenarios discussed in this chapter. Also included are the core processes, business objects, and organizational units that are part of the sales and distribution business process.

5.1   STANDARD ORDER HANDLING SCENARIO

In R/3 ™ parlance, a standard order is a document representing a one-time customer demand for products within standard delivery and accounting parameters. This scenario manages the following activities: 1) helping a customer decide what to buy; 2) processing customer orders; 3) coordinating delivery and related logistics; and 4) producing customer invoices. These are represented in Figure 5-2, which shows a general outline of how the standard order handling process

▶ **Figure 5–2** Value chain: Direct sale to an industrial customer

flows. First, the sales support helps acquire a prospective customer through some marketing channel. Next, the sales process creates various inquiries and ultimately processes the sales order. Credit management conducts credit limit checks, guarantees for open receivables, and generally oversees risk management. Shipping controls deliveries and issues goods. Warehouse management oversees stock placement and removal. Quality management provides the necessary controls for quality assurance, including inspections and checks of deliveries and returns. Transportation involves planning, shipping deadlines, means of transport, and assigning routes. If the shipment involves an international customer, then Foreign Trade tacks export control and declarations to authorities. And finally, billing may take the form of an invoice, credit/debit memo, and rebate processing.

An EPC model of this scenario is illustrated by Figures 5-3 through 5-5. Figure 5-3 shows this business-process scenario beginning by recording sales activities with customers, such as phone calls, meetings, and product presentations. Direct mail campaigns can be planned and monitored. As these activities result in customer inquiries, they are recorded in the system. A quotation, valid for a specified time period, is created on the basis of this inquiry.

After customer acceptance of the quotation, a standard sales order is processed. A standard sales order can also be processed directly from a customer without a quotation. The sales order documents the customer's demand, prices the order, and checks both customer credit and material availability. The sales order function in R/3™ utilizes a configurator to select configured products as well as a "conditions" program to manage complex pricing scenarios. The sales order process sends requirements to manufacturing (Figure 5-4).

This business-process scenario integrates order handling activities with the workflow of downstream delivery and logistics operations. Logistics operations include transportation planning as well as picking, packing, and shipping of products. The credit and material availability checks made during order entry are similarly available in this workflow. As goods leave the plant or warehouse, stock and value adjustments are made in the materials management system. To complete this scenario (Figure 5-5), invoices are processed and sent to custom-

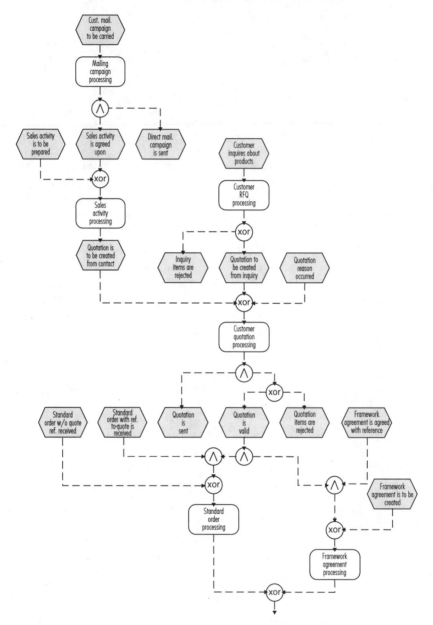

▶ **Figure 5–3**   Analyzing customer demand and creating an order

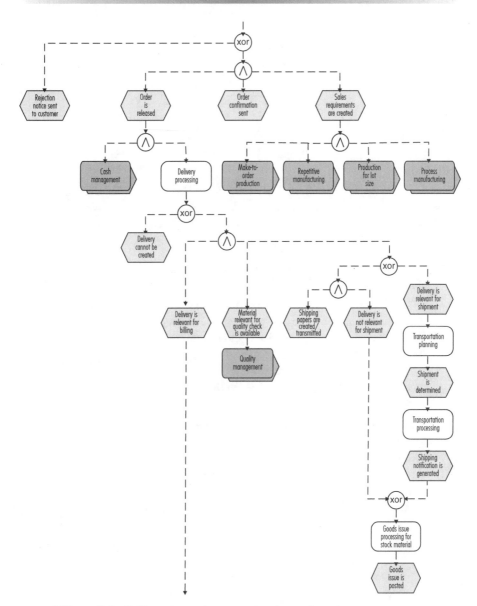

▶ **Figure 5–4** Delivery processing, transportation, and warehouse

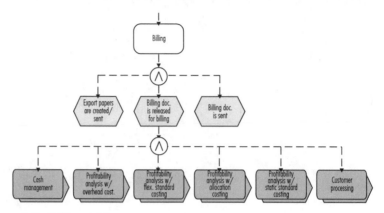

▶ **Figure 5–5**   Billing and finance

ers. The appropriate cash management, accounts receivable, and profitability systems are updated.

In the case of returned goods, for damage or other reasons, the system manages the receipt of these items and processes a credit memo. A subsequent free-of-charge delivery may be processed to replace the damaged goods. If company-owned packaging or shipping materials (e.g., pallets) are included in the original shipment, the system processes a pickup order to retrieve those materials. Damaged or lost packaging is charged to the customer.

Mailing Campaign Processing

We will now examine and link further the main tasks that comprise the standard order handling scenario as outlined in Figures 5-3 through 5-5. The first main task is mailing campaign processing. Direct mail campaigns can be created, using all of the sales information already stored in the system, such as the addresses of customers and prospective customers. Mailing campaign processing involves three events:

1. Determination of business partners: i.e., deciding which customers or prospective customers to target and making an address list
2. Initiation of correspondence: write sales letter, special offer, trade show invitation, etc.
3. Preparation of enclosures for the mailing campaign: create products sample, brochure or documentation

Once these tasks are accomplished, we can begin the mailing campaign.

Sales Activity Processing

Any kind of customer contact—a sales call, a telephone call, or sending a sales letter—is considered a sales activity. When stored as data, different kinds of sales activities can be valuable sources of information for employees in the sales department. Information about one sales activity (e.g., a direct mailing campaign) forms the basis for other sales activities (e.g., telemarketing calls).

Sales activity processing begins by determining what type of activity will take place (see Figure 5-3). Three options are possible:

- Personal—an in-person sales call
- Telephone—a phone sales call
- Written—a sales letter

One of these three kinds of sales activities will lead to the next task: determine business partners and/or a contact person. When we determine this information and enter it into the system, we can then record a description of the sales activity. For example, we may record a short comment about the activity, date and time of the activity, reason, outcome, analysis or status of the activity, and follow-up action. When the outcome of the sales activity is known, it can also be entered as data.

The outcome of sales activity leads to nine possible outcomes, some of which trigger other tasks:

- Unsuccessful sales activity
- Agreed-on follow-up sales activity
- Request for a quotation (RFQ) from the contact—triggers the task customer RFQ processing
- Quotation from the contact—triggers the task customer quotation processing
- Order from the contact—triggers the task standard order processing
- Credit or debit memo from the sales activity—triggers the task credit/debit memo request processing
- Return order from the sales activity—triggers the task returns processing
- Free-of-charge delivery from the sales activity—triggers the task free delivery processing
- Consignment sales order from the sales activity—triggers the task consignment fill-up order processing

All of the possible tasks that follow sales activity processing are included in the sales and distribution business-process scenario.

Customer RFQ Processing

As a result of the mailing campaign sales activity, a customer may inquire by mail or phone about such things as prices, terms of delivery, a description of the products, and so forth. The customer may also enter a RFQ from the company.

A quotation is an offer from a company to sell or deliver goods or services to a customer within a certain period of time and under certain conditions (prices, delivery times, terms of delivery, and material specifications). A quotation can be created with or without reference to a customer inquiry. For example, the company may want to let its customers know about a special offer or a new product. In this case, the quotation is created without reference to a customer inquiry. Alternatively, a quotation is created as a result of a customer inquiry. Inquiries and quotations provide important presales information that can be used to gauge market trends and help plan business strategies.

The task customer inquiry processing leads to two tasks: 1) determine customer inquiry business partner and 2) enter customer inquiry processing items.

These events lead to the next task: check inquiry item. Checking the inquiry item includes four possible events:

- Item is a make-to-order product.
- Item is kept in stock.
- Item is not kept in stock.
- Item is a material that can be configured.

If the last event is triggered—that is, if the item is a material that can be configured—the different parts of the material must be determined.

The next step is to edit the customer RFQ data by incorporating information from checking the inquiry item. Then, the final request for the quotation can be created. After the final request's creation, the next two steps in the chain are 1) monitor the request—because all quotations have a validity date, monitoring the request ensures that the inquiry or quotation is responded to quickly and within the relevant time period, and 2) check acceptance of the request.

The task check acceptance of the request is linked to two possible events: reject request and create quotation from the request. If the request is rejected for some reason, the request for quotation is canceled and the customer inquiry items are rejected (see Figure 5-3). If a quotation is created from the request, the next task in the chain, customer quotation processing, can begin.

Customer Quotation Processing

Both sales activity processing and customer RFQ processing are linked to the task customer quotation processing (see Figure 5-3). Under sales activity, a quotation is created from a contact. Under customer inquiry, a quotation is created because of a request. In both cases, we enter the quotation into the system, triggering the following events: 1) determination of the business partners of the quotation and 2) determination of quotation items.

Next, we ascertain the period for which the quotation is valid. This leads to the following possible steps: 1) check possible prices or taxes of item; and 2) check if item is in warehouse.

Checking the item's possible prices or taxes triggers these events: 1) item has different prices and taxes, or 2) item doesn't have different prices and taxes.

Checking the item for warehouse relevance then leads to these possible events:

- Item is a make-to-order product—two actions are possible. Consult controlling to find out how much it would cost to make the product; add that figure to the quoted prices and taxes. If the product is already in the warehouse, then determine a delivery date.
- Item is a material that cannot be configured—find out what variants of the product are available, then determine delivery date for the product.
- Determine if an availability check is required. If the goods are available, then the process can continue. If the goods are only partially available, then determine whether partial delivery is allowed.
- Item is in stock—triggers the tasks determining delivery dates and determining availability of goods.
- Item is not in stock.

After all the other tasks and related activities in the chain are completed, then we begin the task edit quotation. Editing the quotation involves entering all of the information gained about the quotation—prices, taxes, cost of custom order, delivery dates, availability of goods, determining variants, and so on—into the system. Next, the quotation is created.

Once we create the quotation and enter it into the system, three more tasks follow:

- Transfer quotation to sold-to parties
- Monitor quotation—watch to make sure that quotation is dealt with quickly and within the promised time frame
- Check validity of quotation

In the third case, check validity of quotation is the final step in customer quotation processing. If the quotation is invalid, it's rejected and the process stops. If the quotation is valid, the following four events can take place:

- Standard order processing
- Third-party order processing
- Customer contract processing
- Customer scheduling agreement processing

Standard Order Processing

When a buyer makes a sales order, he or she agrees to accept specified goods and services at specified prices and delivery dates from the seller. Sales orders can result from quotations. If an order does refer to a quotation, the quotation is binding when the validity period and terms of agreement are met.

Standard sales orders carry out normal sales transactions for a customer who orders goods. When a standard sales order is processed, the following tasks are carried out:

- Pricing
- Availability check (if this task is defined in the material master record)
- Transfer requirements to materials planning
- Shipping point and route determination
- Credit limit check

Standard order processing (see Figure 5-4) can begin when an order is placed, without connection to a quotation. In this case, the customer must be identified and then the order is entered into the system. Standard order processing is also, however, directly linked to sales activity processing and customer quotation processing:

- The sales activity processing link triggers the standard order processing when an order is created from a sales contact.
- The customer quotation processing link prompts standard order processing with a valid quotation or the placing of an order that stems from a quotation. In this case, an order arises from the quotation.

Once the order, wherever it came from, is entered into the system, the following tasks occur: 1) determine business partner, and 2) determine order items.

Next, the order must be checked for the following:

- Other prices or taxes—triggers the task carry out credit control
- Batch relevance—triggers the task check warehouse
  Note: A batch is a subset of the total quantity of material held in stock. It's managed separately from other subsets of the same material. Examples of batches are different production lots (paints, dyes, wallpapers, pharmaceutical products), delivery lots, or quality grades of material.

Checking the warehouse leads to these possible events:

- Item is a make-to-order product—two actions are possible. Consult controlling to find out how much it would cost to make the product; add that figure to the quoted prices and taxes. If the product is already in the warehouse, then determine a delivery date.
- Item is a material that can be configured—find out what variants of the product are available. Then, determine delivery date for the product.
- Item is in stock—triggers the tasks determine shipping point, determine route of the order, determine and schedule shipping dates.
- Additionally, check the availability of the order items. If the item is only partially available, first see if partial delivery is acceptable to the customer. Acceptability of partial delivery or full availability of the items triggers the task create sales requirement.
- Item is not in stock.

After all the other tasks and related activities in the chain are completed, then we initiate the task edit order.

Once they're created, the sales requirements either prompt demand management in the area of production planning or, more likely, credit control in financial accounting.

After credit control occurs, one of three tasks is possible: 1) accept order, 2) block order, or 3) refuse order.

If the order is accepted, the next step is to edit text (i.e., make changes) in the system. If the order is blocked, it must first go back to credit control before the task, edit text, can take place. If the order is refused, the customer must be told and the items on order canceled.

When orders are accepted or, for some reason, blocked, the next step is to create a standard order. Four possible actions could follow:

- Transfer order to sold-to parties
- Change or edit the blocked order

- Monitor the order
- Cancel the order

If the blocked order is edited and finally released, the task delivery processing can begin.

BUSINESS OBJECT

▶ *Sales Order*

In today's business environment a sales order can range from a standard document or form, electronic mail, or an XML document processed over the Internet. Whenever a business transaction takes place between two parties the information in the transaction has to be contained in a sales order business object. This business object contains all the information in the SAP™ system relating to a sales order. The data represents the contractual arrangement between a sales organization and a sold-to party (customer) concerning goods to be delivered or services to be rendered. A sales order contains information about prices, quantities and dates. The request is received by a sales area, which is then responsible for fulfilling the order.

The business object sales order is used as a source of information for the following types of business analysis.

Report Subject	Information Delivery
Customer	Summarizes the order quantities and values resulting from business transactions with customers
Customer analysis	Lists breakdown statistics of customer, including period, sales organization, distribution channel and division, customer, and equipment
Product allocations	Used for long- and medium-term planning of sales, production, purchasing, inventory, management, etc.
Salesperson	Contains a list of the key fields and ratios that measure the performance of sales employees
Sales material	Summarizes the order quanties and values for articles or products (material) resulting from transactions with businesss partners
Sales office	Contains the ordering activities and customer transactions by sales office and sales group

Report Subject	Information Delivery
Sales order list	Retrieves detailed information about specific sales orders
Sales organization	Summarizes the ordering activities and customer transactions by sales organization

. . . .

Delivery Processing

Several different tasks in both sales and procurement logistics can set off delivery processing. These include: standard order processing, customer contract call processing, free delivery processing, subsequent delivery processing free-of-charge, consignment fill-up order processing, consignment issue processing, returnable packaging issue processing, customer schedule agreement processing, and purchase order processing for stock transfer. It's also possible that the process begins without any reference to an order.

Standard order processing prompts delivery processing once an order is released (see Figure 5-4). The first task is to monitor the delivery date. Two events may follow: 1) delivery date takes place, or 2) delivery date doesn't take place.

When the delivery date does take place, the next task is to choose the kind of delivery. This choice involves four possibilities:

- Create without reference to an order
- Create from an individual sales order
- Create from delivery-due list (a work list made up of all sales orders and scheduling agreements that are due within a specified period of time)
- Create from stock transport order

The first choice leads to the task determine delivery items. The second choice prompts: open delivery from sales order. The third choice leads to: edit delivery due list. And the fourth choice is followed by: open delivery from stock transport order.

All of these four tasks lead to the next step: open delivery. Once opened, the following task is: carry out credit control. This task connects to finance. One of two things may now happen: credit requirements are fulfilled, or delivery can't be created.

If credit control is successful, a series of tasks follow: determine or transfer delivery route, determine serial numbers of delivery item, and, finally, check delivery items. Checking the delivery items triggers one of two events: 1) item is not in stock, or 2) item is in stock.

If the item is in stock, the next task is to determine the picking location. This leads to checking to see if the item is handled in batches or not. Three possible events follow:

- Item is handled in batches.
- Item is not handled in batches.
- Warehouse management determines delivery batch.

When the item is not batch handled, the next steps are to choose a batch and to check if batch splits are allowable. Batch splitting designates transferring a certain amount of one batch to another. These tasks lead to: determine delivery batch. Now another task in the chain can begin: check availability of delivery item. Here, two possible outcomes exist: 1) delivery items are available, or 2) delivery items are partially available.

If the items are only partially available, the next task is to see if partial delivery is allowed. This leads to: 1) correct the delivery quantity, and 2) reject the delivery item.

If the items are available or partial delivery is allowed, the following task occurs: check out use of warehouse management during picking. This task involves either picking with warehouse management or picking without warehouse management.

Picking with warehouse management involves no other tasks. Picking without warehouse management involves creating a picking list and then carrying out the picking without the help of warehouse management. Picking leads to two events: 1) delivery items are completely picked, or 2) delivery items are partially picked.

After complete picking of items, packing can take place. However, if not all of the items are picked, the results must be edited in the system. This is followed by two activities: 1) create partial delivery, or 2) create full delivery by picking again.

One task follows picking delivery items: pack delivery items. Once done, delivery information is edited, and then a delivery is created. This task triggers seven possible outcomes in sales and distribution (SD) or materials management (MM):

1. Create or transmit shipping papers (SD).
2. Check to see if billing is relevant (SD).
3. Goods issue processing for stock material (MM).
4. Batch goods issue processing (MM).
5. Consignment goods issue processing (MM).

6. Create stock transport order (SD).

7. Release scheduling agreement (SD).

It's also possible to monitor only the delivery without performing any of these tasks.

The second, third, fourth, and fifth events all lead to the task of billing in sales and distribution. In the case of the sixth event, create stock transport order, the next step is to update the order. In the seventh event, release scheduling agreement, the subsequent task is to adapt the agreement quantity.

Goods Issue Processing for Stock Material

In this segment of the logistical chain, goods issue processing for stock material comes after delivery processing in sales and distribution, as shown in Figure 5-4.

Credit control follows, with two possibilities: Either the credit limit is sufficient, or it is not. If there is enough credit, the process continues. Two options follow: post goods issue or select valuation type. If the goods issue is posted, links to project system and sales and distribution occur in the form of project update, delivery processing, local shipping, or printing of goods receipt slip.

It's also possible that warehouse management will remove the goods from storage. This leads to goods issue/removal from storage processing. Another possibility is that the warehouse isn't maintained by warehouse management. In this case, the material is simply issued.

Billing

One of the last tasks in the sales and distribution chain, billing, can be the result of several different sales and distribution functions, from delivery and returns to rebate settlement and third-party order. There is also a link to human resources when any kind of work is performed and later must be paid for. Whatever spurs billing on, the first task is to choose the type of invoice. This activity can include creating the invoice from a single document or from a billing due list. Once either is accomplished, a billing document is created.

The next task is to determine or transfer the billing prices and taxes. Two events may follow: a pro forma invoice and a billing document relevant to accounting. Here, it's possible the billing document is transmitted and then transferred, which leads to the function of project update in project system. Other tasks in other areas may also take place.

The invoice may just be monitored. It may also be checked to see if it has any connection to a volume-based rebate. Finally, controlling may take over the document for its profitability analysis, or finance may use the document for customer invoice processing.

Billing tasks and possibilities are shown in Figure 5-5.

5.2   *CONTRACT HANDLING AND SCHEDULING AGREEMENTS*

The sales logistics chain includes business-process scenarios for the increasingly more complex area of contract handling and scheduling agreements. Businesses require ever-increasing levels of quality and responsiveness from a decreasing number of suppliers with whom they contract. Suppliers require systems that ensure compliance with customer contracts and delivery arrangements. Moreover, customers require that suppliers measure their own performance against these contractual arrangements.

Traditional systems use individual sales orders to manage customer demands, downstream logistics, and accounting activities. An order-based approach assumes that customer demands arrive at the supplier individually, but this is often not the case. The internal mechanisms used by suppliers to fulfill customer demands must support the actual business processes used by each customer.

Sales and Distribution outline agreements scenarios are used to record arrangements with customers to deliver specific quantities or values of goods or services within a predefined time period. The terms specified in the contract can be used as the basis for a scheduling agreement. The scheduling agreement allows you to determine specific delivery quantities and dates within a certain validity period. These scenarios differ in the way customers can specify delivery quantities and dates but are similar in coordinating delivery, logistics, and in producing customer invoices.

In R/3 ™ Release 4.0, business process scenarios for contract handling and scheduling agreement include:

- Customer scheduling agreement handling
- External service agents in customer scheduling agreement
- Customer scheduling agreement handling with delivery order

As with standard order handling, the scenarios for contract handling and scheduling agreements begin by recording sales activities with customers, such as phone calls, meetings, and product presentations. Direct mail campaigns can be planned and monitored. As these activities result in customer inquiries, they are recorded in the system. A quotation, valid for a specified time period, is created on the basis of this inquiry.

After customer acceptance of the quotation, an outline agreement is processed. An outline agreement can also be processed directly from a customer without a quotation. There are three scenarios for processing outline agreements in the R/3™ system:

- Contract handling
- Schedule agreements without release orders
- Schedule agreements with release orders

Contracts specify products and prices but do not include specific quantities or delivery dates. A contract documents terms and conditions controlling subsequent deliveries such as freight, (e.g., FOB delivered) or payment conditions (e.g., net 30 days). A contract may also specify the maximum value of all goods to be shipped. When a customer requests shipment, a release order is processed against the contract. This order is managed similarly to standard order handling, with credit checking, pricing, and use of the R/3™ configurator as well as document printing and subsequent delivery. The products, quantities, and values from each release order are updated on the contract.

Scheduling agreements contain specific products, quantities, and delivery dates. Each line item (individual product) on a scheduling agreement is broken down into delivery requests (subitems). Each delivery is specified by date, week, or month. For standard orders, subsequent delivery and logistics handling are triggered by order line items as each item is associated with one delivery date. In this case, the subsequent delivery and logistics are triggered by each schedule subitem. The processing of scheduling agreements uses the full functionality of standard orders, including checking of both credit and material availability as well as pricing and delivery scheduling.

In the scheduling agreement with release order scenario, deliveries are "held" by the system as unscheduled quantities until the customer requests shipment. This request is processed by a schedule release order. The release order creates a new delivery subitem with the required quantity and date as it concurrently subtracts the unscheduled quantity.

These scenarios integrate customer management activities with the workflow associated with downstream delivery and logistics operations. Logistics operations include transportation planning, as well as picking, packing, and shipping of products. The credit and material availability checks made during order entry are similarly available in this workflow. As goods leave the plant or warehouse, stock and value adjustments are made in the materials management system. To complete this scenario, invoices are processed and sent to customers. The appropriate cash management, accounts receivable, and profitability systems are updated.

In the case of returned goods, for damage or other reasons, the system manages the receipt of these items and processes a credit memo. A subsequent free-of-charge delivery may be processed to replace the damaged goods. If company-owned packaging or shipping materials (e.g., pallets) were included in the original shipment, the system processes a pickup order to retrieve those materials. Damaged or lost packaging is charged to the customer.

5.3   *THIRD-PARTY ORDER HANDLING*

Third-party sales arrangements leverage the relationship between a company and its customers. By managing customer service activities and related accounts receivable functions, an existing infrastructure is utilized to provide a flow of services and products to a customer even when they are not normally sold, stocked, or manufactured by the company. To realize the potential from this type of transaction, however, the systems used for managing the process should be transparent to the customer and streamline costs of fulfillment.

In a third-party sale, a company does not deliver its own products to a customer; rather, it commissions an external supplier to deliver its goods directly to the customer. In addition to processing a sales order, a company must coordinate the customer sale with a purchase from the supplier.

The R/3™ Release 4.0 business-process scenario for third-party handling is represented by the third-party order processing scenario. Just as with standard orders, the third-party scenario begins by recording sales activities with customers, such as phone calls, meetings, and product presentations. Direct mail campaigns can be planned and monitored. As these activities result in customer inquiries, they are recorded in the system. A quotation, valid for a specified time period, is created on the basis of this inquiry.

After customer acceptance of the quotation, a third-party order is processed. A third-party order can also be processed directly from a customer without a quotation. The order documents the customer demand, carries out pricing, and initiates credit checking.

The system creates a purchase requisition detailing the products, quantities, and delivery dates. This purchase requisition is associated with known sources of supply (e.g., purchase contracts or specific vendors), or vendor bids can be processed via RFQs. In either case, a special type of purchase order, a third-party purchase order, is processed and sent to the supplier. This purchase order directs the supplier to ship the products directly to the "ship-to address" identified on the original customer order.

As soon as the delivery to the customer has been completed and the invoice of the supplier processed, billing is carried out for the third-party order. The shipped quantity on the vendor invoice is automatically copied to the billing document sent to the customer. Additional activities in this scenario include customer credit and debit memos and the processing of special vendor arrangements such as volume-based rebates and bonuses.

5.4   *CUSTOMER CONSIGNMENT STOCK HANDLING*

In a traditional vendor/customer transaction, transfer of ownership of inventory occurs with the physical flow of that inventory. Most inventory systems handle this adequately because the accounting of inventory simply mirrors the movement of product. However, a manufacturer may stock spare parts inventory at a customer site to enhance maintenance response time. Or, a manufacturer might not want to pay for an expensive item until it is used in production. To avoid delays in production resulting from a materials shortage, the customer might ask the vendor to stock the material at the customer's facility.

As trading partners work together to increase the overall responsiveness of the supply chain, these types of arrangements are becoming commonplace. Customers try to push the financial burden of maintaining inventories to upstream suppliers and increasingly negotiate for "point-of-use" payment schemes. Customers still maintain the same safety stocks—only now the supplier will "own" the inventory until the customer uses it in production or resells it. To safely and responsively accommodate these practices, a company is required to process the flow of goods in and out of customer-consigned inventories as easily as it processes standard customer orders.

Customer-consigned goods are items stored on the customer's premises for eventual use and/or sale but still owned by the company. When the customer notifies the company that the goods have been issued from the designated consignment inventory, ownership is transferred to the customer, a customer invoice is produced, and the corresponding accounts receivable entry is made. Goods not issued can be returned to the company.

In the R/3™ system, inventoried items are identified in the material master file. Any item can be transferred to a customer location as consigned stock where it is tracked with a "special stock" designation assigned to each customer. Because the same item may be sent to several customers, it is possible to have multiple consignment stocks of the same material—one for each customer. For each customer-specific stock, a moving average price is maintained. This price is used for valuing each issuance (i.e., sale) to that customer.

In R/3™ Release 4.0, the consignment handling business process is represented in the scenario direct sale to the consignment receiver. The scenario begins by recording sales activities with customers, such as phone calls, meetings, and product presentations. Direct mail campaigns can be planned and monitored. In this scenario, customers' demand for product is fulfilled directly from a consigned inventory at their own site. As these stocks are drawn down, the customer may request additional goods. This request is processed with a special type of sales order, a consignment fill-up order. As with a standard order, a consignment fill-up order carries out pricing, initiates credit checking, and determines material availability. The sales order function in R/3™ uses a configurator to select configured products as well as a "conditions" program to manage complex pricing scenarios. The sales order process sends requirements to manufacturing.

This scenario integrates order handling activities with the workflow of downstream delivery and logistics operations. Logistics operations include transportation planning, as well as picking, packing, and shipping of products. The credit and material availability checks made during order entry are similarly available in this workflow. When goods leave the plant or warehouse, stock is transferred to a customer "special stock" inventory location.

Customers notify the company when goods have been issued from the consignment inventory, and a consignment issues transaction is posted. Invoices are processed and sent to customers. The appropriate cash management, accounts receivable, and profitability systems are updated.

Customers may request the company to pick up unwanted or excess goods in the consigned inventory. This request results in the processing of a pickup order with the goods then returned to standard company inventory. Again, in the case of returned goods, for damage or other reasons, the system manages the receipt of these items and processes a credit memo.

5.5   CASH ORDER HANDLING

Order management systems used in the industrial sectors (e.g., by wholesale distributors and manufacturers) divide the order fulfillment process into discrete functions: order taking, credit management, logistics handling, invoicing, and accounts receivable. This breakdown of work corresponds to a standard mode of doing business whereby suppliers receive orders from their customers and use an invoicing and accounts receivable mechanism for handling the financial aspects of the sale.

In an over-the-counter scenario, however, the customer-supplier interaction is different. To begin with, the supplier expects to get paid without going through a traditional accounts receivable cycle (invoice, statement, payment). Second, the customer expects to receive the requested goods immediately.

Cash orders are used to process sales where customers pick up and pay for products at the same time.

This scenario begins when a customer arrives at the company to buy goods for cash. A special order type, a cash order, is used to record the transaction. The total amount of cash received from the customer is entered on the order along with the desired products. The requested goods are issued from inventory and given to the customer. A copy of the order is given to the customer as a receipt, and the invoice is printed and mailed to the customer at a later date.

If customers return damaged goods, the system processes the receipt of these items and produces a credit memo. Optionally, a subsequent free-of-charge delivery can be processed to replace the damaged goods.

5.6   *RUSH ORDER HANDLING*

R/3 ™ processes each stage of the sales fulfillment cycle with a different document. Examples include quotations, inquiries, sales orders, deliveries, and billing documents. Each document contains information for processing the relevant business transaction. Delivery documents are normally created subsequent to the sales order document and initiate the logistics and delivery process. In the case of a "rush order," the delivery document and sales order can be created at the same time. All sales and shipping functions, such as availability check and delivery scheduling, are carried out for both documents at the same time.

As with standard order handling, the rush order handling scenario begins by recording sales activities with customers, such as phone call, meetings, and product presentations. Direct mail campaigns can be planned and monitored. As these activities result in customer inquiries, they are recorded in the system. A quotation, valid for a specified time period, is created on the basis of this inquiry.

After customer acceptance of the quotation, an order is processed. An order can also be processed directly from a customer without a quotation. If the customer requires immediate delivery, a special type of order, a rush order, is used to process the transaction. As with standard orders, rush orders carry out pricing and perform credit checking. The sales order function in R/3 ™ uses a configurator to select configured products as well as a "conditions" program to manage complex pricing scenarios.

With standard orders, the delivery document is created subsequent to the sales order. In this case, the system creates the sales order document and the delivery document at the same time, and the workflow associated with delivery can begin immediately.

The delivery and logistics workflow includes transportation planning as well as picking, packing, and shipping of products. When goods leave the plant or warehouse, stock and value adjustments are made in the materials management system. To complete the usual flow of this scenario, invoices are processed and sent to customers and the appropriate cash management, accounts receivable, and profitability systems are updated. In the case of returned goods, for damage or other reasons, the system manages the receipt of these items and processes a credit memo.

5.7   *MAKE-TO-ORDER SALES ORDER HANDLING*

In the make-to-order sales order handling scenario, a sales order taken in SD that is not covered by finished goods stock in the warehouse leads to the sales-order-based processing of a product. Generally, more than one manufacturing level is involved, and a subset of the components is not covered by warehouse stock but is instead specially manufactured or procured for this sales order.

Production can start directly from sales and distribution, or it can be triggered after requirements planning has been carried out through conversion of a planned order.

Sales-order-based processing distinguishes between the following types of products:

- Nonvariant products
- Single-level products with variants, without order Bill of Materials (BOMs)
- Multilevel products with variants, with or without order BOMs

A nonvariant product is defined uniquely with a material number and is described by a single-level BOM or by a variant of a multiple BOM. In this case, you usually want to start production without having to offset the product's requirements with planning. You can, however, plan single-level BOMs neutrally and offset them using dependent requirements. Sales order processing is no different in this case than it is for other uniquely defined products.

Products with variants, on the other hand, require additional information and master data, such as:

- Characteristics and values
- Classes and object dependencies
- Configuration profiles
- Variant conditions for pricing (optional)
- BOMs and routings with selectable items and operations

In this case, each product is configured to match the customer's needs. To achieve this, the system, using classification criteria, performs a valuation in the sales order. Then, during the subsequent production process, it uses a stored set of rules to select assemblies from a proposed super-BOM. This method of defining a product is interesting particularly when you have complex products with a high number of variants.

This process is also suitable for products that can be described in detail using characteristics with reference to a sales order. In exceptional cases, a variant configured in the sales order can be used as the basis for additional modifications in production just to meet this one customer need. This is known as an order BOM. Order BOMs can only be triggered directly from the sales order. Once the sales order has been posted, they must be processed and adjusted.

5.8 ASSEMBLY-TO-ORDER SALES ORDER HANDLING

The assembly-to-order sales order handling scenario differs from the make-to-order sales order processing scenario as follows:

- The product's components have already been produced and are available in the warehouse.
- Production proceeds in a single step.
- This process is also suitable for products that can be described in detail using characteristics with reference to a sales order.

5.9 EMPTIES AND RETURNABLE PACKAGING HANDLING

Returnable packaging consists of items that sit in the customer's warehouse but are still the property of your company. Customers are not required to pay for returnable packaging unless it is not returned to your company by a certain date. So this function lets you handle the settlement or return of Euro pallets or empties, for example. You can also handle the sale of returnable packaging to a third party this way. Because stocks of returnable packaging are still part of your valuated inventory, you must manage them in your system.

The following conditions apply:

- You must manage returnable packaging stock separately from the rest of your stock so that you can maintain an overview of what the customer has in his warehouse.

- You must manage returnable packaging stock separately for each customer.
- Processing empties and returnable packaging consists of the following separate business processes:
  - Shipment of returnable packaging—returnable packaging is recorded as a separate item in a regular order and shipped to the customer.
  - Pickup of returnable packaging—picking up returnable packaging is handled with a special order.
  - Charges for packaging not returned

Returnable packaging can be billed to the customer if he wants to keep it or if he has damaged it.

5.10   RETURNS HANDLING

This scenario describes returns handling, which can be initiated by the customer or by the external sales force. Causes for returns can include, for example, defective goods, deliveries in error, purchase orders in error, and returns received before the return deadline has expired in the case of a purchase on spec.

Returns can be recorded as part of a customer contact, for example, a phone call. This information then becomes the basis for subsequent returns processing.

When a recall must be carried out as part of Quality Assurance as a result of product deficiencies, a direct mail campaign can be used to notify affected customers. Various situations can arise during returns processing:

- A return is created to handle the process. When the returned goods are received in the warehouse, a returns delivery is created that references this return. The goods issue that is posted for the returns delivery records the receipt of the goods into your stock.
- After the goods receipt, there is a returns check, in which the eligibility of the complaint is checked, and a usage decision is made for the goods (e.g., reprocess, scrap).
- If the customer wants to have the corresponding amount refunded, a credit memo request can be created with reference to the return. When the credit memo request has been approved, a credit memo is generated for the customer.
- If the customer wants the goods to be replaced, a subsequent delivery free of charge is created with reference to the return.

5.11   DECENTRALIZED SHIPPING

Most companies have realized that high levels of customer response cannot be achieved without tightly integrating their logistics, inventory, and order management functions. Software that can unite these functions around a centralized database has been the standard solution. On the other hand, these same companies often manage complex warehouses and distribution centers, which process high volumes of shipments. Optimization of the operations in these locations requires local access and control of high-response systems that are available all the time. The challenge, therefore, is to provide a hybrid approach, which satisfies the requirements of providing integrated data access on a global basis while enabling the implementation of local distributed systems.

Decentralized shipping (not included in Release 4.0) processes the delivery logistics of sales orders on a remote standalone computer without online access to a centralized system. The R/3 ™ system uses a technology, called Application Linking and Enabling (ALE), to implement distributed solutions such as decentralized shipping (see Section 14.5). In this approach, special types of business information documents, called Intermediate Documents (IDOCs), are automatically transmitted between communicating systems. The information transferred on these IDOCs synchronizes the databases on these "loosely coupled" systems. To use decentralized shipping, a company maintains a database that describes the relationships between the centralized order management system and the remote computers used in its distribution centers and warehouses. This database is used by R/3 ™ to automatically generate the IDOCs used in communicating between the host and remote systems.

Sales orders are entered on the host (central) computer. Stock control is also managed on the host system, where the availability of the order items is checked and scheduling for the shipping activities is carried out. Delivery data are transferred to the decentralized shipping computer, where, on the delivery due date, the shipping activities are initiated. Relevant data from the material master records are available in the remote computer. Customer data are transferred from the central system to the decentralized computer for each transaction.

The decentralized computer automatically creates a delivery and initiates picking. Picking can be linked with the warehouse management system. The quantities and batch specifications are confirmed in the delivery. Packaging, weight, and loading data can be printed on the shipping papers. When the delivery is completed, the goods issue for the delivery is confirmed. The data are then transferred back to the host system where order and inventory status is updated, and the delivery is released for billing.

Sales and Distribution Customer Example

Many of SAP™'s customers have found that the integration of sales and distribution applications in R/3™'s logistics chain has improved the performance of their companies. In the rest of this chapter, we take a look at a company whose business engineering efforts have been enhanced by R/3™'s integrated logistics.

Micrografix Corporation, Richardson, Texas

Micrografix Corporation, one of the premier developers and marketers of graphics software in the world, was the first company to develop Windows-based graphics applications for personal computers. Micrografix caters to a wide variety of customers—from very large companies to individuals who order Micrografix products by phone—around the world. The company's two distribution operations are in Texas and the Netherlands.

Micrografix took on reengineering with one main idea in mind—to maintain its strong competitive position in the future. Micrografix competes in a dynamic industry that has recently seen growth rates among individual companies at almost 100 percent per year. The outlook for Micrografix is promising, but all companies must ensure that their internal systems help, not hinder, continued success.

"Micrografix wanted a growth management tool for its domestic and international business," Robert Lytton, director of management systems, explains. "We have to fulfill the commitment to our customers to develop and deliver quality products and services, and at the same time, fulfill the commitment to our stockholders by being a profitable company. It is very important, then, that we make certain our business runs efficiently and effectively."

One important step on the road to increased efficiency was to replace the company's information systems with an integrated system that gave access to online, real-time information. Micrografix chose SAP™'s R/3™ system as the cornerstone of its reengineering effort because of its versatility and ease-of-use for everyone from executives and accountants to someone who works on the loading dock.

Micrografix reengineered by organizing its work processes into "value chains," groups of activities that add value to a company's product for its customers. Supported by the R/3™ system, the company's "value chains" include order processing (where the company takes orders, ships the product, sends out a bill, and processes accounts receivable), materials management (sales forecasts, purchasing, receiving, accounts payable, inventory management, and material requirements planning), and financial controlling ("back-end" reporting on all of the activities in the business).

After the initial phase of implementation, Micrografix saw that R/3™ was delivering immediate benefits. In particular, Micrografix found that R/3™'s integrated sales and distribution applications produced significant dividends. Improvements in this area included maintaining a single customer database and developing a sales tax interface that automatically calculates sales taxes on all orders and invoices.

5.12   R/3 SALES LOGISTICS SUMMARY

The following tables provide an overview to the main scenarios, core processes, business objects, and organizational units that make up R/3 Sales Logistics.

Scenarios

- Direct sale to industrial consumer
- Direct sale to internal consumer
- Direct sale to retail company
- Direct sale to
- Customer order processing MTO
- Customer order processing ATO
- Component supplier processing
- Third-party-order processing

Core Processes

- Material master processing
- Customer master data processing
- Condition processing
- Mailing campaign processing
- Sales activity processing
- Customer quotation processing
- Sales order processing
- Credit limit check
- Outline agreement
- Goods issue processing
- Delivery processing
- Transport

- Foreign trade
- Billing
- Rebate processing

Business Objects

- Sales
  - Customer inquiry
  - Customer quotation
  - Sales order
  - Customer outline agreement
  - Customer complaints order
- Shipping
  - Customer delivery
  - Transport
- Billing
  - Customer billing document
- Sales Support
  - Partner sales activity
  - Mailings

Organizational Units

- Sales organization
- Distribution channel
- Division
- Sales Area
- Plant
- Sales office
- Sales group
- Shipping point
- Loading point
- Transportation planning point

6

Production Logistics

$\mathbf{C}$urrent production planning and control must be developed around processes that can respond quickly and efficiently to rapid change. A number of factors are responsible for this condition: Decreased product development times and shorter life cycles for products have accelerated production rate times; sharper customer focus has intensified demands placed on product quality; and increased competition has forced production to deliver better on price, quality, and delivery times. Now more than ever, a company's competitive advantage depends on planning processes that are flexible and quick to deliver but are focused on quality as well.

Production logistics is the SAP™ solution for a modern production planning and control system. It provides quick deliverability by shortening planning cycles, providing up-to-date information, and increasing the productivity of work processes. It is flexible because it can be used in any sector of industry. All processes can be geared to plant-specific requirements, taking into account different production methods from make-to-order to mass production.

The integration of production logistics with other value chain areas of the business within the overall R/3™ system ensures optimally adjusted processing of all transactions associated with logistics, from procurement and warehousing to sales and distribution. Within this comprehensive integration of applications, the flow of quantities in the logistics scenarios is automatically kept up to date with the flow of values in financial, assets, and managerial accounting. Thus, production logistics offers a high level of performance for the planning and control of the total material flow.

The production logistics application suite conforms to the internationally recognized planning concept MRP II. In this approach, all planning functions—

including business, sales, and production planning—are united into a comprehensive framework. MRP II, however, is not without its shortcomings. First, planning is treated as a process separate from managing actual production activities. For example, MRP II isolates customer sales management from the planning processes. When sales information and processes are not seamlessly integrated into the planning processes, it is difficult to achieve a customer-centric organization. Second, the MRP II approach does not provide explicit support for other current initiatives such as Total Quality Management or Japanese Kanban, a materials management system. Production logistics, along with its links to the entire R/3™ system, is a modern implementation of MRP II that effectively overcomes these two shortcomings. It is built on a common foundation of basic business processes—demand flow management, quality, costing, accounting, and materials and services management—all of which are seamlessly integrated.

Figure 6-1 illustrates the main production logistics scenarios. Also included are the core processes, business objects, and organizational units that are part of the production business process.

This chapter discusses main scenarios that are covered in the production logistics business processes, including: production by lot size, repetitive manu-

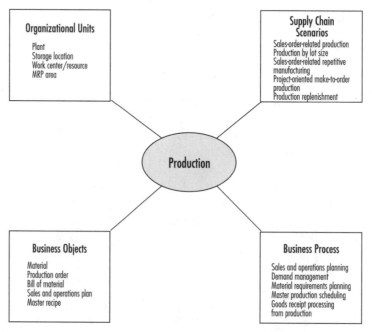

▶ Figure 6–1   Overview of scenario, process, organization, and business objects

facturing, discontinuous/continuous production, regulated production, and project-oriented make-to-order. We'll first examine the production by lot size (noncustomer order-specific production) scenario in detail, and then give an overview of the other main process scenarios. Finally, we will provide an example of how R/3™'s supply chain solution, including its production planning component, has enhanced one company's success.

6.1   PRODUCTION BY LOT SIZE

Production by lot size is a make-to-order strategy that allows a company to produce several customer requirements in one lot. The strategy is to be responsive to customer demands while keeping stock and production runs to a minimum. The size of the lot is determined by various aspects of production. This scenario describes the planning and execution of production, in which multiple requirements are combined and produced under the control of production work orders. It spans the entire logistics chain from enterprise-level business planning to detail production scheduling and tracking. The value chain for this scenario is represented by Figure 6-2.

Described below is a general outline of how a typical production process scenario flows. It begins with the creation and processing of a production work order. Processing of the production order entails checking for material availability, calculating planned costs, and evaluating capacity. Once the order is executed, the quality controls are automatically triggered. Typically, this involves the creation of certain inspection points during production. If defects are found, a quality notification is issued. If not, the goods undergo a final inspection and a quality management order is released. After the lot production process has been completed, goods of an acceptable quality are available for use in the warehouse.

An Event-Driven Process Chain (EPC) diagram of the production by lot size scenario is illustrated in Figures 6-3 and 6-4. In these diagrams, the R/3™ production by lot size business-process scenario begins with the task sales and operations planning, in which a long-term sales plan is developed and reconciled

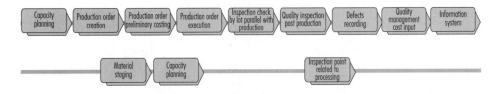

▶ **Figure 6–2**   Value chain: Production by lot size

against a production plan. Sales forecasts and customer orders are introduced into the planning functions via the demand management tasks, which determine quantities and dates for finished products and important assemblies. Customer demands and long-term production plans are integrated, resulting in a master production schedule (MPS). Capacity checking and leveling occurs throughout all stages of planning. The MPS is balanced against aggregate (i.e., rough-cut) capacity.

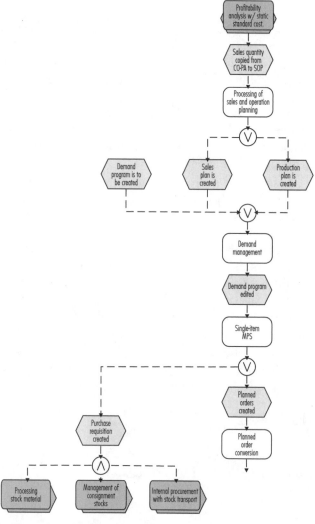

▶ **Figure 6–3**   Processing of sales and operation planning

A detailed material plan is developed via the material requirements planning (MRP) function. Capacity leveling brings this plan into balance with detail plant capacities. The MRP is expressed as a set of planned orders for purchased material, material transferred from another plant, and manufactured items. The requirements both for purchased materials and for material transferred from other plants are passed to the procurement and stock transfer processes. Production activities to be carried out by external service providers generate requisitions and, subsequently, purchase orders, for external services.

Actual production is managed by work orders. Planned orders developed in the MRP function are released into production as required (Figure 6-4). Each work order contains an itemization of all required materials, extracted from the bill of materials, and a sequence of operations to be performed, extracted from the routing. Operations performed by external service providers are identified and integrated. Varying degrees of automated workflow and control are established both to manage work order release and to collect data from production. Material can be issued to work orders manually, automatically (backflushing), and/or via electronic Kanban techniques.

To complete the scenario flow, material is received from the work order. Finally, the work order is confirmed and closed out (settled). The entire scenario flow is then integrated to costing and quality processes.

Processing of Sales and Operation Planning

Four main tasks constitute the noncustomer, order-specific production. The first is sales and operation planning, which specifies sales quantities for the long and medium term and plans a rough approximation of the production activities necessary to achieve these objectives.

In this process, the setting of a sales planning date begins the chain. Once the date is set, the next task is to specify the planning object. This leads to two possibilities: 1) plan a product group or 2) plan an individual product (see Figure 6-3).

The next tasks are simply to specify 1) a plan version and 2) origin of sales volume. Determining the origin of the sales volume can come from six different sources:

- Automatic forecast
- Product group sales plan
- Product group master plan
- Sales volume entered manually
- Sales volume from sales information system
- Sales volume from profitability analysis

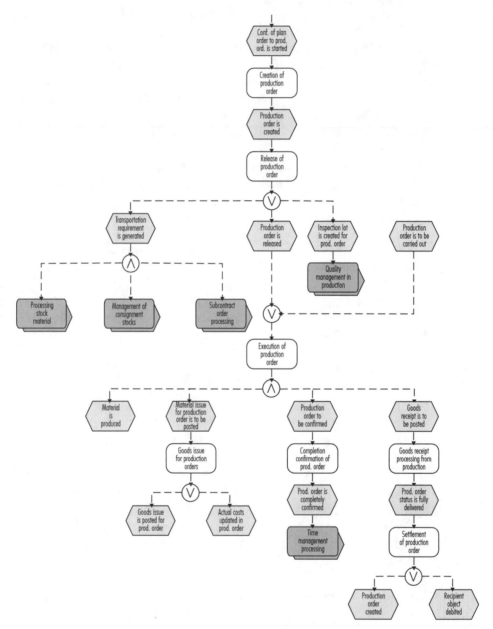

▶ **Figure 6–4**   Execution of production order

If the sales volume is forecasted automatically, the forecast comes from the area of procurement, where forecast values are created.

When the origin of sales volume is specified, the next task is create sales plan. Creating a sales plan can lead to demand management, which is the last task involved in sales and operation planning.

It's also possible to create a production plan based on the sales plan. In this case, a few more steps must occur before demand management can take place. The first step is to specify a category for the production plan. Five possible actions exist:

- Take production plan from product group.
- Create production plan manually.
- Create production plan with a view to direct distribution.
- Create production plan with target stocks.
- Create production plan with supplies from target days.

All of these events lead to examining capacity data. Capacity planning offers an overview—sometimes approximate, sometimes detailed—of the ability of a plant to produce something during a specified period of time. It's possible that the production plan is processed during this planning phase with or without capacity data. After processing, there's a creation of the production plan. At this point, demand management can take place.

Demand Management

The creation of a demand management program begins the next phase of the logistics chain. Demand management entails determining quantities and dates for finished products and assemblies. The results of sales and operations planning can be used as a basis for demand management. Demand management also includes developing strategies for the planning and producing or buying of a product.

After the creation of the demand management program, demand management categories for planned independent requirements are then determined. Three possibilities exist:

1. Create planned independent requirements (i.e., requirements such as quantities and dates are planned for future, not actual, sales).
2. Create customer independent requirements (without sales and distribution).
3. Take over customer independent requirements (from sales and distribution).

In the first case, create planned independent requirements, the type of planned independent requirements is determined and selected, and the origin of the requirements data is specified. Five events may follow:

- Requirements data taken from sales plan
- Data taken from production plan
- Data entered manually
- Data taken from forecast
- Data taken from reference requirements

In the second case, creating customer-independent requirements without sales and distribution determines the type of customer-independent requirements, which then are selected and entered into the system.

The third case involves a direct link between production planning and sales and distribution (especially standard order processing). In this case, all data about customer independent requirements is simply taken over from sales and distribution.

Now, planned independent requirements can be created.

BUSINESS OBJECT

▶ *Material*

A material order may represent any good that is the subject of business activity. A material may be used in manufacturing, consumed, traded, or produced. A material master record is structured according to organizational units (plant, plant storage area, warehouse complex, and distribution chain). Different departments of an enterprise have different views of a material (for example, Materials Planning, Purchasing, Warehouse Management). Materials made up of several constituent parts can be described with the aid of a BOM, a formal list of the components that make up a product or assembly. Materials for which a change in requirements has occurred are recorded in the planning file and used for requirements planning.

The material business object is used as a source of information for the following types of business analysis.

Report Subject	Information Delivery
Customer	Summarizes the order quantities and values resulting from business transactions with customers
Inventory controlling	Retrieves the current stock levels for a variety of stock types and monitors the flow of materials in and out of inventory

Report Subject	Information Delivery
Kanban	Evaluates Kanban supply areas, such as Kanban quantities, replenishment times, and number of replenishment operation
Material usage	Provides statistics on the quantities of materials or assemblies consumed by a plant within a given time period
Operation	Contains metrics for measuring the performance of specific work centers within a production process and provides information regarding the capacity, throughput, and reliability for work centers within specific plants in a predetermined time period
Production order	Provides information on the flow of materials in production at your company
Stock requirements analysis	Displays the availability of a material for the MRP point of view
Quantity flows (warehouse management)	Monitors the flow of goods into and from one or more storage units
Vendor evaluation	Compares and ranks vendors by quality of goods they produce, the timeliness of their deliveries, the quality of their service, and the price performance of their products as compared with other vendors of similar products

Material Requirements Planning (Single-Item MPS)

The main task of MRP is first determining which material is required, in which quantity and at what time, and then creating the necessary order proposals.

In our logistics chain, material requirements planning begins with a single item. (See Figure 6-3, Single-Item MPS.)

The first task is to determine the category of the planning run. The planning run refers to the carrying out of the material planning, including all of the materials and assemblies selected for a particular plan. Two choices are possible: carry out single-level planning or carry out multilevel planning.

Once the level of planning is selected, the next task is to determine the category of the results processing. Two events can follow: process results immediately and create dependent requirements automatically.

The next task is either to determine scheduling or to determine planning type. Two kinds of *scheduling* are available: basic data schedule for planned orders and lead-time schedule (capacity loads aren't taken into account) for planned orders. In addition, two types of *planning* are also possible: 1) net change (a planning run where only those materials that have already changed since the last planning run are planned again) and 2) net change for future planning.

Completion of schedule or planning type determination prompts the next task: carry out MRP run. The planning results may already exist; if they do, then the next step is MRP results processing. If the planning results do not yet exist, then carry out the MRP run by one of the following means:

- Create capacity load.
- Create automatic dependent requirement.
- Create automatic purchase requisition.
- Create planned order automatically.
- Create scheduled quantity automatically.
- Create direct purchase requisition automatically.

Carrying out the MRP run triggers two other possible events:

- Create MRP list —This action also leads to MRP results processing. An MRP list is the MRP controller's most important tool. The MRP controller is the person responsible for a group of materials in a plant or company. The MRP controller's list is a record for each material, including information about all future stock and requirements developments calculated during the planning run.
- Process planning results immediately.

The event process planning results immediately leads to five other possible events:

- Carry out comparison—Here, a basis for the comparison must be determined. The comparison may be with the MRP list or with the stock/requisition situation.
- Create purchase order proposals manually—This action leads to creating three other things manually: the scheduled quantity, the planned order, and the purchase requisition.
- Process purchase order proposals manually—This action leads to four possible events: process scheduled quantity further, process direct procurement purchase requisition, process purchase requisition further,

and process planned order further. These four events all lead to tasks in procurement.

- Save planning result—This action leads to creation of an MRP list, which, in turn leads once again to MRP results processing.
- Carry out statement of order—This action leads to capacity adjustment.

Many different tasks in production planning trigger a planned order not converted via an MRP list, which is the case with our single-item MRP. Others include MRP results processing, interactive MPS, single-item MPS, MPS sales order, MPS project, and planned order processing. These all lead to the manual creation of a planned order.

Without the MRP list, a category for the planned order conversion must be determined. Categories include these actions:

- Convert planned order into purchase requisition.
- Convert planned order into purchase requisition by multiple processing.
- Convert planned order into production order.
- Convert planned order into production order by multiple processing.

The first two tasks lead to purchase requisition processing for stock material in procurement. The last two lead to the creation of production orders in Production Planning.

Creation, Release, and Execution of Production Order

Three tasks can trigger the carrying out of a production order: schedule processing, release of the production order, or printout of production order (see Figure 6-4).

The first task, schedule processing, includes choosing individual processing via production orders. The second, release of the production order, entails either partially or fully releasing the production order. The third task is simply printing out the order. All of these lead to the next task: execution of production order (see Figure 6-4).

Execution of the production order involves preparing and issuing the material. Three events are possible: 1) not posting material issue, 2) posting material issue, and 3) issuing material physically.

If the material issue is posted, a category of withdrawal posting must be determined. This leads to further tasks: 1) carrying out backflush (complete the confirmation of production orders); and 2) carrying out issue of production orders (issue goods for production orders). If the material is physically issued, the first task is to pick the material. Once done, the operation can be carried out.

It's also possible, however, that the material must first be produced. This leads to two possible tasks in procurement: delivering material physically and receiving goods from production.

Once the operation is carried out, the next task is to begin to enter actual data. Three events can follow: no entry of actual data is provided, completed confirmation for operation is carried out, and wage entry is carried out.

The completion of the confirmation of the operation leads to completion of confirmation of production orders. The third task, carrying out wage entry, is the Production Planning link to Human Resources.

6.2   *REPETITIVE MANUFACTURING*

In MRP II systems, production work orders help manage production. Created automatically by the planning logic within the MRP system, each work order provides a detailed list of necessary materials and operations. Production personnel use this information to manage production.

In many high-volume environments where the same or similar products are produced over an extended period of time (days, weeks, etc.), work orders introduce an unnecessary and therefore unwanted level of complexity to production control and management. Production is controlled through use of a schedule, which lists the sequence and run times for every product produced on each production line. Although this approach seems uncomplicated, the system must ensure that the appropriate materials are dispatched to the production lines at just the right time. Interactive rescheduling is required to accommodate variations in actual production or customer demands.

Repetitive manufacturing refers to production of identical or similar products on high-volume production lines. Instead of work orders, production schedules are used to manage production. These schedules keep personnel on each production line informed about which products to manufacture and in what sequence.

The repetitive manufacturing scenario in SAP™ release 4.0 (and earlier) describes the planning and execution of production in a repetitive environment. It spans the entire logistics chain from enterprise-level business planning through to detail production scheduling and reporting.

This scenario begins similarly to production by lot size. It starts with sales and operations planning. Sales forecasts and customer orders are introduced through the demand management processes, and customer demands and long-term production plans are integrated, resulting in a master schedule. A detailed material plan is developed via the MRP functions, and the requirements both for purchased materials and for material transferred from other plants are passed to the procurement and stock transfer processes.

Production schedules contain a list of the sequences and run times for every item produced on each production line (plant personnel are told to run a particular sequence for a specified time). Completed production of each item is reported to the system. Material issuance is then computed from the bill of materials of the produced item and is automatically posted out of inventory (retroactive posting of material issues). On a predefined basis (usually weekly or monthly), the production schedule is closed.

Material issues are backflushed. "Backflushing" refers to an automatic method of posting material and production costs to an underlying cost structure (cost object for repetitive manufacturing) as production is reported through a predefined step in the production process. On a periodic basis, this cost object is posted and closed out.

This scenario is fully integrated to the quality system: inspection strategies are established for each product, and inspection work flows are triggered when material is reported out of production.

6.3   *MAKE-TO-ORDER PRODUCTION*

MRP II systems separate sales and production management. In these systems, customer demands are reconciled with production at one point—the master schedule. The master schedule is often treated as a "firewall," which formally separates production from sales and demand management activities. After the master schedule is set, production activities are planned, tracked, and costed without regard to the individual customer requirements. This process is appropriate in make-to-stock environments (where customer requirements are satisfied from inventory) but is inappropriate for make-to-order production where customization is required. In order to manage customer-driven manufacturing more profitably, manufacturers require systems that can plan and track the actual costs of production on an order-by-order basis.

The make-to-order production scenario describes a strategy for individually managing the production associated with specific customer sales orders. Production and procurement costs are tracked to individual sales orders. This tracking results in detailed reporting and analysis of the planned and actual costs for each order. This scenario follows the same flow as production by lot size, beginning with sales and operations planning all the way down to the confirmation and closing out of the work order.

Each sales order generates an internal "cost object" for planning and tracking actual costs of production. The system plans costs by "exploding" the BOM and routings for each stage of production associated with the final end item. Actual costs are tracked on work orders during production and are posted to this cost object.

6.4   PROCESS MANUFACTURING

Traditional manufacturing systems such as MRP II were originally designed for discrete manufacturers. Because the characteristics of process and discrete manufacturers are different, attempts to adapt traditional systems to the process manufacturer were met with two challenges:

- Business vs. plant management—The traditional approach isolates business management from plant management and process control. For the process manufacturer, however, the production process actually drives other business activities. Therefore, production and business processes must be integrated into a unified framework.
- Capacity-based planning vs. material-based planning—The traditional materials-oriented approaches leave capacity checking and leveling to the end of the planning process. To optimize the large investments in capital assets, business and production planning in process industries needs to be capacity oriented.

In the past, problems with traditional approaches could be overcome as long as the manufacturer could either shape customer demand and response expectations or maintain enough lead time to replan production and balance output with customer demand. In most industries, these options are no longer viable. As manufacturers integrate their businesses into high-performance supply chains, the production planning and execution activities must integrate into demand management, procurement, maintenance, and other business systems.

The SAP™ R/3™ scenarios for process manufacturing manage the planning, execution, and control activities for process-oriented manufacturing. In SAP™ R/3™ Release 4.0, the Reference Model contains different scenarios for companies that use batch- and recipe-oriented manufacture of products in process industries, including:

- Continuous production
- Discontinuous production
- Regulated production

The continuous production scenario describes the process whereby the product is manufactured in a continuous process over time. In continuous production, the entire line is devoted to the production of the order. Conversely, in discontinuous production, it is possible to manufacture the order in stages, and several products can be manufactured on the same line. Regulated production scenarios are largely associated with the pharmaceuticals industry, which requires that the process orders meet rigorous quality standards and legal requirements (see Section 6.6).

These process manufacturing scenarios begin with sales and operations planning. Data from the production systems are included to yield cost and profit projections. Through the demand management processes, detailed sales forecasts and customer orders are brought into the planning cycle, and long-term production plans and a master schedule are generated. Capacity leveling brings the master schedule into balance with aggregate plant capacities.

Material flow is then computed via the MRP functions, and capacity leveling brings this flow into balance with detail plant capacities. Requirements for purchased materials are passed to the procurement processes. These purchase requisitions along with planned production orders represent the material flow plan.

The actual production is managed with the process order. The process order contains the detailed recipe data and workflow instructions to manage production. Varying degrees of automated workflow and control are established to manage recipe dispatching, downloading of instructions to automated process control equipment, and the subsequent monitoring of production.

To complete the scenario flow, material is received from or issued to production and the process order is completed and closed out. The entire scenario flow is integrated to costing and quality processes. All production data, along with the recipe, are archived for regulatory or other uses.

6.5   PROJECT-RELATED "ENGINEER TO ORDER"

Traditional approaches to managing production based upon MRP II concepts have not proven successful in manufacturing environments of complex one-of-a-kind products. The reasons for this failing include the following:

- The work orders used by MRP II are individually scheduled and managed without support for coordination between operations on different work orders (e.g., operation 25 on work order A-100 cannot start until operation 10 on work order B-50 has begun). Engineer-to-order manufacturers use project management techniques for scheduling, activity coordination, and job costing.

- MRP II divides production of the finished product into smaller units, using a BOM. Engineer-to-order manufacturers manage production by breaking down total production into work packages specified in a work breakdown structure. These structures do not correspond one-to-one with the units defined in the BOM.
- MRP II isolates engineering, maintenance, and other customer-related activities from production. Engineer-to-order manufacturers require that production and nonproduction tasks be managed together.
- MRP II uses standard costs, whereas engineer-to-order manufacturers require actual costs.

Project management systems are not designed well for managing production. They do not support inventory management, material requirements planning, or the dispatching and tracking of work within the factory.

The engineer-to-order manufacturers require a system that synthesizes the best of both approaches. They require the combination of the MRP's ability to manage work orders, inventories, and material requirements planning and the project-oriented approach's ability to handle work coordination, budgeting, and actual costing.

The project-related, engineer-to-order scenario—also known as project-oriented make-to-order production in Release 4.0—describes a process for managing the production of complex items such as aircraft, ships, or large industrial equipment. A substantial portion of both the lead time and total value-added activity associated with these types of products is found in nonproduction activities such as engineering, design, work scheduling, and job costing. This scenario, therefore, integrates those activities into the overall production process, using the R/3™ project system.

This scenario integrates R/3™'s project system with components of its production and sales systems. Projects are defined by using work breakdown structures and networks. A work breakdown structure (WBS) is a hierarchical model of the tasks to be performed in a project. The WBS is the basis for organization and coordination of the project. It contains the work, time, and costs involved in each task. An initial WBS is developed for preliminary planning (i.e., during the customer bidding process) and can be extended dynamically throughout the life cycle of the project.

Networks are used to model detailed activities involving people, capacities, materials, production resources, tools, and services needed for the project. Networks can also describe comprehensive relationships between activities. Networks are linked to the WBS and, therefore, provide an additional level of detail in expressing the overall work breakdown.

This scenario begins by establishing a project structure to quote a customer job. As the project structure is defined, detail cost plans are developed and integrated into a budget. A plan works bottom-up from the detail, and a budget is developed top-down. Capacities are also checked. Project details are rolled up into a customer quotation.

A customer order can be posted by a special type of sales order (engineer-to-order) that references the project. The project is then released for processing, using the WBS and network controls. Down payments, billings, and additional customer payments are tracked to the appropriate WBS element. Costs and material issues are posted to networks or WBS elements directly. The system tracks the availability of budgeted funds. Costs are "settled" (transferred to the general ledger, cost center, or directly to the profitability system) on a periodic basis and/or at the end of the project.

Manufactured items are itemized on the sales order and are managed by using the make-to-order production scenario. Production work orders are either created manually or generated by the system. These work orders are linked to the appropriate WBS element. In this way, production is managed by traditional work orders, with actual production costs and milestones posted to the assigned WBS element.

6.6 QUALITY MANAGEMENT FOR GOODS RECEIPT FROM PRODUCTION

In most industries, high-quality products and services are no longer differentiators, because most businesses now design their operations and processes to ensure high quality. Even so, traditional manufacturing and logistics software approaches have no standard support for quality. Most companies have had to add specific functionality on top of their existing systems to overcome this lack. This approach is problematic. Just as manufacturers must build quality into the very foundation of every business process, a software system must incorporate support for quality measurement and improvement into its basic architecture.

In R/3™, material that flows out of the production process is recorded as a "goods receipt." In R/3™ Release 4.0, this scenario is called regulated production. This scenario integrates the goods receipt transaction into an enterprise-wide quality system. The scenario is used in manufacturing environments, where specific characteristics (beyond the usual material and lot number) of produced material must be recorded to the system to provide the proper identification of inventory batches. This scenario is usually a requirement for process-oriented manufacturers, such as chemical, food, beverage, and pharmaceutical companies. It can be used in any environment to support quality improvement programs, for example, by integrating test and inspection plans into the receiving process and using this data to monitor production and to improve quality.

The scenario begins with the goods receiving function. Material can be reported from production, using the goods receipt transaction in order-based, repetitive, or process manufacturing scenarios. Each material item in the system can have predefined inspection criteria associated with it. These include information on how to create inspection lots, what sequence of operations define the inspection process of each lot, what measurements need to be taken and recorded, and what criteria should be used to accept or reject material.

R/3™ uses this data to generate an order, called the quality management (QM) order, which is used to control the inspection process and record results. The order can activate problem notifications and generate follow-up activities. The disposition of material in the quality department is tracked via the QM order.

When all results are recorded, the QM order is closed (the technical term is "settled"), which moves the inventory lot into the stock-keeping area or the next step in production. Characteristics associated with each lot are created from the results recorded in inspection. All activities charged to the QM order are transferred to the cost management system.

Production Logistics Example:
Autodesk Incorporated, Sausalito, California

R/3™'s integrated production planning approach has improved the performance of one company, Autodesk Incorporated. Autodesk Incorporated employs some 1,900 people in the development, manufacturing, and distribution of its world-renowned computer-aided design (CAD) and multimedia software. The company's facilities include ten sales offices in the United States and five development centers in the United States and Switzerland. Autodesk also has subsidiaries in 20 countries in North America, Europe, and Asia-Pacific, the three major areas it serves. Autodesk is a $400 million company, growing at a rate of 20 percent each year.

Autodesk's goal is to maintain its growth rate and at the same time continue to ship products within one hour of receiving a customer order. But the software firm's rapid growth and globalization had stretched its business system—a small information system originally developed for a small startup company—to the limit.

"The information system we had couldn't handle our growth, the multiple order codes that constitute all our product permutations, or our guarantee to ship within 24 hours of an order. Additionally, it wasn't making critical operating information available to our executives on a timely basis for their analysis and decision making," says William Kredel, Autodesk's chief information officer.

In its search for a new business solution, Autodesk had a clear idea of what it wanted and needed. "We wanted real-time information on the state of our business, so that at any time of the day, our executives could see our revenue position, our expense position, our cash position, what products were selling, what customers we were selling to, and in what regions," Kredel says.

Using SAP™ software as a catalyst to redesign its business model, Autodesk reengineered 25 major business processes, "which included a total of some 240 subprocesses," according to Kedel. The system's multilanguage, multicurrency capabilities, and international tax support were important to the company, as was its open architecture. "We definitely believe in open systems. We ship our own products on multiple platforms—UNIX, DOS, and Windows."

The company's new order process is just one example of its successful reengineering effort. "Orders are now priced at the time they are entered," Kedel says. "We can quote the price to the customer on the phone, including shipping costs and sales taxes, which is something we couldn't do before. This pricing is completely accurate and includes things like discounts by customer, by channel, and so on." The system has also helped the company reduce the number of order codes it used—from 12,000 to just 1,500—and track information more efficiently.

Kedel explains: "When we introduce a new product, we can track it on a minute-to-minute basis to see how it's selling and what the average selling price is. We can see how many products we're giving away as evaluation copies, and when those evaluation copies are scheduled to turn into real licensed copies. We can determine the effect a marketing program is having by region. And we have the capability to look at individual cost centers, as well as compare overall costs across all regions, to compare, for example, the cost of manufacturing in Singapore vs. the U.S."

The next step is to develop the software in the European and Asia-Pacific regions and to standardize the operations of all Autodesk's subsidiaries, which currently operate very differently. "This will satisfy two of our objectives in installing the system—to make it easier for our customers to do business with Autodesk and to enhance global visibility. It will make our business processes similar around the world, so that our multinational customers will have one view of Autodesk."

Future plans include enabling customers to remotely access its system themselves to look at what products Autodesk has installed, what the serial numbers are, and what might be upgraded. Another plan under development is to move distribution of Autodesk's product to CD-ROM and, later, to electronic distribution, so the company can ship products to customers over the information highway. The overall goal is to improve cycle times across the business. "If we can develop our software faster, if we can ship it faster, if we can deliver it faster, if we can resolve problems faster, we will gain market share," Kedel says.

6.7   *R/3 PRODUCTION LOGISTICS SUMMARY*

The following tables provide an overview to the main scenarios, core processes, business objects, and organizational units that make up R/3 Production Logistics.

- -

Scenarios

▶ Sales-order-related production with production order

▶ Production by lot size

▶ Repetitive manufacturing

▶ Sales-order-related repetitive manufacturing

▶ Project-oriented make-to-order production

▶ Production replenishment using Kanban

▶ Continuous production

▶ Regulated production

▶ Discontinuous production

▶ Packaging

- -

Core Processes

▶ Material master record processing

▶ Material BOM processing

▶ Routing processing

▶ Work center/resource processing

▶ Sales and operations planning

▶ Demand management

▶ Material requirements planning

▶ Master production scheduling

▶ Planned order conversion

▶ Creating/processing production order

▶ Release of production order

▶ Execution of production order

▶ Confirmation of production order

▶ Production order settlement

▶ Goods issue for production orders

▶ Goods receipt processing from production

- -

Business Objects

▶ Production planning
  - Sales and operations plan
  - Planned independent requirement
  - Planned order
  - MRP list
  - Dependent requirements
▶ Production control
  - Kanban production control
  - Run schedule header
  - Production order

- -

Organizational Units

▶ Logical system
▶ Plant
▶ Storage location
▶ Work center/resource
▶ MRP area

7
Procurement Logistics

It is still common in business today for the flow of material to be controlled and managed by autonomous departments. Except for a few batch-type interfaces upstream (e.g., materials planning) or downstream (e.g., quality and accounting), a company's procurement activities used to be isolated from inventory logistics, production, and accounting functions. Now with shorter lead times, increased global operations, and more stringent quality requirements, isolated functions hinder the flow and overall performance of the procurement supply chain.

Procurement logistics, also known as Materials Management (MM) in R/3™ terminology, has a full range of integrated functions that help optimize such functional areas as purchasing, inventory management, and warehouse operations. For example, each time an inventory item is received into or issued from inventory, the system automatically updates stock quantities and values, and reduces inventory control. The high level of automation in R/3™ procurement logistics simplifies such time-consuming tasks as determining the optimum source of supply, analyzing and comparing vendor pricing, issuing purchase orders, managing the authorization process for purchase requisitions, and processing invoices for payment. Moreover, the high level of integration with production planning, inventory management, and accounts payable ensures an equally high degree of accuracy in order processing and facilitates the smooth flow of material necessary for manufacturing or internal consumption. Figure 7-1 illustrates the wide range of procurement logistics business processes supply chain scenarios, organizational units, and business objects that are discussed in this chapter.

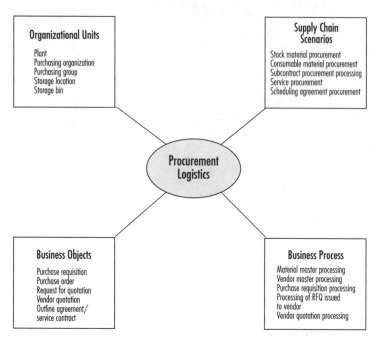

▶ **Figure 7–1**   Overview of scenario, process, organization, and business objects

For the sake of clarity, we examine in depth one business-process scenario, processing stock material, which will serve to illustrate the general processes of procurement logistics. Next, we provide an overview of other important scenarios, followed by customer examples.

7.1   PROCUREMENT OF STOCK MATERIAL

The Procurement of stock material scenario demonstrates how material flow is planned, expedited, and monitored by the R/3 ™ system. An efficient supply chain requires all stock planning and operational activities to be integrated into a uniform business-process flow. The material requirements planning, inventory, production, and procurement processes must all work together to orchestrate a smooth flow of high-quality material. Moreover, due to increasing competition, organizations must have the capability to adapt these processes to ever-changing workflows.

The procurement of stock material business process scenario acts as a central component of R/3 ™'s logistical chain. This scenario is concerned with forecast-

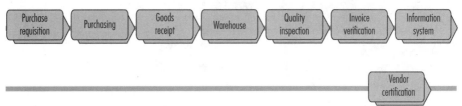

▶ **Figure 7–2**   Value chain: Procurement of stock material

ing and material requirements planning; tactical, operational, and execution functions of procurement communication; supplier integration to accounting and quality systems; and automated workflow and document management. These are incorporated into the value chain example of procurement logistics shown in Figure 7-2.

Represented in Figure 7-2 is a general outline of how a typical procurement process flows. The value chain depicts the subsequent workflow of converting the proposed supply plan for purchased material into commercial arrangements with suppliers, monitoring the status of these purchases, and receiving the items into inventory. Workflow events are configured to each company's requirements by taking into consideration the degree to which automated or manual controls are required. These steps include:

- Approving the planned requirements and generating a requisition
- Associating the requirement with a preplanned "source of supply" (contract or delivery schedule)
- Creating RFQs and obtaining bids from suppliers
- Issuing a purchase order
- Sending the purchase order to a supplier
- Generating an EDI purchase order
- Receiving a shipping notification from the supplier
- Receiving the items into inventory
- Issuing items to production or to maintenance orders
- Receiving items from production

Figures 7-3 through 7-5 illustrate this chain in a more detailed EPC diagram.

Our scenario begins when some kind of new requirement occurs—for example, someone wants to buy something—which triggers the task of purchase requisition processing (Figure 7-3).

Purchase requisition occurs when someone asks or instructs the purchasing department to buy a material or service by a certain date. If the purchase requisi-

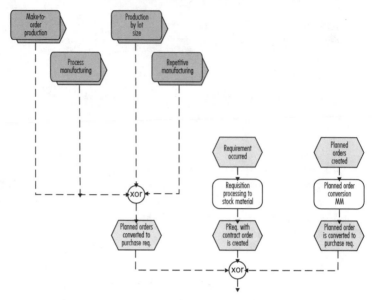

▶ **Figure 7–3** Procurement of stock material: Requisition processing to stock material

tion has a source of supply, the next step is purchase order processing. If not, a few more activities are necessary to begin purchase order processing.

First, vendor RFQ processing takes place. (A vendor is an outside supply source of materials and services.) Under this task, the inquiry is sent to the vendor and the quotation arrives.

Once the quotation arrives, vendor quotation processing begins. This task entails selecting a quotation. After that, the next task begins: purchase order processing. A purchase order includes such data as terms of delivery and payment and detailed description of the item.

If the purchase order is transferred—in other words, sent to the vendor—it's likely that the vendor will then ship the ordered item. Once the item arrives, goods receipt processing makes the next link in the chain. At the option of the company, goods receipt functions can interact with quality processes. In such a case, inspection operations are introduced into the process workflow. These operations include posting the material to blocked stock or placing it in storage. There's also a link to quality management if the material is posted to stock in the quality inspection department.

Materials that end up in storage are eventually delivered, a task that is the responsibility of sales and distribution (SD).

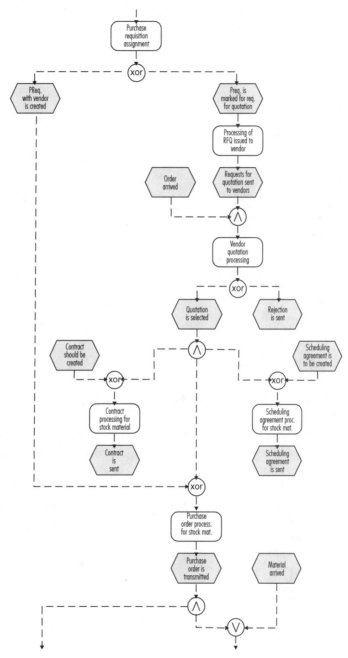

▶ **Figure 7–4** Procurement of stock material: Vendor quotation processing

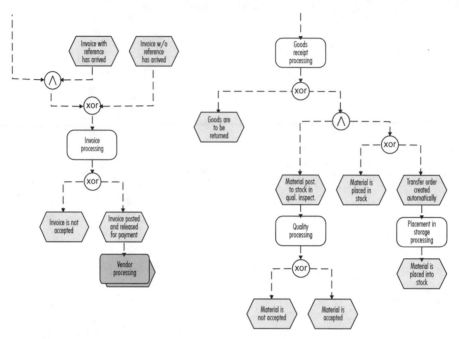

▶ **Figure 7–5**   Procurement of stock material: Goods receipt processing

Material Requirement Planning

The primary entry point for this scenario is the forecasting and MRP processes. The MRP uses a variety of deterministic or statistical methods to anticipate future demand for each stock item. The supply plan for these items is balanced with current demand and is consistent with the company's inventory investment and strategy. Hence, the materials planning incorporates "demand" information into the procurement activities. For example, information about current demand can consist of reservations for material required by a given functional area (e.g., when a production process requires a given quantity on a given day). The material reservations are collectively used to identify demand for a material at a given time.

Requisition Processing to Stock Material

When a new requirement for material is identified, the result is a purchase requisition (see Figure 7-3). A purchase requisition is a formal request that instructs purchasing to produce a material (or service) in a given quantity by a certain date. An item can be requisitioned in two ways: with a source of supply or without.

- With: There are existing contracts or buying history with a supplier, or the material can be sourced internally (i.e., from an existing plant).
- Without: The purchasing department must find a supplier on the open market by using a bidding process.

If the purchase requisition has a source of supply, the next step is purchase order processing. If not, a few more activities are necessary to begin purchase order processing. First, vendor inquiry processing takes place. (A vendor is an outside supply source of materials and services.) Under this task, the inquiry is sent to vendor and the quotation arrives. Once the quotation arrives, vendor quotation processing begins. After that, the next task, purchase order processing, begins.

Processing of RFQ Issued to Vendor

Companies receive quotations from different vendors by sending out a Request for Quotation (RFQ). A quotation contains a vendor's pricing and conditions for certain goods or services. A request for quotation can be created with reference to a purchase requisition or can be entered manually.

An RFQ is used to communicate requirements for a material or service to potential suppliers. In this process, requirements specified in authorized purchase requisitions for which no source of supply has been identified are copied into the RFQ. (The RFQ can also be entered manually.) The buyer specifies the deadline for the supplier's quote or bid. When the RFQ contains all items required, including desired quality and the delivery date, the buyer then enters the address information (either from the vendor master record or manually) for each potential supplier. An RFQ is created for each vendor, but the items within each RFQ are identical. The buyer can specify a code to monitor all RFQs belonging to a single bidding process. Finally, the RFQs are sent to the respective vendors. When the deadline for the submission of quotations passes (or when all vendor quotations have been received), the process "vender quotation processing" is triggered.

Vendor Quotation Processing

Vendor quotation processing occurs after the vendors have responded to the previous request for quotation and have sent their quotations back. Once their information has been entered into the system, it is then possible to compare bids. Price comparison is the most important step of vendor quotation processing.

This task leads to three possible events: 1) select quotation, 2) information record processing, and 3) subcontractor information record processing (see Figure 7-4).

If the quotation isn't selected, a rejection notice is transferred. If the quotation is selected, three tasks may take place: 1) purchase order processing for stock material, 2) purchase order processing for subcontracting, and 3) purchase order processing for consumable material.

BUSINESS OBJECT

▶ *Purchase Order*

The business object purchase order is a request or instruction from a purchasing organization to a vendor (external supplier) or a plant to deliver a quantity of material or to perform services at a certain point in time. The business object defines a request to a supplier (external vendor or internal plant) to deliver a material or service in a specific quantity at an agreed-on price and date.

A purchase order (PO) consists of a number of items, for each of which a procurement type is defined, as for subcontracting, consignment, stock transfer, or service.

The business object purchase order is used as a source of information for the following types of business analysis.

Report Subject	Information Delivery
Purchase order	Provides detailed information about specific purchase orders, such as client, purchasing document number, or creation date
Purchasing organizations	Measures the performance of procurement channels within your company responsible for procuring products or raw materials, managing the relationship with suppliers, and negotiating terms of purchase with suppliers
Purchasing groups	Measures the performance of buyers or purchasing agents within a company responsible for procuring a class of parts, products, or raw materials and managing the relationship with suppliers

Purchase Order Processing for Stock Material

Purchase order processing of stock material begins as a result of a number of different tasks in the areas of procurement (materials management) and production (production planning) logistics. It falls under the responsibility of warehouse management. In this case, we'll examine how the previous two tasks—vendor quotation processing and vendor RFQ processing—trigger this step.

In vendor quotation processing, a quotation and data about the order item are first selected and then transferred for vendor data processing.

In the case of vendor RFQ processing, three possible events can occur:

- Creation of a purchase requisition with a source of supply
- Creation of a purchase requisition with a vendor
- Creation of a purchase requisition without a source of supply
  (following this, a source of supply and a vendor must be determined)

All three lead to selection of data about the item, transfer of the order item, and processing of vendor data.

It is possible that a demand for the item exists but no source of supply is yet available. If this is the case, we determine a supply source and vendor and then select a category for the order item (for example, normal). Now, vendor data processing can begin.

Vendor data processing includes processing all vendor-related information and then checking or entering the material. Once completed, we determine stock material with a master record. Stock material is something that's always kept in stock (for example, a raw material) and has a material master record, allowing companies to manage and keep track of the amount of material they possess. Determining stock material leads to five possible actions:

- Enter order as detail data
- Maintain goods released control
- Process purchase order conditions
- Specify key acknowledgments
- Enter additional item data

All five are linked to the next task: enter supplier schedules. After this, we create the purchase order. A purchase order includes such data as terms of delivery and payment and detailed description of the item ("What kind of material is it?" "How much has been ordered?" "When is it to be delivered?" "How much does it cost?"). In this phase, the goal is to process purchase orders as quickly as possible, using reference information from previous tasks, such as purchase requisition processing.

Now, one of three things can happen: 1) monitor order, 2) transfer order, or 3) process information record. If the order is transferred, it triggers the next task: send a delivery letter.

Goods Receipt Processing

Goods receipt processing follows the sending of a letter to a vendor asking for the delivery of an ordered item. Goods receipt processing begins when the ordered material arrives or a material arrives with a shipping notification. At this point, two events occur: checking material slip and determining storage and removal (Figure 7-5).

By checking the material and shipping slip, we can see whether the shipment is correct or needs to be returned. Once we determine the purchase order and material storage arrangements, we adjust purchase order dates and select valuation type.

First, it's possible that the goods receipt can't be posted, and the process stops. However, other events can also take place:

- Material posted to warehouse stock—opens two possibilities:
  - Warehouse management moves material into storage—triggers next task, storage processing of goods receipt
  - Warehouse management doesn't maintain warehouse (i.e., warehouse is independently managed)—material is simply placed in stock
- Material posted to quality inspection stock
- Material posted to blocked stock

In all three cases, two tasks follow: inform purchasing and print goods receipt-and-issue slip.

7.2 PROCUREMENT OF CONSUMABLE MATERIALS

In most systems, purchased materials are received into inventory and then issued to production, work orders, or other cost centers within the company. In these systems, costs are associated with each item in inventory and subsequently posted to the appropriate job order or cost center when the material is issued from inventory.

In a job-oriented environment, however, it might be desirable to charge material expenses directly to a job but still track the status of the material through use of an inventory-based approach. In other words, companies would like to be able to use the requisitioning, purchasing, and tracking capability of a standard inventory system, but they would also prefer to bypass the mechanisms of using an inventory-based accounting system to charge expenses to a job order or cost center.

Inventory control systems track the quantity and value of each material. In this way, the flow of value (i.e., accounting) is synchronized with the physical flow of material. In R/3 ™, there exists a special class of material, "consumable material," whose values are not tracked in the inventory system. Instead, the costs of consumable materials are expensed directly to a job or cost center when the material is received from a supplier. Therefore, for these items, the accounting flow is decoupled from the physical flow of material. The system continues to track the item through inventory, but it does not post any further accounting transaction when the item is used in production, maintenance, or other operational areas. The costing systems deal with the allocation of these costs independently from inventory accounting.

In R/3 ™, inventoried items are identified to the system with a material number in the "material master file." Thereafter, the quantity and monetary value of items are tracked and accounted for in the system. Consumable materials are tracked for quantity only, and their value is not accounted for in the inventory system. Instead of being carried in inventory, the costs of these materials are expensed directly to a cost center, job, or other entity at the time the materials are received into the company. These items can be:

- Required as input to the manufacturing process for make-to-order or project-oriented production
- Used as a replacement item in the maintenance of an asset or customer equipment
- Used on a job or project

The primary entry point for the procurement of consumable materials scenario is when material is requested by an operational system, for instance, production or maintenance. The request is handled in the form of a requisition. Requisitions can be generated automatically or manually. Automatic requisitioning occurs when consumable materials are associated directly with a job; that is, when the consumable item is listed on a bill of materials for a production or maintenance order.

This scenario controls the subsequent workflow of converting the requisition into a commercial arrangement with a vendor, monitoring the status of the purchase, receiving the item into the company, and handling the appropriate accounting and costing aspects of the transaction. When the material is received into the company, the purchase costs are posted directly to the order or cost center associated with the source of the original requisition. This workflow includes:

- Approving the requisition
- Associating the requisition with a preplanned "source of supply," that is specific vendor, contract, or delivery schedule
- Creating RFQs and obtaining bids from suppliers
- Creating a purchase order or call-off against a purchase contract
- Sending the purchase order to a supplier or generating an EDI purchase order
- Receiving a shipping notification from the supplier
- Receiving the items at the appropriate point of use
- Processing vendor invoices
- Settling special arrangements such as bonuses or volume-based rebates

The accounting is posted automatically to the appropriate account or cost entity at the time of receipt. This procurement process is also integrated with cash management and budgeting.

7.3   PROCUREMENT OF CONSIGNMENT MATERIALS

In a traditional vendor/customer transaction, transfer of ownership of inventory occurs at the same time as the physical flow of that inventory. Naturally, most inventory systems handle this adequately, because the accounting of inventory mirrors the movement of product.

There are always exceptions, however. For instance, a manufacturer may stock spare parts inventory at a customer site to enhance maintenance response time. Alternatively, a manufacturer might not want to pay for an expensive item until it is used in production. To avoid delays in production resulting from a materials shortage, the customer might ask the vendor to stock the material at the customer's facility.

As trading partners work together to increase the overall responsiveness of the supply chain, these types of arrangements are becoming commonplace. Customers will try to push the financial burden of maintaining inventories to upstream suppliers and will increasingly negotiate for "point-of-use" payment schemes. Customers will still maintain the same safety stocks, but now the supplier will "own" the inventory until the customer uses it in production or resells it. To accommodate the needs of these consignment practices, a company will be required to track vendor-owned inventory as if it were its own.

Consignment materials are items that are owned by a supplier but stored on the company's premises. They are not valued on the company's books until they are formally issued from a specially designated inventory called consignment stores. This transaction transfers ownership of the consigned materials to the company. Consignment materials can be used as inputs to production, resold, used in maintenance or engineering operations, or simply transferred into standard company inventory. R/3™ is designed so that all materials—standard stock, consignment stock, and consumable material—can be managed consistently with a common set of transactions. In this scenario, however, special functionality is required to automatically handle vendor payables and the valuation of inventory as it passes from consignment.

In R/3™, inventoried items are identified to the system with a material number in the material master file. These items can be:

- Required as input to the manufacturing process
- Received as output from production
- Reserved as a spare part
- Resold to a customer
- Used as a replacement item in maintenance

An item can be managed as a company's own stock, as consigned material, or both. When managed as consigned material, the inventory is tracked with a "special stock" designation assigned to each vendor. Because the same item can be purchased from several vendors, it is possible to have multiple consignment stocks of the same material—one for each vendor. For each vendor-specific stock, a moving average price is maintained. This price is used for valuing each withdrawal or transfer to company stocks. Withdrawals of consignment material can be preplanned by means of reservations, and all movements involving consignment material are clearly identified as such at the time of posting. Batch management and quality/inspection functionality work for consigned inventory exactly as they do for standard stock material.

As with normal stocked material, the primary entry point for the procurement of consignment materials, or procurement on a consignment basis (Release 4.0), scenario is the forecasting and material planning processes. The material planning processes use a variety of deterministic (i.e., MRP) or statistical (i.e., forecasting) methods to anticipate future demand for each item. The supply plan for these items is balanced with demand and is consistent with the company's inventory investment strategies. Material reservation requests in any area of the company (e.g., in the plant maintenance or field service areas), are integrated as a "demand" to which the planning system responds.

This scenario controls the subsequent workflow of converting the proposed supply plan for purchased material into commercial arrangements with suppliers, monitoring the status of these purchases, receiving the items into stock, and issuing the material out of "consignment stores." This workflow includes:

- Approving the planned requirements and generating a requisition
- Associating the requirement with a preplanned "source of supply" (contract or delivery schedule)
- Creating RFQs and obtaining bids from suppliers
- Creating a consignment purchase order
- Sending the purchase order to a supplier
- Generating an EDI purchase order
- Receiving a shipping notification from the supplier
- Receiving the items into "special stock" consignment stores
- Issuing items from consignment stores to production or maintenance orders
- Transferring consignment stores to normal company inventory

Vendor invoicing occurs automatically when material is issued from consignment stores. Receiving functions can integrate the quality system because preplanned inspection operations can be introduced into the receiving workflow. This scenario is integrated with cash management and funds control.

7.4   PROCUREMENT OF SUBCONTRACT WORK

Outsourcing gains a manufacturer access to a subcontractor's specialized skills, manufacturing expertise, or work force. It is also an important alternative in helping manufacturers cut costs and lead times. To realize the potential from outsourcing, a subcontractor must be integrated into the logistics flow of the company. Otherwise, the costs of maintaining a separate logistics systems to manage outsourcing could offset the potential economic benefit. Subcontract logistics—reserving, issuing, and receiving material—along with documentation and accounting should be integrated and managed with the same systems used for standard procurement and internal materials management. Subcontract orders are used to manage the outsourcing of manufacturing processes in which the company provides some or all of the materials to the subcontractor.

In SAP™ R/3™ Release 4.0, subcontracting procurement is covered in the procurement via subcontracting business process scenario. The scenario begins with forecasting and materials planning. These activities use statistical or deterministic methods to calculate material requirements. The planning system fills the requirements by generating a supply plan.

This scenario controls the subsequent workflow of converting the proposed supply plan for outsourced material into commercial arrangements with subcontractors, monitoring the status of these purchases, provisioning and issuing component materials to the subcontractor, and receiving the manufactured items into stock. These steps include:

- Approving the planned requirements from the planning system and generating a requisition
- Associating the requisition with a preplanned "source of supply" (contract or delivery schedule)
- Creating RFQs and obtaining bids from suppliers
- Creating a subcontract purchase order
- Sending the purchase order to a supplier
- Issuing component material to the subcontractor
- Generating an EDI purchase order
- Receiving a shipping notification from the supplier
- Receiving the items into stock

If a company maintains stocks of materials on the subcontractor's premises, these are identified to the system as "vendor special stocks" when they are issued to the subcontractor. In this case, the material still belongs to the providing company but is not considered available on-hand inventory.

Company-owned material that is consumed by the subcontractor is identified on each subcontract purchase order. After receipt of material from the subcontractor, the quantities and values of the component material provided by the company (and consumed in the production process) are automatically posted out of inventory. The inventory value of the produced (and received) material equals the net purchase order value of the produced material plus the value of the component materials posted out of inventory. With receipt of the subcontractor's invoice, the previously posted consumption of material can be corrected to account for any overusage or underusage.

This scenario handles vendor invoices and accounting as well as management and settlement of special supplier financial arrangements such as bonuses and volume discounts. Receiving functions can integrate the quality system because preplanned inspection operations can be introduced into the receiving workflow. This scenario is also integrated with cash management and funds control.

7.5   STOCK TRANSFER PROCESSING

An efficient flow of material within a company is essential to improved supply chain performance. As companies are forced to achieve higher levels of supply chain performance, an inefficient logistics system for handling intersite inventory transfers becomes a bottleneck. Many companies use multiple and incompatible systems for handling different methods of processing inbound materials to a stocking location or plant. For instance, items purchased from external suppliers might be handled in a purchase order module, whereas another stock transfer module might handle intersite transfers. In these cases, individual logistics activities such as generating material requirements, reserving inventory for shipping, or processing in-bound receipts are handled differently in each system.

In the R/3 ™ system, a common set of logistics activities are implemented to handle inbound transfers or purchases from vendors. These include materials planning, requisitions, reservations, material issues, and inventory receipts. These activities are performed similarly regardless of the scenario in which they are used.

R/3 ™ is a multisite inventory management system. These sites are called "plants" in R/3 ™ and can include warehouses, manufacturing facilities, or distribution centers. R/3 ™ can automatically plan the transfer of material from one plant to another, monitor the status of these transfers, and post the related financial transactions. "Transport orders" are used for transfers of stock between plants. These orders allow for the preplanning of delivery costs. The procurement price of each inbound transfer is the valuation of the material at the issuing plant plus the additional costs of delivery.

Order policies, maintained in the material master file, help the planning system automatically determine:

- What item to order
- From which plant to order
- Quantity to order
- When to place the order (based on transit lead time)

The planning system determines transfers at the same time it generates the material plan for purchased and manufactured items. In this way, in one operation, an integrated supply chain plan is generated.

The stock transfer processing scenario controls the subsequent workflow of 1) converting the planned transfer into a transport order (a special type of purchase order), 2) monitoring the status of the transport order, 3) reserving the material at the issuing plant, 4) issuing the material, and 5) processing a goods receipt at the receiving plant. When the issuing plant posts the goods issue transaction with reference to the transport order, the quantity withdrawn from stock at the issuing plant is listed as stock in transit at the receiving plant. When the receiving plant posts the receipt transaction with reference to the transport order, the inventory control system reflects the stock now on hand, and stock-in-transit and the open purchase order quantity at the receiving plant are reduced.

7.6   EXTERNAL SERVICES MANAGEMENT

Traditional purchasing systems were designed to procure material for inventory. Although the basic cycle of requisition, approval, purchase order, and invoicing is similar for the procurement of goods or services, the details are very different. It is unwieldy to record services performed into a system that is defined to post inventory. However, services are generally charged off to a cost center or work order on completion, whereas materials are recorded in an inventory control system at receipt. An optimal procurement system handles the management of outside services. Many services are performed in support of manufacturing or maintenance operations. Therefore, the external management of services systems should be fully integrated into the operating systems that manage production and maintenance. The external services management scenario is used to manage the procurement of services from external suppliers.

This scenario begins with the requisition process. Requisitions can be created manually or generated automatically from maintenance or production orders. These orders create the requisitions for external services when an operation on the order is indicated to be performed by an external supplier.

The requisition moves through the approval cycle and can be associated with a known source of supply, such as a specific vendor or preexisting service purchase contract. The requisition can be converted into an RFQ and bids sent to various suppliers. A "service purchase order" or "order release" (against a contract) is created and sent to the vendor. Transactions are posted when services are performed and/or approved.

This scenario integrates invoicing and accounting functions as well as management and settlement of special supplier financial arrangements such as bonuses and volume discounts. It is also fully integrated with cash management and funds control.

7.7   R/3™ PROCUREMENT LOGISTICS SUMMARY

The following tables provide an overview to the main scenarios, core processes, business objects, and organizational units that make up R/3™ Procurement Logistics.

Scenarios

▶ Stock material procurement
▶ Consumable material procurement
▶ Consignment processing
▶ Subcontract procurement processing
▶ Stock transfer processing
▶ Service procurement
▶ Internal procurement
▶ Scheduling agreement procurement

Core Processes

▶ Material master processing
▶ Vendor master processing
▶ Material disposition
▶ Purchase requisition processing
▶ Purchase requisition assignment
▶ Processing of RFQ issued to vendor
▶ Vendor quotation processing
▶ Scheduling agreement processing
▶ Contract processing
▶ Purchase order processing
▶ Entry of services rendered
▶ Shipping notification/confirmation processing
▶ Goods receipt processing with reference
▶ Inspection lot creation
▶ Inspection lot completion
▶ Results recording
▶ Invoice processing with reference
▶ Goods issue processing

Business Objects

▶ Purchasing

  – Purchase requisition

  – Purchase order

  – Request for quotation

  – Vendor quotation

  – Outline agreement/service contract

  – Shipping notification

  – Purchasing info record

Organizational Units

▶ Logical system

▶ Plant

▶ Purchasing organization

▶ Purchasing group

▶ Storage location

▶ Warehouse complex

▶ Storage type

▶ Storage bin

▶ Valuation area

MATERIALS MANAGEMENT EXAMPLE

Many SAP™ customers have testified to the importance of logistical chains connected to procurement logistics MM in generating increased company performance. The following are two examples of SAP™ customers that have benefited from R/3™'s integrated logistical chains.

Chevron Corporation, Tulsa, Oklahoma

Chevron is a $32 billion company ranked number 11 on the Fortune 500. The company began the roll-out of its new business reengineering program—Advanced Financial Information System (AFIS)—at Warren Petroleum, a billion-dollar business unit headquartered in Tulsa. Warren employs about 1,000 people and is the largest extractor, refiner, and seller of natural gas liquids in the United States. Ten remote plants are spread across Oklahoma, Texas, Louisiana, and New Mexico.

As part of its continuing effort to reduce costs, the company conducted an internal study that showed how much it spent annually on its core financial processes. Chevron calculated that reengineering those business processes and moving to a client/server financial information system could reduce costs by 25 percent.

Chevron had already reduced its costs by more than a billion dollars, but the company wanted to cut costs even more in its drive to become the least expensive, best-class producer of oil and gas. Chevron's AFIS project targeted the firm's core financial processes: purchasing, service contracts, accounts payable, fixed-asset accounting, intercompany accounting and consolidation, general ledger, financial reporting, and capital project tracking. The company's previous system was a 30-year-old patchwork suite of 200 home-grown subsystems running on a mainframe.

sive, best-class producer of oil and gas. Chevron's AFIS project targeted the firm's core financial processes: purchasing, service contracts, accounts payable, fixed-asset accounting, intercompany accounting and consolidation, general ledger, financial reporting, and capital project tracking. The company's previous system was a 30-year-old patchwork suite of 200 home-grown subsystems running on a mainframe.

"The system wasn't integrated, the applications functioned like silos," James Zell, Chevron's AFIS project manager, says. "It wasn't flexible enough to meet our changing requirements, particularly when we restructured our operations into strategic business units. And it was costly to maintain." Information wasn't available in a timely or easy-to-access way. Data were accumulated in a variety of ways from separate, nonintegrated systems, resulting in expensive and time-consuming analysis.

Rather than automating things the way they were, Chevron focused on reengineering its processes. To do so, it assembled a team of 30 people to analyze and redesign its main financial processes in the most efficient way possible.

"We developed a vision of how all these financial processes should work by analyzing best-practices in a number of industries," Zell says. Then, Chevron looked for a software to match that vision, finally deciding on SAP™'s R/3™ system.

The company began its worldwide roll-out of AFIS at Warren Petroleum. Today, some 250 users—often 100 on line at the same time—are connected to the client/server information system at Warren, which links headquarters with ten remote plants across five different states.

Says Linda Manning, manager of change management and training for the AFIS project, "Warren has completely reengineered its financial processes to capture data at source. Whenever data is received, it goes into the system immediately and is available immediately throughout the entire system for viewing." Thus, purchased materials received at a warehouse are reflected in financials right away. Moreover, both current and historical financial information are available to users on the network almost instantly.

"The savings in paperwork processing compared with the previous system are tremendous," Manning says. "Previously, when goods were received, we got an invoice at the plant. People made copies, filed them, and eventually sent the invoice along to headquarters for payment. At headquarters, these invoices then had to be searched out and matched against the purchase order and goods-receipts document."

Chevron's next step is to generate payment without waiting for an invoice. "If you have a purchase order and know the price and all applicable sales taxes, then once you get notification of goods received, you just pay the vendor without waiting for an invoice," Zell explains. "That has the potential of saving us a lot of money."

Critical financial information is also now available for analysis immediately, whereas before it took a month or more to get to cost or expense centers. "The information they received on how they ran their business was not current or timely," Manning admits. "Now, purchasing managers can see how much business they are doing with a vendor and how much they owe that vendor. Cost center managers can examine month-to-date information on expenses and compare that information to planned budget. Finance managers can look at accounts payable ledgers and see the status of invoices. And so on."

In Chevron's case, reengineering included bringing technology into new areas, for example, putting a PC into the warehouse for the person receiving goods. That, of course, involved a "tremendous amount of change" for everyone in the company. Manning credits the success of the training part of reengineering to the support of upper management.

"The president and financial vice president at Warren were very supportive," she says. "They were also very visible, and there was a constant flow of communication to the people who were expected to use the system. The message was: it's coming, it's important, we need to do this, we support it, and we need you to support it as well."

Chevron's Warren plant has already seen 20 percent savings in the way it does business. The next phase of the company's AFIS project is the simultaneous roll-out of the system to Chevron's corporate headquarters, pipeline company, and domestic refining and marketing companies. The final goal is to reengineer all of the corporation's main financial processes at Chevron's 15 different operating companies within five years. The result: ultimately linking 2,000 users worldwide.

Westcoast Energy, Inc., Vancouver, British Columbia

Westcoast Energy, Inc., is a leader in Canada's natural gas industry. The largest processor, transporter, and distributor of natural gas in Canada, Westcoast Energy's range of interests includes natural gas transportation pipelines, distribution systems, power generation, gas processing, and marketing.

Before the mid-1980s, Westcoast Energy was the only company that could buy gas in northern British Columbia and resell it to distribution. Industry deregulation came a few years later, just as Westcoast was buying utilities across Canada and expanding its activities in the areas of distribution and power generation. Both changes forced the company to reengineer its business processes.

Westcoast's biggest challenge was to bring all of its business activities together, which would include installing new computer systems and overhauling the flow of business processes. The company created Team SPIRIT (Strategic Process Improvement through Redesign, Integration, and Technology), a group of 60 representatives from senior management, IT, finance, materials management, engineering, processing, transmission, and outside consultants.

The first task of Team SPIRIT was to redesign almost all of Westcoast's pipeline business processes and deliver up-to-date, on-line information to staff along 1,600 miles of pipeline stretching from the British Columbia-Yukon border to the British Columbia-United States border. It chose SAP™'s R/3™ client/server system to help it link the large geographical area. Sixteen months later, Westcoast Energy had reduced cycle times in materials procurement (from 23 days to 12 days) and in the financial month-end closing (from 12 days to 6 days).

The move from periodic financial reporting to on-line, real-time information reduced processing time and freed managers and analysts from taking the time to gather decision-making information. They now have the time and tools to analyze results earlier and in greater depth. The elimination of extra steps in processes will result in savings of between $2 and $3 million a year.

Says Art Williams, president of Westcoast Energy, "The success of the Team SPIRIT project is fundamental to the long-term effectiveness and success of our company."

8

External Accounting

Many of the current business practices, processes, and conditions discussed earlier—changes in information technology, corporate restructuring, business engineering, and so forth—have created radically different financial and accounting needs within a corporation. Add to this already existing backdrop such other issues as the emerging technologies of electronic commerce and the increasing reliance on business partners, third-party producers, and outside vendors, and it is not surprising that businesses now quickly embrace highly complex economic processes as the result. Compounding these problems are the ever-increasing demands on accounting, not only to be integrated with all company processes, but to become more of a management tool for all company departments. Companies today want more coordination and control from their accounting systems; they want shorter response times and timely decisions based on strategic planning; and they want an accounting system that can plan, control, and monitor operations.

The SAP ™ R/3 ™ accounting system is geared toward meeting these demands. It is divided into key areas such as financial accounting, asset management, and management accounting (controlling). All three areas not only facilitate the storage and recording of data but allow management to monitor, control, and plan key business transactions on the basis of up-to-date accounting information. Integration of information is once again a key element of new enterprise systems. The accounting system allows access to information in each phase of a corporate organization—from development to key logistical operations. It also provides important links to and from vendors, customers, and financial institutions.

To be most effective, financial accounting must satisfy both internal and external accounting requirements. Internal requirements—that is, profit center accounting or profitability analysis—are handled by controlling (see Chapter 10). External accounting processes—such as providing accounting disclosures and information to shareholders, creditors, and the public—are primarily contained in financial accounting.

External accounting reflects the changing relationship between companies and outside vendors or suppliers. Along with the ability to process standard accounts, external accounting must be prepared for the many possibilities that arise from special circumstances. For example, in addition to standard customer processing or vendor processing, external accounting must also be able to handle a one-time invoice, a one-time customer account, or a payment made from a head office to branches or subsidiaries of a customer.

This chapter explains the business processes related to external accounting. Figure 8-1 illustrates the wide range of processes and scenarios discussed in this chapter.

Figure 8-1 represents the core work in financial accounting. We begin by first detailing a scenario from vendor processing and then explain other key processes. The chapter concludes with an illustrative customer example.

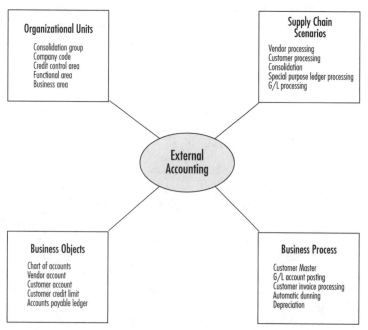

▶ **Figure 8–1**   Overview of scenario, process, organizations, and business objects

8.1   VENDOR HANDLING

Reflecting the growing interconnectivity between companies and outside suppliers, the R/3™ accounts payable manages the accounting data of all of a company's vendors. A vendor is defined broadly as any business partner toward whom there exists outstanding payables for received goods or services. Services may include, for example, goods delivered, certain services performed, or a transferred right. Accounts payable is also an essential component of the purchasing system, where purchase orders, deliveries, and invoices are managed for each vendor and used in the evaluation of vendors.

Key areas of accounts payable revolve around integration of information, cash management, and payment procedures. In regard to integration, items posted in accounts payable are simultaneously posted and managed in the general ledger (a financial accounting ledger that is defined for the generation of closing reports as required by law; see Section 8.5). Hence, all postings to vendor accounts are made simultaneously to the general ledger. Different general ledger accounts are updated depending on the transaction involved (payables, down payments, etc.). Items are also posted automatically in each of the operational transactions throughout the system, which ensures that appropriate functions (i.e., invoice processing) are updated throughout the system.

Accounts payable must be closely linked to cash management and forecasting. Due-date forecasts and other standard reports enable accounting to keep track of the open items. The values from the invoices are also handed over to cash management, ensuring optimum liquidity planning. Moreover, dunning procedures are supported by the dunning process, which allows vendors to be dunned for any outstanding receivables (e.g., the repayment of a credit memo).

Payables are settled by the payment program, which supports all the standard payment methods, both those in paper form (checks and transfers) and in electronic form (data exchange via disk and telecommunication). The payment program also supports payment methods that are specific to certain countries. The processes in external accounting involve a full range of business correspondence types, such as balance confirmations, account statements, notices, which users can adapt to suit their requirements. Finally, for documenting individual transactions, there are balance lists, balance audit trails, journals, and other evaluations.

The value chain illustrated in Figure 8-2 describes the processes involved in vendor processing.

This chain explains the basic flow of a vendor handling process. First, processing a vendor invoice begins. It can be "parked" until all information is collected. Once all information is in, then the invoice is posted into the system. If the vendor requires down payments, a payment request is created. Payments can be requested automatically or manually. Payments may be made or received. If

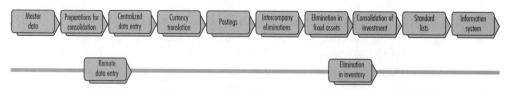

▶ **Figure 8–2**   Value chain: Consolidation

vendors fall behind on making payments, they may be reminded via payment reminders or dunning notices.

A more-detailed EPC diagram of this process scenario is illustrated in Figure 8-3. The diagram begins with an invoice sent from a vendor. Invoices can be either entered into the system via data entry, scanned into the system using an interface to an archive system, or transferred through electronic data interchange (EDI). The invoices are documented and then exported to financial accounting. The vendor's records are accessed through the vendor master record, which contains all vendor information and controls the posting transaction as well as the processing of posting data. If no master record exists, one is created. Next, the invoice data undergoes vendor invoice processing. The system immediately checks all entries for errors and suggests corrections. Once all necessary information is completed and entered, the invoice is then posted.

This event triggers either down payment release and invoice payment release or is sent to overheads management with allocation costing for further processing. In our scenario, the next step involves a down payment. Down payment information is stored in the system according to individual requests. After the down payment is released, the task "automatic payment" is then triggered. This task involves creating payment proposals, editing payment proposals, and posting payment documents. Here, terms of payment, method of payment, bank selection, and payment forms are determined. The R/3™ system also supports manual payment settlement for such items as original invoices or electronic pre-process (e.g., a bank statement for outgoing payments). Finally, payment is either sent or posted for further processing (e.g., by central budgeting).

Vendor Master Record Processing

The basic data object in vendor processing, the vendor master record, contains the link to the general ledger and to information on individual vendors. At the same time, it provides the connection between purchasing and accounting functions in the R/3™ system. Master records have a three-level structure that can be

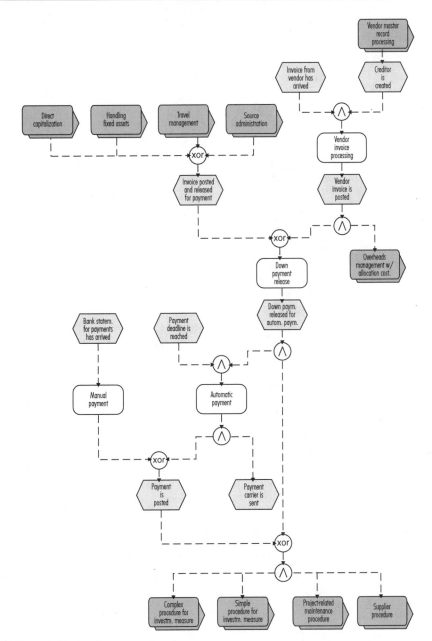

▶ **Figure 8–3**   Vendor processing

customized according to individual organizational structures. In general, each master record consists of:

- General data
- Company code data
- Purchasing organization data

General data consist of basic information such as company address, telephone, fax, and so forth. Items also entered into the master record include bank information, company number, corporate group, industry branch, country, language, and so on. Company code data include individual account information concerning the vendor. Account information contains a record of correspondences, dunning procedures, and important information concerning the agreed-upon payment terms and method of payment (such as check, electronic fund transfer, etc.). Company code data have links to the general ledger, which is updated automatically when postings are made to the specific vendor account. Finally, purchasing organization data revolve around information on requests for quotation, purchase orders, and invoice verification. These data also have links to other enterprise process areas (e.g., procurement).

Master record processing entails creating a new master record for each individual account group. First, a number assignment type is assigned to the account. Two possibilities exist: internal and external. Internal is generated by the system itself; external is determined by the user. In either case, to prevent duplication of information, the system allows only one number to be assigned to the account. Next, information required for transaction processing is entered into the new master record. All necessary information for master records is predefined into the system through a customized user interface.

Once the master record is created, further processing can occur on an ongoing basis. The data in master records can be accessed by using separate functions for creating, changing, and displaying data. Authorizations for these functions can be assigned depending on the area of responsibility of the particular employee. For this process, master records from one account group are allocated to a certain vendor type, which can then be broken down according to different criteria.

There are also other support options throughout the system to help in the processing of master records. These include, for example, an automatic duplicate check, which ensures that no redundant data are entered in the system, and a copy function, which copies data from an existing master record into a new one or transfers an entire group of master records of one company code to another.

Vendor Invoice Processing

"Business as usual" has changed dramatically in recent years because of the innovative usage of new enterprise architecture technologies such as the Internet. Such innovations make it critical to examine invoicing for reports.

A vendor invoice can be sent to a company in a variety of ways, such as manual entry, EDI, or scanning. The data are then documented and exported to financial accounting for processing. This event triggers the task vendor invoice processing.

This task involves some form of data entry, such as preliminary document entry. Invoices may or may not have a vendor master record. If the invoice does have a master record, the document header and a variable number of purchase order items are entered for each document. Other line items, such as input tax postings, are then created automatically by the system. If an invoice arrives from a vendor whose master data has not yet been entered in the system, invoice data cannot be entered into the system until a master record for that vendor is created (as described above).

Once the amount payable is entered into the system, it is then allocated to a company code. The company code is defined as the smallest organizational unit for which a complete, self-contained set of accounts can be drawn up for purposes of statutory reporting (see Section 8.5). After the company code has been determined, the offsetting entry is then made. This item can be posted to two areas: either to a fixed assets account or to a current assets account. In either case, the system then carries out an automatic procedure that checks whether the posting document has been entered correctly. This "balance check" ensures that the debit amount of the document matches the credit amount. If the balance is zero, then the vendor invoice is posted. If not, then the process is reversed step by step so that the user can correct his or her entries.

After the invoice is posted, the system then issues a payment. Payment can be carried out either automatically or manually.

Down Payment Release

Understanding payment processing is crucial for adjusting to changes in business conditions, liquidity problems, and general relationships with vendors. Of course, these processes are very different across the world, making it all the more important to grasp the core business scenario.

The payment program generates down payments to vendors. In the first step of this process, a down payment request is entered (see Figure 8-3).

This request contains all specifications needed for a down payment and a due date by which the down payment must be made. The down payment request is stored as a document, but this document does not change or update any account balances. Also, at any time the system can display an individual request, all requests for a specific vendor, or all requests entered thus far.

The system automatically creates the actual down payments. When a final settlement is posted, the system will refer to any down payments already made. After an incoming invoice is posted, it can be used to clear one or more down payments completely or partially. The payment program then pays the invoice amount minus the down payments that were cleared. Down payments can be presented as either gross amounts (including tax on sales/purchases) or net amounts (without tax) in both the vendor account and the general ledger account for down payments made. In either case, the system guarantees that the amounts will be reported accurately in the balance sheet at net value.

Automatic Payment

As consumers, we have all recognized the trend away from manual payments. Automatic payments in businesses are often related to sophisticated transactions that can take months to execute or can involve multiple currencies. The automatic processing of payment transactions in Accounts Payable is designed to facilitate the payment process.

Automatic payments are carried out in three steps:

1. Create payment proposal
2. Process payment proposal
3. Post payment documents

First, the payment program creates a payment proposal list based on the specifications in the customer master record and the invoice documents.

Next, the proposal either undergoes editing or processing, or payment is triggered directly. If desired, it can be processed by several clerks at the same time. The payment proposal can be modified as required, for example, if a proposed payment method or selected bank is changed. The system generates a log of the payment process so that users have a record of the whole transaction, which they can use to check payment transactions at any time. The system has an automatic due-date determination function, which runs continuously in the background. This function generally pays invoices as late as possible without incurring any monetary loss; it also calculates the highest cash discount possible and pays accordingly. In addition, the payment programs support a wide range of different specifications and forms of payment. For example, the user can specify multilevel terms of payment by entering various combinations of dates and due dates.

In the last step, the payment program generates payments with matching documents based on the processed version of the proposal. Payable items are cleared and linked to the payments. The system then prints out the required forms and/or creates a disk for data medium exchange. This data medium can also be processed via the data medium management function, which provides the user with an overview of all pertinent data, such as house bank, clearing house, amount paid, and so on.

The payment program also supports all commonly used methods of payment (checks, transfers, bills of exchange, postal checks) as well as numerous country-specific methods, such as the check/bill of exchange procedure, the POR Swiss Postal system, LCA and LCC in France, or Ricevuta Bancaria in Italy. Ten different methods of payment can be selected for each vendor. In each case, the system will identify and use the most cost-effective method.

Manual Payment

For a variety of reasons (regional customs, industry practice, etc.), many businesses choose to make manual payments. Manual invoice processing is an additional option for processing payments. With this method, original invoices or documents are derived from an electronic preprocess and require further editing.

The simplest procedure for manual document processing would, for example, entail specifying a document number on the document medium being processed. No matter what the procedure, however, the following information must always be entered manually:

- The general ledger account number for the bank
- The payment amount
- Any charges/fees
- The document number

If the totals in the specified invoices (after deduction of cash discount, if applicable) match the entered payment amount, the document will be posted and the payment will be cleared with the invoices. The cleared items will then contain the payment document number and the clearing date. Again, a check is run automatically in the background to determine whether the clearing and the payment clearing were within the set tolerance limits.

If the available information is insufficient, the business will need to search according to a predefined set of search parameters (i.e., reference number, posting number, invoice amount). After the transaction and all necessary checks have been run, the system displays the payment posting again and any correspondence requests that had to be generated.

BUSINESS OBJECT

▶ *Customer Account*

The customer account business object records the transaction figures that represent value movements as periodic totals. It is used for reporting purposes in the accounts receivable ledger. A customer account contains the information a company code requires in presenting the actual value of the business transactions carried out with a customer. Receivables against customers are simultaneously recorded in a general ledger account by assigning a reconciliation account to the customer account.

The business object customer account is used as a source of information for the following types of business analysis.

Subject	Information Delivery
Balanced items	Lists the clearing transactions made to a customer account in a given time period; clearing entries (i.e. payments) and associated cleared items (i.e. invoices) are displayed together
Current balance	Provides the closing balance of a customer account in the current fiscal year and displays both the balance of standard transactions and the total balance of standard transactions and special ledger transactions
Key date balance	Supplies a customer account balance for a given key date
Open items	Lists the open items in a customer account for a given key date
Period balances	Lists the posting period totals per customer account for the current fiscal year as well as the transactions and sales period
Account statement	Supplies the postings made to a customer account in a given time period

8.2   CUSTOMER PROCESSING

The Customer processing business scenario describes how financial transactions are managed for standard customers. This scenario serves two general functions.

On one hand, it provides basic data for effective credit management. On the other hand, it supports all traditional accounts receivable techniques, making them simpler and more efficient.

First, with regard to credit management, the customer processing scenario is fully integrated with sales and has links to controlling and cash forecasting. This integration ensures an efficient flow of accounting information. When, for example, a sales order is taken, this triggers a credit check in financial accounting. A preset credit limit is established into the system via customer credit management. Later, when sales sends out the customer order with an invoice, the invoice will be posted automatically in the accounting system. During this process, cash management and forecasting are updated continuously, in real time, for optimal liquidity planning. In this way, all persons handling credit management, liquidity planning, and contribution margin accounting always have accurate and up-to-date information.

Second, account information is monitored and managed according to well-accepted accounts receivable practices. As in vendor processing, the primary mode of documenting data in customer processing centers on a master record. In accounts receivable, this is called a "customer master record," which is like the vendor master record in most ways. The customer vendor record has a three-part structure that allows for the determination of general data concerning the customer (address, telephone, etc.), company code data (form of payment, due dates), and sales data (order processing, shipping, invoicing, etc.). The customer master record can be edited, customized, and processed as discussed earlier. Moreover, if a customer is also a supplier to the company, the system will link the vendor and customer records. It will also ensure that vendor payments are offset against customer receivables.

Outgoing invoices and credit memos are created either automatically or manually. If the invoice has been created in the R/3™ system, then the appropriate billing system (e.g., through sales) prepares and posts outgoing invoices. If the invoice has not been created in the R/3™ system, then it must be recorded manually. Items can be entered manually or can be created from sample documents or existing accounting documents.

Incoming payments can also be processed manually or automatically. If agreed on with the customer, all invoices can be automatically collected according to their due date via the payment program. The payment program also supports electronic account statements, lockboxes, check deposits, and so on. Manual processing is typically performed for such paper-based transactions as checks, transfers, and bills of exchange. Many special features, however, such as electronic account statement, manual account statement, and manual check deposit, help dramatically reduce manual entry work.

In today's fast-paced business world, many transactions are cash-flow driven. Companies want to get their money quickly, making "dunning" or "reminders" a key part of financial transactions. Customer processing is therefore often cited as a key process to optimize in new enterprises. Faster payment results in a more effective process and greater savings.

To that end, dunning notices for customers whose accounts have fallen into arrears are sent to remind them of their financial obligations. The dunning program automatically handles all dunning procedures. The dunning program includes:

- Dunning levels (based on number of days the account is in arrears)
- Dunning texts (corresponding in language and content to the degree of dunning level)
- Vendor dunning (especially for debit balances because of a credit note)
- Optional interest on arrears and charges
- Payment-due deadline printed on dunning letter

The dunning process consists of generating dunning and editing the dunning proposal. In edit mode, the dunning levels can be changed, and items can be released or blocked. Once the dunning proposal has been accepted, dunning notices are printed. In addition to dunning notices, accounts receivable provides a variety of correspondences, from payment notices and balance confirmations to bill-of-exchange charges statements.

Customer processing is integrated with the following other scenarios:

- Sales logistics and order entry
- Project-related, engineer-to-order production
- Payroll processing (Germany, international)
- Budgeting (local, central, local/central)
- Zero-based budgeting
- Incremental budgeting

8.3   OTA VENDOR PROCESSING

The "power to transact" is an important business concept with roots in technology and business practices. This scenario is a good example of how to work with the exception, the one-time account. It is often the case that companies work with a number of suppliers from whom purchases are made only once. In SAP™ terminology, these are called one-time accounts (OTA). These accounts are treated differently in the system than standard vendor processing, primarily for purposes of a more simplified approach to master data processing.

Because OTA accounts do not require an individual master record, a common master record is created for all OTA vendors. Unlike the standard master record, the OTA master record does not contain specific account information (i.e., name, address, or bank data). Rather, this information is supplied when the OTA invoice is entered into the system. This is typically referred to as "one-step invoice processing."

The process for this scenario then follows the standard vendor processing with one notable exception: it does not support down payments. As with standard vendor processing, the system checks for invoices erroneously entered more than once. Incomplete invoices can be "parked," or put aside until the missing information is entered. Once the invoice is posted, the cost accounting, forecasting, and controlling are all simultaneously updated. Moreover, OTA vendor processing supports manual and automatic payment and all the above-mentioned common methods of payment.

The OTA vendor processing scenario is typically activated for:

- Recording and posting vendor invoices as one-step invoices
- Vendor dunning procedures
- Processing bank statements for outgoing payments

Finally, the OTA vendor processing scenario applies equally to one-time customer accounts as well.

8.4   *CREDITOR SUBSIDIARY/HEAD-OFFICE PROCESSING*

Creditor subsidiary/head-office processing is designed for vendors with head offices and subsidiaries who are customary suppliers of services and goods. Because purchases typically are made from subsidiary (or branch offices), whereas payments are made to the head office account, this scenario also differs from standard vendor processing.

First, two sets of master records are kept for both the subsidiary and head office accounts. They are, however, linked together so that invoices posted to the branch account automatically update the head office account.

Second, modifications can be made to both the subsidiary and head office accounts as needed. For example, correspondences can be created or modified for either account. Also, payments can be flexibly defined for subsidiaries and head offices.

Receiving and posting vendor invoices, managing down payments, and processing vendor payments are the same as described above in vendor processing. Moreover, the functions in this scenario are integrated with procurement functions. Finally, posting can be simultaneously updated in the general ledger, cost accounting, cash forecasting, investment management, and budgeting systems.

8.5   *GENERAL LEDGER PROCESSING*

R/3™ simplifies external accounting processes and procedures as a result of its general ledger system. The general ledger is a financial accounting ledger that is defined for the generation of closing reports as required by law. It provides clear and comprehensive structures for the organization and documentation of accounting, flexible yet integrated posting system procedures, and highly automated processes for day-, month-, and year-end closings.

Basic structural categories of the general ledger consist of:

• Company code
• Business area
• Chart of accounts

The company code, as defined earlier, represents the smallest organizational entity of external accounting. A company code is like an organizational object that is moved from one process to another. In the general ledger, for example, the company code is an independent accounting unit that maintains its own profit and loss statement and balance sheets. In a centralized company, the company code typically represents the tax-related view of the company. In a decentralized company, the company code may represent individual divisions within autonomous business units. In both cases, financial accounting maintains a complete, self-contained accounting system that includes all postings and closing records.

A business area is a classification concept wider in scope than a company code. It helps depict internal structures for external segment reporting. The business area is used to analyze balance sheet items and profit and loss statements for product divisions, regional structures, profit centers, and the like. It is essentially an evaluation tool that can show broader views of data taken from different company codes.

Chart of accounts is a classification system and evaluation tool that records values or value flows. There are three chart of account functions represented in the system: 1) corporate chart of accounts, which concerns all accounts throughout a corporate grouping; 2) local chart of accounts, which fulfills country-specific legal requirements; and 3) operational chart of accounts, which contains the accounts currently used in day-to-day transactions within the system. The various levels of chart of accounts make it possible to process posting data at the various levels within a company hierarchy.

General ledger account postings are well organized and integrated with other areas. General ledger account postings are always made from the originating point of entry or area of a company, ensuring that all business transactions requiring posting are entered only once. Standard software, such as SAP™ R/3™, provides support for data maintenance, automatic posting, authorization codes, and validity checks. Postings can be permitted or blocked for each individual user according to account, company code, or business area. Moreover, postings can be integrated with procurement, assets accounting, and controlling, this allowing data from subsidiary ledgers to be posted simultaneously within the general ledger. Subsidiary ledgers can be integrated on the basis of master, transaction, or reporting data. Thus, each posted business transaction automatically updates all affected operational evaluations.

Most importantly, the general ledger contains a calendar that permits fiscal year flexibility; for example, year-round closing capabilities. During the fiscal year, daily closings can be completed without additional posting activity. Once data are posted, the system can report on account balance for the day or for several posting days. Monthly closing can help prepare year-end closing. Programs are available for creating a sortable posting journal, updating the balance audit trail with reconciled items, and archiving documents. Year-end closing may be based on month-end closings, or it may be undertaken at year end. A number of programs will automatically generate annual balance sheet and profit and loss statement, in keeping with country-specific statutory requirements. Standard reports can also be called up at any time for evaluation and analysis. These can be generated for account statements, line item journals, general ledger account lists, balance sheets, profit and loss statements, and so forth.

8.6   SPECIAL-PURPOSE LEDGER HANDLING

Special-purpose ledgers provide an evaluation system for areas not answered directly in the general ledger accounts. In special ledger processing, there are numerous options for analyses and reports that supplement traditional accounting applications. This process shows how various account assignments based on companies or company codes can be transferred to special ledgers for analysis and reporting. Special ledgers can be created according to time (year, month, etc.), type (account, cost center, region), specified comparisons (actual values, total values, budget) or internal and external requirements (local ledgers, consolidation). The key areas of special ledger functionality are integration, planning capabilities, and reporting.

The business value of special ledgers lies in the information from different business areas, R/3™ applications, or even third-party data. Special ledgers are typically derived from various business areas and processes such as invoicing, asset transfers, receivables, cash receipts/disbursements, individual account closings, and statistical activity types. Specified data may be transferred immediately or periodically to a special ledger, which is automatically updated. These data can come from processes in procurement or postings from financial accounting. The special ledger also can be derived from third-party systems using a standard interface.

A special-purpose ledger is an instrumental component in planning and controlling. The desired information that will be used for comparison purposes—that is, sales totals versus personnel costs—is stored in business objects with planning attributes. These planning parameters are based on general data (e.g., transactions, quantities) and used to compile information over a set period of time (usually days or weeks). Company-specific distribution keys can be created for different planning objects. Once defined, these keys can be used repeatedly for different planning periods or plan versions.

Finally, special-ledger processing is useful for understanding which reports on specified company areas or requirements can be done. The special ledger compiles various transactions in such areas as vendor invoices, individual account closings, depreciation, receivables, and interest. It then generates reports through one of two information system programs: report painter or report writer. The report painter uses a graphic report structure to display report lines, columns, and so on. The report writer is menu driven and can be used to evaluate totals records and other specified material. Both aid in reconciling and checking data, and generating check paths for internal and external auditing. Both report programs can be written for management reporting, individual account closing, consolidated financial statements, or statistical reporting, to name a few.

8.7   CONSOLIDATION

R/3™ consolidation deals with the ways in which companies summarize financial information from different subsidiaries and joint ventures in various currencies and countries. The consolidation business process scenario is designed for companies with multiple legal entities that want to create consolidated financial statements for statutory and management reporting purposes. R/3™ consolidation is especially applicable to diversified multinational companies.

In the R/3™ system, local financial systems are structured along corporate guidelines. Data in local systems is reconciled for intercompany balances, local currency translation, and valuations/adjustments required by group accounting rules. Consequently, local management possesses financial statements of the company from both a local and a corporate group view. Seldom are all related data available in R/3™. Due to local infrastructure characteristics and the fact that some entities in a company may not have an R/3™ system, business data can be taken from local databases and such spreadsheets as MS Excel™. After the data are collected, they are then transferred to consolidation.

The consolidation of a multilevel corporate group is performed using either step or simultaneous consolidation. Step consolidation refers to the process in which individual companies are consolidated step-by-step according to a multilevel corporate hierarchy of defined subgroups. (Subgroups are defined according to meaningful categories such as region or business unit or to individual hierarchy levels of a multilevel enterprise.)

In simultaneous consolidation, no hierarchies of ownership relationship are required. The total percentage of ownership of a consolidation group's investee is computed, and the percentage of group ownership is used to identify the total group's portion of the investee equity. Because the percentage of ownership of a full consolidation group is used to compute the group consolidation adjustment for any one investee, consolidation of the total group is made simultaneously.

In consolidation, companies report their individual financial statements to a consolidated entity, which treats each company as a unit of consolidation. Consolidation is the process of collecting and reconciling the financial statements of companies into a single consolidated financial statement that accurately portrays the financial circumstances of all companies as a whole. Companies carry out consolidations to merge financial statements for meeting certain legal requirements as well as to aid in internal decision-making. Consolidation scenarios allow for the following types of business analysis:

- Intercompany payables and receivables
- Intercompany expense and revenue
- Income from investments
- Intercompany profit/loss in inventory
- Intercompany profit/loss in transferred assets
- Consolidation of investments

Actual consolidation can be performed once the following are available to the consolidation system:

- Individual financial statements
- Currency translations
- Intercompany balance verification

All necessary standardizing or reclassification entries (e.g., reclassification of finished goods into unfinished goods for purposes of corporate group reporting)

Once the above are made available, intercompany eliminations may be performed. Eliminations include payables and receivables, expenses and revenues, income from investments, profit/loss inventory, and transfer of fixed assets.

Actual consolidation also consists of consolidation of investments. Numerous aspects of consolidation of investments are covered in R/3™, which are reflected in Table 8-1.

Table 8–1　　Consolidation of Investments

Business Case	Definition
First consolidation	The first inclusion of a company into the consolidated financial statements
Step acquisition	An increase of an investment in a company by directly acquiring additional shares
Change in indirect investment	The group's share in a company changes without a change in the direct investment percentage (usually the case when additional shares are acquired in the company's parent as a result of step acquisition)
Increase/decrease in capitalization	The capital stock and the investment's book value increases or decreases without a change in the investment percentage
Transfer	A parent company sells all or some of its shares in a subsidiary to another company within the group
Subsequent consolidation	Reflects the adjustment of the minority shares and/or the amortization of a good will and hidden reserves that need to be made because of changes in capital structure

Consolidation information supports a general understanding of how a business is working. This business process shows how the legal requirements are fulfilled. From a management perspective, it's important to see the trees as well as the forest; hence, the emphasis is on extensive reporting functions. Reports are generated with multiple versions defined to compare the results of different consolidation scenarios. These scenarios may be driven by alternative consolidation methods or currency simulations.

The consolidation business process shows how a business system is graphed into the standard R/3™ Blueprint. WR Grace and BMW have been innovative in supporting the consolidation process, using ActiveSheets for SAP™ R/3™. ActiveSheets provides a useful interface for analyzing and managing R/3™ consolidation data. This link allows live communication between consolidation data and Excel spreadsheets. Users can work within Excel and access live data, such as company account information, from financial accounting. It provides additional calculation, formatting, and print options. Changes to consolidation in the R/3™ system are automatically updated in Excel. The decision-making steps are modeled in a separate business process.

8.8   R/3™ EXTERNAL ACCOUNTING OVERVIEW

The following tables provide an overview to the main scenarios, core processes, business objects, and organizational units that make up R/3 External Accounting.

Scenarios

▶ Vendor processing

▶ One-time vendor processing

▶ Customer processing

▶ One-time customer processing

▶ Consolidation

▶ Handling of closing

▶ Special purpose ledger processing

▶ G/L processing

Core Processes

▶ G/L account master record processing

▶ Vendor Master

▶ Customer Master

▶ G/L account posting

▶ Vendor invoice processing

▶ Customer invoice processing

▶ Manual clearing

▶ Clearing

▶ Manual payment

▶ Down payment release

Core Processes (continued)

▶ Automatic payment

▶ Automatic dunning

▶ Automatic clearing

▶ GR/IR clearing account maintenance

▶ Depreciation

▶ Reclassification receivables/payables

▶ Execution of year-end closing

▶ Fiscal year change

Business Objects

▶ Ledgers

    – General ledger

    – Reconciliation ledger

    – Consolidation ledger

    – Accounts payable ledger

    – Accounts receivable ledger

▶ Accounts

    – G/L account

    – Vendor account

    – Customer account

    – Customer credit limit

▶ Accounting documents

    – G/L account document

    – Accounts payable document

    – Accounts receivable document

▶ Chart of accounts

Organizational Units

▶ Logical system

▶ Consolidation group

▶ Company

▶ Company code

▶ Credit control area

▶ Taxes on sales/purchases group

▶ Functional area

▶ Business area

Customer Example: Syntex Corporation, Palo Alto, California, and Maidenhead, England

Founded in 1944, Syntex Corporation is an international healthcare company. Operating worldwide in the research, development, manufacturing, and marketing of human and animal pharmaceutical products and medical diagnostic systems, the company sells pharmaceutical products, including medicines to treat arthritis pain, inflammation, and allergies, as well as medicines for cardiovascular, cerebrovascular, gynecological, viral, and skin diseases, and oral contraceptives. Syntex also produces health products for food-producing animals. Its medical diagnostics business includes products for drugs-of-abuse testing, therapeutic drug-monitoring, infectious disease diagnosis, and measurement of endocrine concentrations.

Like many others in the pharmaceutical industry, Syntex faces increasingly tough government regulations related to new drug applications and the complexities and size of clinical trials, while it strives to invest in the development of new medicines. To better deal with these pressures, the company examined its structure and organization to identify ways to "reduce costs, maximize sales opportunities, advance the research and development pipeline, and increase attention to cash flow."

A cost restructuring plan recommended that Syntex create shared services, especially with its European operations, in such areas as finance, distribution, and data processing, to reduce costs and improve efficiency.

Ronan Byrne, director of European Financial Services Organization at Syntex, explains: "It was clear that consistent, shared systems in each country could help management be more responsive to the ever-changing marketplace. In general, they [countries] have similar needs but were using different systems and procedures. The new approach will also make employees more effective in their jobs. A central database for all areas of the business will eliminate local, paper-based reporting, as people will be able to access all the information they need via personal computers. For example, a salesman visiting a doctor in any European country will be able to use his laptop PC to access data on that individual's prescribing habits and other relevant market information before the meeting takes place."

Other company goals include improving returns on research and development. Syntex has 500 researchers in the United Kingdom alone, and centralized systems will allow it to cost drug development projects more effectively and to better control the 20 percent of revenues invested in research and development.

Syntex's business-process redesign required major technical, organizational, and, perhaps most importantly, cultural change in the company. Focusing on the human aspects of process change at its European Financial Services Organization, based in Maidenhead, U.K., the company created a central service center and combined people of different nationalities and cultures to respond effectively to the needs of clients in other countries. One of the biggest challenges Syntex faced was introducing new cultural and management changes to the company.

"In the past, Syntex had a high degree of decentralization in its management approach," Byrne says. "However, the changes in our operating environment have made it necessary to adapt and [to] create more consistency and coordination throughout the organization." Business processes found in the R/3™ Blueprint support this goal and make communication and coordination much easier. Again, the concentration on the human aspects of process design makes it important to clearly communicate how business processes work. This comprehension helps people adapt better.

As Byrne explains, "Managers who were previously responsible for their unit's financial reporting and accounting have transferred these tasks to the centralized organization, which now produces standardized, on-line and on-screen financial reporting for statutory, corporate, and unit management use.

"This initially created some concern among the line managers who felt they were losing ownership of their information and were concerned over who would have access to it. The European Financial Services Organization reassured them by demonstrating the high security levels and access restriction capabilities inherent within the SAP™ software, which meant that no one else in the organization can see information about a unit before its manager does, or without the appropriate authorization."

In the initial phase of implementing R/3™, Syntex saw that business reengineering didn't just involve installing a new computer system; rather, it was also creating new ways of working. "We've learned a lot about the management of change, which we will apply to the next phase of the project. It's not just a new IT system—it's changed the way people operate," Byrne says.

Such changes include on-line, on-demand data that has shifted the way many people work. "The big dream for accountants is not to be faced with the 'month-end,' and we are approaching this situation because the systems are updated all the time. The system will change accountants' role in the organization because they will have more time to assist management as general advisors who can stand back and look at the business and how the numbers can help," Byrne explains.

In the long term, Syntex expects greater integration of its processes throughout the business. For example, finance and manufacturing operations will be able to share data and applications. The company also expects to improve its sales order processing and, in turn, deliver better customer service and fill orders faster—all helping to reduce costs and make Syntex more efficient.

Byrne's vision is a one-stop European information center or data warehouse that will provide consolidated information and drill-down capabilities to anyone in the company at anytime.

The success of the European project has impressed the company's American headquarters so much that it, too, will base its business engineering project on the R/3 ™ Blueprint. Byrne admits that although such an undertaking will be a major organizational change for Syntex, it's worth the effort in terms of world-wide consistency of information across operational areas from accounting to product management.

9

Organization and Human Resource Management

In many industries, such as business consulting or software development, the human assets typically exit the company every evening. Having modern and flexible human resource processes makes better use of these assets and can make the difference in whether a company thrives over time. This chapter is devoted to helping business decision makers comprehend the core R/3 ™ processes related to organization and human resources, which are crucial for building a flexible organization with a strong information technology base.

During the latter half of this century, the area of human resources has grown markedly, a statistic that reflects the increasing focus in business on employee development and empowerment. Because human resources has grown to such a degree and continues to evolve in so many directions, few areas of business require as wide a range of expertise from its managers. Today's human resource personnel are expected to know the full range of compensation and benefits plans, ranging from pretax plans (such as 401k) to retirement plans to health forms. They are expected to be conversant in areas of employment and labor law, such as sexual harassment, hiring practices, termination of employment, and relations with organized labor. In addition to these areas of expertise, they also need to have a good background in traditional business and administration, as well as psychology or sociology. In some businesses, human resource personnel often are expected to be knowledgeable in public relations (newsletters, brochures, etc.), training, education, and even safety procedures. Other areas of expertise typically include travel management, payroll processing, manpower planning, and contract reviews.

Given this sprawling range of duties and responsibilities, or perhaps because of this sprawl, record keeping and data management have become an increasing concern for human resource management. Hence, add to the above responsibilities a knowledge of information systems for the tracking of company personnel, the documenting of all personnel transactions, and the managing of all relevant human resource data.

Too often this last responsibility only further burdens an already overextended human resource department. Only poor information systems, however, cause problems. In poor information systems, software typically does not match up well with individual company requirements, is not open to other systems within or outside (i.e., third-party vendors) the organization, or is not easily customized to conform to an organization's functional needs.

The processes that make up the SAP™ organization and human resources areas effectively avoid these pitfalls. Especially diverse in their broad range of applications, these processes reflect the wide variety of responsibilities that have become the norm for human resource departments.

Human resource systems cover the following areas:

- Human resource organizational management (job description, ergonomics, work-place assessment, salary/wage structure)
- Personnel planning (labor market, requirements planning, recruitment planning, etc.)
- Recruitment (internal job advertisements, temporary staff, external job advertisements, selection procedures, employment contracts)
- Work-force planning and administration (introduction and training, labor and social legislation, reorganization due to internal transfer, terminations, dismissals, retirement)
- Personnel development (performance appraisal, employee-suggestion system, wage/salary policy)
- Personnel training and further education (training of new employees, employee training program)
- Social benefits (social facilities, leisure activities, employment protection)

Integration of all organization and human resource processes enables companies and organizations to carry out all the above-mentioned human resource management activities. The process blueprint describes the functions that 1) are prescribed by law or collective agreement; 2) are required for keeping personnel data; 3) handle the wide range of payroll accounting procedures and methods (including those that are country specific); and 4) facilitate and simplify the entering, maintaining, retrieval, processing, and presentation of personnel data.

In addition to the personnel management business-process scenario that will be described in detail, other independent scenarios—for example, training and

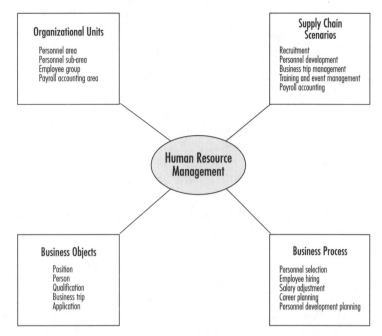

▶ Figure 9–1   Overview of scenarios, process, organizations, and business objects

event management, travel expense accounting, time management—illustrate the full range of functions and activities found in the organization and human resource processes. Figure 9-1 illustrates the main human resources processes, organizations, scenarios, and business objects.

After describing the main scenarios in human resources, this chapter concludes with a real-life business example.

9.1   RECRUITMENT

As companies experience greater growth and evolve to meet market demands, they are faced with a constant pressure for hiring the best available talent in the marketplace. In an increasingly competitive job market, the necessity of having clear goals and processes for the hiring of new talent has never been greater.

This process requires planning strategies that are designed to meet both the present and future needs of a company. Recruitment strategies must be devised that consider dynamic labor force conditions as well as prospects for internal career growth. Other important issues such as personnel, succession or evolu-

> **Figure 9–2**   Value chain: Recruiting new employees

tion planning, career planning, and training must all be factored in when planning for an organization's present and future personnel growth and development. Moreover, the planning stages must be so integrated that all of the hiring activities—from writing job descriptions to documenting procedures—become an effective process.

In the case of R/3™, the ability to integrate archived data into other R/3™ areas—such as personnel administration, financial, or cost accounting functions—allows for better planning across all functional areas. Moreover, various applications within the module are designed to facilitate such tasks as processing job applications, recruitment, and creating job specifications and qualification profiles. The R/3™ system supports the entire recruiting process, from the personnel search to the processing of the recruitees and the administration thereof to the choice and employment of the right person. Figure 9-2 illustrates the main processes involved in the Recruitment business process scenario.

The value chain describes the process flow of recruitment in the SAP™ system. The process begins when a company recruits new employees as a result of a vacancy in the organization and a recruitment request is entered. Typically the Human Resource department issues the recruitment request for the purpose of searching for prospective employees who are suitable for the job opening.

The next stage in the process is the job advertisement, which entails obtaining information on the job opening, the current job market, or the financial resources for the advertisement. Once applications are received, the next stage of recruitment begins. This process involves sorting out external and internal employee applications, gathering personal data, and notifying applicants of the receipt of their application. All applicants are kept in a pool that is regularly monitored for the job opening or any others that may arise in the organization. Applicants who are rejected are sent notification.

Selection of applicants first involves screening of the applicants for meeting the criteria of the job opening. Applicants who meet the requirements are short listed and then are interviewed, tested, and the like, depending on the needs of the job and organizational methods and goals for employment. The applicant is then selected, rejected, or placed on hold. In the first instance, the applicant is offered a contract. In the other instances, the applicant is put on file for possible openings later on. Figures 9-3 and 9-4 provide a more detailed diagram of the entire recruitment process.

Creating a Search

When a company experiences the need for recruitment, a search contract is created in order to handle these needs and document the entire process. A recruiting demand occurs when a company has vacancies, and this vacancy will be filled by new, externally recruited employees. The vacancy and the position will determine the type of contract. With the search contract, the responsible department, (for instance, the personnel department), claims ownership of the process of filling the open position.

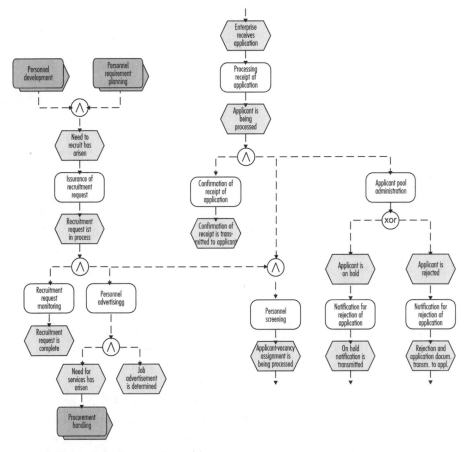

▶ **Figure 9–3**   Personnel recruiting

Tracking the Search Process

The person responsible for the search will need to have information and facts related to the search process from time to time. The following are the information types available:

- The number of open and already filled search positions

- The number of open positions for which a candidate has already been found

- The amount of budget, and information about the activities, for example, advertising, publication of positions

- Other activities related to the direct search process

When this information is made available, a determination can be made whether the search process is open or closed. For example, the search contract can be closed when all open positions are filled, or when there's no budget to continue the search.

Job Description

The department responsible for the search is also responsible for creating the job description, which also describes the vacancies. In order to write the job description, the department must have information about the vacancy, about the internal/external job market, and the financial resources available to conduct the search process and to fill the position. When the relevant information is available, the exact specification of the job position is determined.

In many countries, there are special requirements for personnel. For instance, in the United States hiring foreign employees requires a personnel search process, which demands from the authorities an exhaustive search of available talent in the market. In other words, it is very important at the beginning of the search process to have all the information about the exact requirements of a position. For instance, at Component Software, we need people to be able to speak the German language. This requirement compels us go beyond the local pool of talent and look elsewhere for candidates to fill the particular need. The language requirement also has a direct impact on the financial resources needed to conduct that search.

BUSINESS OBJECT

▶ *Employee*

The employee business object is determined on the basis of a work contract or a contract for services. In the R/3 ™ system, an employee is considered anyone who contributes or has contributed to the creation of goods and services within the enterprise. The employee business object constitutes the main focus of interest for the majority of human resource subareas. All business processes within these areas relate to the employee.

The employee business object is used as a source of information for the following types of business analysis.

- Flexible Employee Data
- Employees who have Entered and/or Left the Company
- Family Members
- Birthday List
- Service Anniversaries
- Vehicle List
- Employee Directory
- List of Maternity Data
- Education and Training
- Telephone Directory
- Employees with Powers of Attorney
- Time spent in each pay scale area/type/group/level
- Defaults for Pay Scale Reclassification
- Reference Personnel Numbers
- Severely Challenged
- HR Master Data Sheet
- Atts./Absences for Each Employee
- Absence/attendance data: Calendar view
- Attendance Check
- Atts./Absences for Each Employee
- Overview of Absence and Attendance Data
- Time Statement Form
- Working Times of Time and Incentive Wage Earners
- Remuneration Statements
- Payroll Accounts
- Payments and Deductions
- Bank Details
- Remuneration Statements
- Payroll Accounts
- Employee History Report
- Garnishment History

- Listing of Customizing Tables
- Garnishment Statistics
- Benefits Dependents List
- Grievance Summary
- Tax Infotype Summary
- Filling of tax interface tables from payroll and third party remittance

Employee Application Processing

When a company receives an application, the data for the applicant and the application are entered into the R/3™ system. The dependencies for entering new applicants into the system relate to the applicant's job status. For example, the applicant may be a company employee, an external applicant, a first time applicant, or an applicant that has applied to the company before. Depending on these factors (and others), employee application processing determines which type of personal data has to be entered into the system or which data already contained in the system needs updating.

Confirming the Application Receipt

In this process, the applicant receives a letter in which the company confirms the receipt of the application. The system supports the automatic generation of the reception letter, whereby the standard text can be individually adapted for every case. The confirmation letter can be either printed and sent as regular mail, sent as a telefax, or sent electronically as an email to the applicant. With the email confirmation, the applicant is given an application number and a password in which the applicant can call up the status of his or her application via the Internet at any time.

Preliminary Personnel Choice

In preliminary personnel choice, the company searches through the applicants for the vacant position and checks each applicant to see if he or she has the basic requirements to fill that position. The test for the basic requirements can be supported by the R/3™ system by a profile comparison between the requirements for the position for which the applicant applied and the qualification profile of the applicant. If the applicant fulfills the basic requirements, the vacancy will be associated with the applicant and he or she will be brought into the secondary pool of candidates.

Personnel Processing

In personnel processing, the person responsible for the position (typically a department head) checks the applicants and judges them according to various personnel methods, which may include:

- Analysis of the application (resume)
- Grading of application materials and resume
- First interview
- Testing

The types and the sequence of methods are not only dependent on the vacancy but also on the standards of each company. The results of the personnel choice is documented into the system. Depending on the results of the choice process, the person responsible for the position makes the decision about the further status of each and every applicant. Figure 9-4 shows that there are three possibilities:

1. The applicant is offered a contract for the vacancy.
2. The applicant is rejected.
3. The applicant for the vacancy is put on hold.

Employment Agreement Offer Processing

Here the qualified applicant will receive a written contractual offer from the company. The contractual conditions are specified within the offer. The employment agreement is printed out and a company representative presents the contract and offer to the applicant.

Applicant Status Check

When an applicant for a vacancy is rejected or put on hold, the results of the preliminary search process are documented in the applicant file. This information is sent back to the personnel department.

Preparation for Employing the Applicant

If the applicant accepts the contractual offer, the company can begin to prepare for his or her employment in the organization. Here, the acceptance of the contractual offer is documented, the employee's department head is informed, and the applicant file is converted into a personnel file.

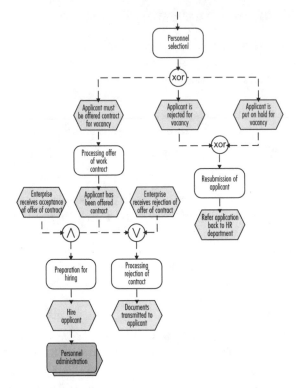

▶ **Figure 9–4**   Personnel processing

Rejection of Offer

If the applicant rejects the contractual offer, the event is recorded into the system, and the would-be boss is informed of the rejection. The applicant status is reset to rejected.

Applicant Pool Administration

All applicants are administered in a central applicant pool. The personnel department regularly checks the status of applications in process and applications that have been put on hold or rejected. The personnel department decides which of the applicants continue to be of interest to the company.

Putting an Application on Hold

If it is clear that an applicant would be considered for employment in the company at a later point in time, an offer can be made that allows the application to be placed on hold. The applicant receives a letter from the company in which he or she is informed of this decision.

Rejection of Application

Here, the applicant is informed if and when the company decides that it cannot offer a position of employment. In addition, the applicant receives his or her complete resume and application materials from the company.

9.2   BUSINESS EVENT HANDLING

Human resources typically is made responsible for the planning, administering, and managing of business events, ranging from small training seminars to major conferences. In today's market, this responsibility usually entails working within tight budgetary constraints, overseeing a wide range of business activities (from accounting to marketing), managing several business events at once, and utilizing an admixture of internal and external resources. These obstacles become even more difficult when projects are not designed, conducted, and evaluated properly, which can result not only in poor management of resources but in poorly rated events as well.

Designed to monitor all phases of the business event process, this business-process scenario covers:

- Data processing and participant administration
- Marketing
- Billing
- Business event planning
- Participant administration
- Personnel development

Data on each participant, whether internal or external, are tracked and recorded in the system. A master data file on each participant is created, and a number is assigned to the participant. The participant is classified according to organizational unit, company, or status such as partner or external participant. A booking priority is established, which will either book potential participants immediately or place them on a waiting list. It is also possible to determine the entire daily event schedule of the participant according to the date, time, and title of each event. Finally, links to personnel planning (cost planning, organizational management, etc.), payroll, and time management can be chosen.

The business event handling business process scenario has marketing functionality for large conferences and conventions that extend outside the company. It supports mailing campaigns, customer profiling, budgeting, and so on. Customers can be targeted according to group criteria, such as sales, region, or branch. Other customer information, such as partnership agreements and histories, can be used for managing quotas and budgets.

Billing may be customized according to the following participant data:

- Cancellation deadlines
- Pricing scales
- Discounts
- Package deals

Also, payment information such as credit memos, deadlines, and process quotas can all be created and monitored.

The seminar and convention management process supports business event planning and administration. In addition to managing budget and requirement specifications, it maintains data on resources, instructors, time schedules, costs, and so on. It allows for the rescheduling and rebooking of entire events. Personnel can be tracked and profiled according to event information. This process helps determine such informational areas as qualification profiles, employee potential, team profiles, and future training needs.

9.3   BUSINESS TRIP MANAGEMENT

Business travel is expensive. There are expenses not only for the person making the trip but also for those who are responsible for planning, approving, and accounting. Generally, attempts to control travel expenses result in bottlenecks and excessive paperwork. This situation occurs often because the document flow is controlled manually or because data links to related business areas are poor or nonexistent. Moreover, redundant data are too often the result of travel expense control systems. In other words, costs to control travel expenses can exceed potential savings.

The Business trip management business process scenario exploits the benefits of an integrated business system by providing access to data throughout the human resource, payroll, accounts payable, and costing systems. The first step is to establish the organization procedures and guidelines for travel (transportation, lodging, and meals). These then manage the document flow, authorization, and accounting allocations for travel expense. These procedures can provide a mix of central or decentralized control. Employee-specific data are then established. These data link individual employees to the organizational plan. Such data include allowable expenses, authorization levels, and standard cost distribution templates. The organizational and employee master data together establish controls for automating trip planning, document flow, and accounting.

The next step in this scenario manages applications for travel. Trip data are checked and sent on for electronic approval. Advance payments can be processed for each application. After the trip, the employee provides required documentation. The trip data are again checked by the system and supplemental data, as required, are entered into the system. Financial and cost distribution is generated and posted to the system. Payments are authorized and passed on to the accounts payable or payroll systems. The system manages:

- Lump sum accounting per employee
- Lump sum accounting per trip
- Statutory compliance with Germany, Austria, and other countries
- Currency conversion
- Trips with multiple stopovers and customer visits
- Employee-specific proportional cost distribution

9.4 TIME MANAGEMENT HANDLING

Modern work scheduling strategies have changed the way companies view time management. Novel scheduling approaches such as flexible hours, alternating 40- and 30-hour work weeks, 3- and 4-day "weekends," and new work incentive programs, such as those that pay overtime after 35 instead of 40 hours have radically altered the face of the traditional work week. The high number of variables that can exist within a company in regard to pay scales and scheduling makes it increasingly more difficult for company information systems to keep pace with the sheer amount of data to be processed.

The time management processing scenario includes the following capabilities:

- Daily work schedule for long-term work schedules
- Flexible daily work schedules
- Time data maintenance system
- Error recovery for updating data on individual employees
- Time evaluation tool that calculates overtime for each employee

- Incentive wage functionality
- Plant data collection system for cost controlling

The time management handling business process scenario provides a comprehensive tool for planning, recording, and allocating employee time. The system defines and generates a company's work calendar, taking into consideration general, regional, and local public holidays. Individual employees are assigned to work schedules that contain overtime rules and personnel alternatives. The system records exceptions to the work schedule such as absences (e.g., accruals for sick leave or vacation), overtime, or personnel substitution, while recording employee absences (incident tracking).

Front-end recording systems that collect actual employee time and attendance data can be interfaced to the system using a standard interface. The R/3™ system evaluates and formats the received data, determines the compensation for overtime, and prepares the data for payroll processing. The scheduled work hours are validated against actual hours reported. The labor cost-allocation function computes costs from hours and posts labor costs to projects, cost centers, and work orders. Variances between scheduled and reported hours are used in the labor cost-allocation routine.

9.5　 *INTERNATIONAL PAYROLL PROCESSING*

Paying employees correctly in a multinational environment is a complex and critical function, especially when one considers the numerous, applicable taxing authorities and other factors impacting employee net compensation. Failure to comply with the complex web of regulations in a timely manner subjects an enterprise to potential government penalties as well as employee dissatisfaction.

Traditionally, payroll processing existed as an accounting function isolated from other business operations with inflexible procedures and policies. In the current global business environment, payroll processing often involves multinational tax-, benefit-, and garnishment-related laws and regulations. In this environment, with changes within one or more national borders having the power to impact personnel and payroll issues on an individual and class basis, a payroll system must automate the workflow processes while providing the flexibility to adapt itself on an ongoing basis. Integration to other application areas is critical to effective use of management's human resource tools.

The German payroll calculation, for example, is more sophisticated than others. In addition to extensive federal legislation, a payroll system must take into account variances between industries and must accommodate union and multi-state requirements. Ongoing legislative and regulatory changes add further complexity; therefore, the system requires flexibility to adapt to such changes while maintaining simplicity in operation.

The international payroll accounting business process scenario provides a comprehensive tool for payroll processing in multinational environments. The scenario for German payroll accounting operates within the complex structures of German legislation and collective bargaining, including:

- Processing garnishments (e.g., priorities, transfers)
- Determining reduced work hours and bad weather premiums
- Providing public service functionality
- Maintaining supplementary insurance
- Processing certificates
- Calculating gross-to-net payroll, including retroactive adjustments
- Generating direct deposits

Standard payroll processing occurs monthly, using basic data as updated for employee status, tax-based data, social insurance data, payment data, and time management data. Reduced work hours as well as garnishments are taken into account. Payroll for public service entities differs from that of private industry, resulting in a different gross-to-net calculation as required by law. Data posted after payroll period closing automatically generate retroactive calculations.

Results of the payroll calculation are stored in a database that is used to generate:

- Payroll slips
- Company-specific evaluations
- Data transfer exchange for direct deposit
- Payroll certificates

Data are automatically transferred to general ledger and cost accounting systems. Simulated gross-to-net or net-to-gross calculations are also available.

Another scenario example is the "Payroll Processing—International," which provides a comprehensive tool for international payroll processing. It includes:

- Calculating gross payroll independent of country-specific functionality
- Responding to garnishments and other payment obligations through third-party remittance
- Outsourcing defined functions (e.g., net pay calculation or remote check printing)
- Establishing rules for overtime calculation, benefit, or accrual transactions

- Producing checks in one or multiple currencies
- Retroactively calculating date sensitivity payroll adjustments
- Distributing earnings to employee accounts

Because the payroll process is a calculation function, all the processing of basic data is performed first. Basic data include employee status, company- or subsidiary-specific data, payment, and time management data for individual employees.

This scenario will run each designated employee group at once, processing either a gross calculation or a full gross-to-net calculation. The gross-to-net calculation is provided as a standard feature for many different countries around the world.

Late entries generate a retroactive calculation (i.e., a retroactive adjustment to a payroll period). Special payroll calculations, such as bonus payments, can be processed separately or integrated into the standard payroll calculation. Payroll data are available for producing checks as well as integrating with accounts payable to allow for checks or electronic transfers to responsible third-party payors (outsourced payroll services) automatically. Data are then transferred to the general ledger and cost accounting systems.

9.6   SALARY ADMINISTRATION

There is perhaps no other area more potentially ripe for internal conflict than a company's compensation structure. A fair and equitable system, however, is not always easy to achieve. On one hand, a company must strive to provide equitable salary ranges for its people on the basis of job titles or levels. On the other hand, incentives must be built into the process to promote higher performance levels among its employees. Add to this often tenuous balance the typical budgetary constraints, and salary administration can be a difficult challenge for human resource managers.

Modern management is increasingly conjoining pay and performance at every level in the organization in order to encourage employee participation in the achieving of corporate goals. In line with this practice, the personnel and salary administration scenarios aid in the structuring and managing of salary and reward compensation packages. They assist the salary administration and review process by providing both for standard, across-the-board salary changes and for individual compensations and exceptions. It can also analyze the effects of salary increases or decreases on organizational units and subunits.

A compensation administration matrix can be developed based on salary range and performance level. The salary range is defined by the current salary level as compared to employees in similar positions. The performance level is a rating system based on various appraisal information and qualitative criteria. This matrix sets low-to-high performance criteria against current salary level data, resulting in a simple selection of predetermined dollar amounts. Such a system ensures both a standard procedure for salary raises and a solid criterion for rewarding performance.

In some cases, it is necessary to single out an individual for superior or inferior performance. An override capability allows for these exceptions to be entered into the system, documented, and processed. The changes can be then calculated into the system for determination of their effects on budgetary concerns. Moreover, an overview of department or group salary information is available for review or salary adjustment.

9.7   BENEFITS ADMINISTRATION

The number of alternatives for employee benefits is practically unlimited in today's global market. In the United States alone, information systems must be able to handle group health insurance, traditional major medical, preferred provider organizations, HMOs, cafeteria plans, dental insurance, vision care, Section 125 (pretax plans), COBRA (continuation of coverage)—just to name some of the options available. In addition to these many plans, benefit programs have to be devised for part-time, full-time, exempt, nonexempt, and retired employees.

As benefit programs become more complex, benefit plans require the integration of administrative, human resources, and payroll systems to manage these complex programs. A benefits management system that streamlines the administrative process maximizes employee net compensation while minimizing company costs. Traditionally, enrolling employees into benefit programs is a labor-intensive function. Efficient administrative systems should provide the technology for direct employee access for enrollments and inquiries.

The benefits administration scenario provides a comprehensive tool for administering human resource benefits. The first step is setting up each benefit plan. Within each plan, multiple cost and coverage options are defined; for example, based on the number of dependents covered, the amount and type of coverage provided, or the desired deductible. Eligibility rules are established through predefined criteria such as job class, length of employment, or employee status.

The scenario's integration to personnel administration and the plan coverage determine the benefit costs, based on salary, years of service, age, and location. Employees can then select their participation in benefit plans from the costs and coverage available to them. Deductions are activated through an automated process integrated to the payroll process calculation.

Benefits administration can be configured to support any benefit program. It includes the following options:

- Medical programs
- Dental plans
- Vision care
- COBRA processing
- Standard reporting
- Spending accounts
- Vesting
- Coverage options
- Cost planning

The system provides step-by-step guides for developing, defining, and maintaining benefit plans. Benefit groups can be defined according to exempt, nonexempt, part-time, and retired status. Eligibility can be determined for whatever benefit plan is entered into the system. Multiple eligibility rules based on predetermined criteria (minimum work hours, waiting period, service, etc.) are defined and automatically verified by the system. Moreover, the system allows for maintaining specific information on each employee, such as eligibility status and dependent and beneficiary information. This information is updated centrally and is available both to the end user and the individual employee.

Standard reporting includes statements for employee enrollment and confirmation, eligibility reports, lists of participants, and premium reports. Nondiscrimination, ERISA 5500, reports are also possible, as well as enrollment tracking and reporting for COBRA plans.

Finally, the cost planning feature allows for the definition of multiple coverages, the costs for which can then be determined for both employee and employer. Calculations are based on a number of predefined variables, including age, salary, and years of service.

9.8   PERSONNEL PLANNING AND MANAGEMENT

Certainly one of the key responsibilities of human resources revolves around the hiring of new employees and managing their organizational growth over time. Referred to as "corporate fitness" are a whole battery of processes that support management's understanding of not only how to hire employees but how to keep them fit, productive, and happy over time.

The personnel planning and management business process scenario (for SAP™ Release 4.0B, see the employee management scenario) helps a company create its own organizational structure, a system that can then be used as a basis for planning personnel costs, needs, and the like. The business-process scenario for personnel management begins with the creation of a job description and continues on to training and overhead management.

One of the first tasks in personnel management is the development of an organizational plan. In the organizational plan, the overall task of the company is divided into as many subtasks as required to perform an overall task. This division into subtasks and the subsequent combination of the subtasks result in the definition of jobs. The various jobs have to be grouped together in an overall structure and linked to one another. Personnel planning and development results in organizational units, jobs, positions, work centers, and tasks.

The organizational plan is a collection of different types of information that together provide a comprehensive view of the structural and human resource environment in a company. Organizational plans form the basis for personnel planning and development. They contain the fundamental information about a company that is essential for optimal performance.

An organizational plan requires the following information:

- Organizational structure currently in place
- Individual positions performed and the reporting structure or chain of command that exists among the positions
- Different types or classes of jobs that are performed
- Work centers (actual physical locations) where jobs and positions are carried out
- Different tasks performed while fulfilling a job or position

The organizational plan can be a representation of an entire company with all its national and/or international branches, or it can be restricted to an individual area within the company. Once the organizational plan is defined, it can be edited or revised according to changing employment structures. This reorganization typically is followed by the creation of a particular job description.

The main purpose of job descriptions is to create clearly defined areas of responsibility without any gaps or overlaps. The job description contains binding information on where the job is situated in the organizational structure, what functions the job has, and what responsibilities and competencies a job entails. The job description should also specify what requirements a job places on its incumbent (holder). Finally, a job description can assist in promoting cooperation and mutual understanding among employees, in training new employees, and in establishing the need for employee training.

Organization planning also entails "tracking" employees through the life cycle of organizational change and personnel. When a determination is made for filling a new job or position, or an event such as the alteration of an employment contract occurs, the personnel management scenario is designed to continually update employee data and monitor employee status within the company. Updating is essential for not only assuring that an individual receives due process within the organization, but that the company's actions are defensible and non-discriminatory in the case of legal disputes. In personnel management, employee statuses are used to give an overview of all the important changes that have occurred to a company employee and to document the most important steps an employee has taken. Events such as termination, hiring, organizational changes, and the like, are processed and logged. The processes of filling positions (staffing assignments) and recruitment are influenced and triggered by the employee status. Hence, the employee status can be a useful tool for conducting internal searches to fulfill staffing needs, as well as for overall career planning and development.

If staffing assignments are used in conjunction with personnel planning and development, then all the positions that exist in a company are available in structured form in personnel planning and development. In this case, the positions to be filled merely have to be flagged as "vacant" in personnel planning and development to trigger work-force requirements and recruitment.

Work-force requirements are determined by calculating what is required in terms of time, quality, and quantity to achieve particular business goals. It is the task of the recruitment system to ensure that these requirements are met in the hiring of new employees. External recruitment obtains the necessary personnel from among the work-force potential existing outside the company. External recruitment involves such tasks as:

- Creating external job advertisements

- Processing letters of interest and resumes

- Checking references

- Revising selection procedures

- Reviewing employment contracts

Finally, the role of personnel cost planning is to assist a company in its decision-making processes by providing a basis for determining future personnel policy. In personnel cost planning, it is possible to:

- Determine up-to-date, actual personnel costs
- Forecast future personnel costs
- Plan personnel costs expected in the future (on the basis of changes that might occur in the organizational and/or salary structure)

Personnel cost planning records both actual and projected costs. Actual costs are compared with target costs to evaluate future personnel policy decisions. The basis for planning can consist of projected pay, basic pay, or payroll results. In the personnel cost planning scenario, a distinction is drawn between a cost forecast and cost planning. In the case of a cost forecast, it is presumed that the factors that influence the costs (e.g., number of employees, wage structure) will remain unchanged. Cost planning, on the other hand, takes into account organizational changes and other factors that are not typically associated with human resources/payroll accounting. These variables are linked with the cost planning and controlling, which allow for more accurate assessments of future costs.

Personnel cost planning can also be used for simulating different scenarios to better assess personnel options. Various alternatives such as deductions, pay scale agreements, or taxation can be simulated in order to show graphically the total effects of all personnel events on costs.

9.9   R/3 PROCUREMENT LOGISTICS OVERVIEW

The following tables provide an overview to the main scenarios, core processes, business objects, and organizational units that make up R/3 Procurement Logistics.

- -

Scenarios

- ▶ Recruitment
- ▶ Personnel development
- ▶ Business trip management
- ▶ Benefits administration
- ▶ Training and event management
- ▶ Payroll accounting

- -

Core Processes

- ▶ Planning of organizational plan
- ▶ Personnel selection
- ▶ Employee hiring

Core Processes (continued)

▶ Employee transfer

▶ Employee leaving

▶ Salary adjustment

▶ Career planning

▶ Individual personnel development planning

▶ Calculation of remuneration

Business Objects

▶ Travel management
  - Business trip
  - Trip provision

▶ Payroll accounting
  - Wage type
  - Payroll accounting
  - Evaluation class

▶ Time management
  - Period work schedule
  - Absence/attendance type
  - Time quota
  - Time type
  - Employee time balance
  - Time recording
  - Time evaluation

▶ Recruitment
  - Application
  - Job advertisement

Organizational Units

▶ Organizational plan

▶ Personnel area

▶ Personnel subarea

▶ Employee group

▶ Payroll accounting area

Customer Example: The Wellmann Group, Enger, Germany

The Wellmann Group is a leading European manufacturer of kitchens and provider of kitchen products. Headquartered in Enger, Germany, the company produces over 1,000 kitchens a day, and its product range covers such famous kitchen brand names as Tielsa, Gruco, GEBA, Euro-Lanzet, Wellblock, and Wellpac—to name a few. Founded in 1953, the company now employs over 2,700 people, owns nine European subsidiaries, and sells its products to over 40 countries worldwide.

In 1993, The Wellmann Group chose SAP™ as a software solution to help with problems it had encountered, especially in the areas of financial accounting and payroll. The company had a number of obstacles to overcome. For one, company growth had made payroll and cost accounting more difficult. By 1993, it had eight different production centers, located in different German federal states, which made payroll accounting more difficult because of the resulting differences in pay scales. For another, a recent merger between the GEBA company and The Wellmann Group had created a situation in which an entirely different system needed to be converted and integrated into the new payroll system.

A four-person project team consisting of three Wellmann employees and an SAP™ consultant implemented the new human resources system in 18 consulting days, two of which were spent on wage accounting and the remainder on salary accounting. Three members of the project team attended training courses on the system and then trained employees at The Wellmann Group. In the end, the newly implemented system 1) simplified payroll for 2,700 employees; 2) created a smooth system for data communication with financial and cost accounting; 3) maintained an efficient payroll accounting in accordance with the various pay scales; and 4) allowed for the future integration of the system with production planning, materials management, and sales and distribution.

According to Juergen Wortmann, head of payroll at The Wellmann Group: "Our personnel administrators have unanimously accepted the R/3™ system because it rationalizes their work immensely."

Moreover, the addition of the time management with the payroll module in most of its production centers has had similarly favorable results: "We have already linked up almost the entire company," says Wortmann. "As a result, evaluations are now processed faster, and the benefits are particularly apparent in Enger, where we currently work with 150 time programs. Incentive wages no longer pose a problem, either, because R/3™ allows us to work much more effectively and more productively."

10

Business Planning and Controlling

Companies typically create new business designs in order to analyze and improve their internal business processes. Because one of the main goals of this process is cost reduction, business planning and controlling become crucial areas for managers. Managers require detailed financial accounting and process verification information that will help them track the use of monetary resources. On the basis of this information, they can then make informed decisions on how to optimize those resources.

Conventional cost accounting methods are usually sufficient for exacting analysis and monitoring direct costs concerning manufacturing operations (e.g., wages, materials, or equipment rates). These methods, however, are often inadequate for controlling such indirect costs as sales or administration. Consequently, companies may have successfully optimized their production potential, whereas their indirect areas lack cost control. For example, although the reduction of manufacturing penetration may cause a reduction in direct manufacturing costs, external procurement can cause indirect costs to increase. An increase in product services and a greater number of potential buyers may also cause indirect costs to escalate. Moreover, new products may require high development expenditures and comprehensive quality assurance. Finally, a need for customer education may require additional efforts from sales and service areas.

Conventional cost center accounting typically structures costs by using the company's organizational structure and areas of responsibility (i.e., departments). Although this practice allows for the determination of where costs accrue in the company, it does not specify what resources were used or how. Thus, because of limited data, measures of cost optimization are frequently reduced to only local improvements on the cost center level.

By contrast, a process-oriented view considers costs on the basis of process organization across functions. Thus, costs are debited to a business process based on its resource usage. This method, in turn, allows managers to better plan resources and to evaluate optimization measures on a companywide basis.

The business planning and controlling scenarios in R/3™ afford such a process-oriented view. They provide conventional cost center accounting capabilities but supplement these by allocating cost center costs to business processes. Integration with the value flow patterns of the SAP™ systems (logistics, sales, and financial accounting activities) helps give managers a companywide view of where costs accrue and for what purposes they are used.

The main processes, process scenarios, business objects, and organizations, involved in R/3™ revenue and cost controlling are illustrated in Figure 10-1.

These business planning and controlling functions comprise all activities required for cost and revenue accounting. Cost accounting valuates internal exchanges of goods and services and, depending on the method of results analysis, also valuates sales or changes in inventory (imputing). A number of account assignment objects—cost centers, orders, projects, cost objects—are used to allocate costs down to the profitability segments. The values for the different objects are shown as cost and revenue elements.

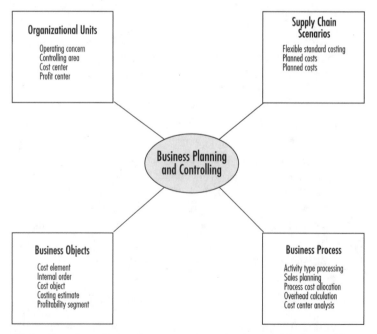

▶ **Figure 10–1**   Overview of scenarios, process, organizations, and business objects

The four business scenarios included in this chapter are defined as follows:

- Cost object controlling—A part of product cost accounting that focuses on the economical creation of a product (cost object). It supplies key information for planning and monitoring of product costs. Product cost controlling attributes the costs incurred in a company to its output units (products, product groups, or orders).
- Profitability analysis—Carries out a profit analysis. As a profitability analysis, it is the last step in the cost-element-related settlement process. For sales management, the costs attributed to the revenues are assigned to the revenues differentiated by market segment.
- Profit center accounting—Not part of the settlement process. The goal is to implement a structure according to profit responsibility. All profit-relevant accounting transactions are projected onto this structure. In addition, selected balance sheet items can be identified with profit centers in the sense of an investment center.
- Overhead cost management—Plans, allocates, controls, and monitors indirect costs.

10.1   *COST OBJECT CONTROLLING*

Cost object controlling is part of a product cost controlling process that determines the costs that accrue in producing a product or performing a service. It helps provide base information for the following business operational functions:

- Price setting and price policy
- Stock valuation controlling of costs of goods manufactured
- Production cost management
- Inventory valuation
- Profitability analysis
- Profit center accounting

Product cost controlling in R/3™ involves two processes: order-neutral product costing and cost object controlling.

Product costing involves estimating the costs of a material or costing object before an order to commence manufacturing is placed. A tool for planning costs and setting prices, it calculates the cost of goods manufactured and the cost of goods sold for each product unit. Products can be tangible goods or intangible goods (services). Along with providing information for inventory valuation and profitability analysis, it helps calculate the variances in cost object controlling.

Cost object controlling involves the order-specific preliminary costing, simultaneous costing, and final costing of a cost object. In cost object controlling, the costs that accrue in manufacturing a product are collected for a cost object. Depending on the type of enterprise, different cost objects are used in R/3™, such as production orders, make-to-stock orders, or sales orders. The purpose of these cost objects is to:

- Determine the actual cost of goods manufactured for a product
- Determine and explain variances between the actual cost of goods manufactured and product costing
- Valuate the work-in-process inventory
- Compare a cost object's revenues with its costs

Cost object controlling is applicable for a number of manufacturing environments, such as repetitive manufacturing, process manufacturing, and engineer-to-order.

The cost object controlling business process scenario (illustrated in Figures 10-2 and 10-3) describes business planning and controlling for order-related production.

The scenario begins with the creation and preliminary costing of a production order from a production-by-lot-size process. Cost object controlling calculates and analyzes the planned and actual costs for each production order. Costs are planned for internal and external activities, overhead, and material usage.

If planning indicates profitability, the order is released and actual production begins. For each production order, all goods receipts are processed and posted to relevant cost controlling assignments. Simultaneous costing allows for the calculation of each variance and provides information for the comparison of planned and actual costs of each production order.

After the material has been manufactured and all actual costs have been assigned to the production order, period-end closing begins. During period-end closing, actual costs are compared with the calculated target costs for each order. These actual costs are then passed on to other objects in R/3™.

Period-end closing consists of four steps: calculating overhead, calculating work-in-process, calculating variances, and settling orders. These steps must be carried out in this sequence. The settlement process passes the work-in-process for each order to financial accounting and profit center accounting, the production variances and scrap costs to profitability analysis, and the remaining costs either to a price difference account or to stock, depending on the price control of the material manufactured.

For this process to function properly, master data and basic data must be entered into the system. These data are provided by the processes process cost

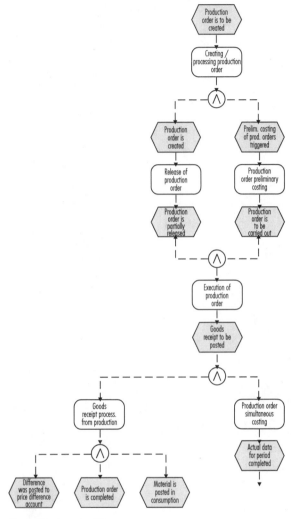

Figure 10–2   Cost object controlling

and revenue element, process cost center, and process activity type in cost accounting. In logistics, it is necessary to set up BOMs, routings, and work centers that serve as the link between cost accounting and logistics.

The planning and preliminary costing of production orders during the production process are not part of the annual planning process. Instead, these are done automatically and in real time as soon as a new order is opened for production.

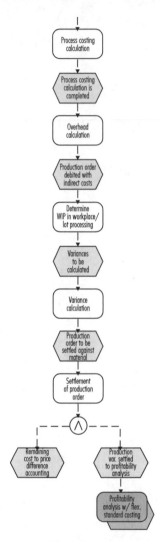

▶ **Figure 10–3**　Period end closing and final costing

Production Order Preliminary Costing

In this phase, managers plan the costs for internal activities, external activities, material usage, and overhead for each production order. Essentially, this phase works as a tool for planning costs and setting prices. Planning the cost of executing a production order is necessary in order to calculate the variances and to compare the planned and actual costs for each order. Order-related preliminary costing is not necessary if variances are calculated and settled periodically.

The order is costed automatically when the task *create production order* is initiated (on the basis of the planned order from quantity planning in production planning). The planned costs calculated in plan price iteration are made available for calculating the flow of activity quantities in production.

The task *preliminary costing of production order* causes the operations of the routing to be valuated with the costs from the cost center.

Preliminary costing is accomplished by using the exploded quantity structure. The BOM items are likewise valuated with the material prices from procurement.

Other agents resulting from this process include the automatic creation of purchase requisitions for external activities and nonstock materials and automatic creation of a reservation list for stock materials.

Production Order Simultaneous Costing

The planned costs of the order can now serve as a basis for deciding whether or not to manufacture the product. If the planned costs indicate that the product will be profitable, actual production can begin with the task *release production order*. The physical execution of the order is accompanied by the task *production order simultaneous costing*.

This phase ensures that each posting that is relevant to cost controlling is assigned to both a cost element and a production order. This assignment is necessary in order to calculate the variance and to compare the planned and actual costs of each production order.

In simultaneous costing, the debits to the production order are found with actual costs. Details on the origin of these debits (such as through confirmations) or the interfaces to the other corporate areas/applications become visible when the function *production order simultaneous costing* is broken down. This function is based on an event-controlled process chain that describes the function in great detail.

Once the material has been manufactured and all actual costs have been assigned to the order, the order is delivered to stock in procurement in the task *process goods received from production*.

This process sets off a number of actions:

- The material stock is debited with the price defined in the price control in the material master record.
- The production order is credited.
- The difference between the debit and the credit is posted to a price difference account in financial accounting.

This concludes the production process and completes the loop between the production process *order-related production* and the controlling process *cost object controlling with order-related production.*

Now we can proceed to the period-end closing steps in controlling.

Period-End Closing and Final Costing

Once the processes of overhead calculation, determine WIP, and variance calculation along with a variance analysis have been carried out, the production order is settled to stock (settlement of production order), and the production variances and scrap costs are settled to profitability analysis.

In this phase, it is possible to calculate overhead on the basis of the actual costs incurred. Here, the cost centers or internal orders are credited, and all production orders are debited with the overhead costs that can be attributed to them.

In addition, work-in-process can be measured. The balance of work-in-progress is calculated by using either the actual costs incurred or the planned costs for the confirmed operations. Moreover, variances and scrap can be calculated and settled for each order. In variance calculation, one can determine the cause of the variances between the target costs (calculated in the standard cost estimate for the material manufactured) and the actual costs for the order. The value of the confirmed scrap can also be calculated. One can also assess further variances between the target costs and the actual costs for the order and between the target costs for the material and the planned costs for the order.

Finally, with settlement, the work-in-process for each order is passed on to financial accounting and profit center accounting, production, variances, and scrap costs are passed to profitability analysis, and the remaining costs are posted either to a price difference account or to stock, depending on the price control of the material.

Once the complete plan and actual data are available, then managers can analyze the product costs in the information system.

10.2   PROFITABILITY ANALYSIS

Profitability analysis in R/3™ breaks down product- and market-oriented activities to fundamental cost accounting information, such as identifying which products or markets have the highest contribution margin or outlining how the profit from a certain customer order is structured. This information is designed to improve cost accounting in the areas of sales, marketing, business planning, and product management. It is especially applicable for companies involved in manufacturing, trade, or service industries.

In profitability analysis, cost-of-sales accounting techniques provide continuous information on contribution margins. Sales and profit planning are used for business planning, and cost estimating procedures measure the performance of all business activities. Costs and revenues are fully integrated into controlling and can be allocated not only to individual products but also to different areas of responsibility.

Profitability analysis takes into account company-specific aspects by supplementing the traditional concept of the *cost object* (the activity units of the value-added process to which costs can be allocated according to origin). In profitability analysis, all profit-related criteria can be used as tracing factors to assign quantities, costs, and revenues. The characteristics of these criteria are combined to create multidimensional *profitability segments*. A profitability segment is the basic accounting assignment of profitability analysis. For profitability segments, an operating result is shown by comparing costs and revenues.

Characteristics for forming profitability segments can be related to the following categories:

- Customer (customer, country group, industry)
- Product (product, product range, range of goods, form of manufacturer)
- Activity (order type, order size, credit worthiness)
- Organization (sales representative's territory, distribution channel, profit center)

Depending on whatever characteristics are defined by the user, profitability segments may be used to compare revenues, quantity/value components, sales deductions, and costs.

In addition to providing valuable cost accounting information, the profitability segment is an integral part of planning in profitability analysis. The entire planning scope includes:

- Sales quantity planning of a profitability segment (planning object)
- Calculation of planned gross/net revenues by valuating the sales quantity with the values stored in the sales system (revenues, discounts, value-based rebates, etc.)
- Profit planning by transferring the costs planned in R/3™ controlling (for example, cost of goods manufactured, indirect cost-center costs)
- Planning by stages of all fixed costs

By virtue of the combination of individual characteristics, each profitability segment reflects a very specific planning unit. For example, a planning unit may consist of the planned sales/planned contribution margin of the range of goods "men's outerwear," of the customer group "department stores," in the sales region "Boston," for "month nine." It is possible to plan sales quantity data for any user-defined profitability segment, instead of having to plan on a product/customer level or to define a general planning level. Each company can therefore carry out its sales quantity and profit planning based on its individual organizational processes.

Profitability analysis enables each company to individually define the scope, type, and sequence of the planning process. The following types of planning are supported:

- Automatic planning—Calculated according to previous year or from other systems such as sales, material requirements forecasting, or external projection planning systems
- Bottom-up planning—Based on sales quantities planned on a lower level, which the system automatically aggregates through the individual planning levels
- Top-down planning—Distributes comprehensively planned objects, such as product ranges, to the individual products or customers by means of system algorithms
- Time-based distribution—Company-specific, time-based distribution, seasonal cycles, sales-quantity-dependent time series, and production-dependent time series

Planning data are integrated with various partial plans from other areas for companywide business planning. To deal with the interdependencies among the partial plans, R/3™ follows the model of "multistage planning," where existing plan data from certain partial plans can be used as a basis for planning in other areas. There are both integrated interfaces for activity-related updating of planning data in other applications and tools to periodically transfer partial plans in their entirety.

10.3   PROFIT CENTER ACCOUNTING

Profit center accounting serves internal management of decentralized company units or profit centers. A profit center is the management-oriented subdivision of a company that serves the purpose of internal control. Profit centers show operating results that have been determined through cost of sales and/or period accounting.

Profit center accounting supports a company organization on the basis of:

- Products (profit centers, product groups)
- Regional markets (locations)
- Function (production, sales, service)

An operating result is determined for each individual profit center. By transferring certain balance sheet items and showing key figures (e.g., cash flow or percentage return on sales), profit centers can be expanded into something more like "responsibility centers."

Based on the assignment of balance sheet items, the profit center manager is also responsible not only for the profit/loss in his or her profit center but also for the invested capital. Key figures can be calculated to place the profit center's profit/loss in relation to the invested capital (return on investment). By showing tied-up assets, the profit center thus acts as an investment center as well.

Profit center accounting is not only fully integrated with the operative applications but is also integrated in real time with all operative systems. This integration eliminates costly review or reentry of data. Actual data are transferred from the following applications:

- Financial accounting—Transfer of primary costs and revenues from *customer invoice processing*
- Sales and distribution—Transfer of revenues and sales deductions (freight, discounts) as well as reserves (e.g., from rebate agreements) via invoice data transfer
- Procurement—Transfer of all costs from goods movements (consumption postings, materials receipt, invoice receipt, price changes/revaluation, inventory differences)
- Asset management—Availability of all profit-related data from the creation, utilization, and sale of capital goods
- Controlling—Availability of all secondary allocations between controlling objects with mapping to the associated profit center (job order settlement, assessment/distribution, activity allocation, repostings, calculations of imputed costs, surcharges)

Period accounting data are used for showing operating results in profit center accounting. In the context of general closing operations, the following balance sheet items are transferred automatically at the end of an accounting period:

- Receivables and payables
- Stock of materials (raw materials, semifinished and finished products)

- Asset portfolios (acquisition costs and accrued depreciation)
- Work-in-process inventory

In addition to automatically determining balance sheet items, the system offers the option of manually assigning balance sheet items from financial accounting to profit center accounting.

After data transfer has been completed, profit center accounting can then assess and distribute certain costs. These costs are collected online from central areas (such as administration cost centers) to a "service center" and assessed or distributed to the actual profit centers at the end of the accounting period. This process is especially applicable for distributing the transferred balance sheet items. For example, capital invested in certain raw materials could be distributed to all the profit centers that use these materials.

Finally, an extensive reporting system is integrated with the data-supplying system components. Typical analysis requirements are supported by a large number of standard reports, which include:

- Profitability reports with plan/actual comparison
- Quarterly reports
- Comparison of "current period" and "cumulative periods"
- Key figure reports

In reporting, existing internal sales can be eliminated on any aggregation level. The system allows flexible navigation between reports and a breakdown of the individual lines by the type of origin object (cost center, orders, projects, etc.). Moreover, drilldown makes it possible to access detailed information, such as the cause of specific profit variables (e.g., cost center accounting).

Logistics data for a profit center can be reported directly from the R/3™ logistics information system, as the profit center is anchored in the logistics master data (e.g., via customer order, purchase order, production order). This capability makes it possible to display additional information, such as orders on hand or production throughput times by profit center. Additional logistics key figures can be used to support decision making.

The reports from the logistics information system together with the profitability reports of profit center accounting can be included in a single detailed report. Figure 10-4 illustrates the overall flow of information contained in R/3™ profit center accounting.

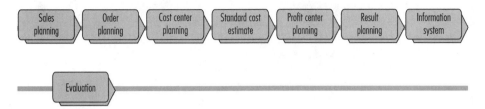

▶ **Figure 10–4**   Value Chain: Profit center accounting

BUSINESS OBJECT

▶ *Cost Center*

A cost center is an organizational unit within a controlling area that represents a separate location of cost incurrence. The definition can be based on

- Location
- Functional requirements
- Allocation criteria
- Activities or services provided
- Area of responsibility

Cost centers are combined into hierarchical decision, managerial, and responsibility groups. They support differentiation of the assignment of overhead costs to organizational activities based on use of the relevant areas (cost determination function). They also support differentiated controlling of costs arising in an organization (cost controlling functions).

The cost center business object is used as a source of information for the following types of business analysis:

- Plan/Actual Comparisons
- Actual/Plan/Variance
- Drilldown by Partner
- Drilldown by Activity
- Actual/Plan/Commitment
- Actual/Plan/Commitment
- Projection
- Fiscal Quarter Comparison
- Fiscal Year Comparison
- Variance Analysis
- Cost Centers: Planning Overview
- Cost Centers: Activity Prices

- Cost Centers: Actual Line Items
- Cost Centers: Commitment Line Items
- Cost Centers: Plan Line Items
- Co Documents: Actual Costs
- Co Plan Documents
- Cost Centers: Master Data Report
- Cost Elements: Master Data Report
- Activity Types: Master Data Report
- Cost Centers: Rolling Year
- Average Costs
- Cost-object Comparison
- Internal Business Volume
- Actual/target from Summarized
- Period Drilldown Actual/plan
- Cost Component Split
- Activity Types: Period Drilldown
- Activity Types: Scheduled/plan
- Area: Actual/budget/commit

- -

10.4   OVERHEAD COST MANAGEMENT

Overhead cost management plans, allocates, controls, and monitors indirect costs (i.e., costs that are not directly assigned to cost objects). Planning indirect costs in overhead cost management allows standards to be defined, which enables control of costs and assignment of values to internal activities. All indirect costs are charged to the cost centers where they were incurred or to the jobs that led to their occurrence.

Overhead cost management is structured as follows:

- Cost element and revenue element accounting—Identifies costs and revenues, delimits the costing-based outlay costs and opportunity costs, reconciles cost accounting and financial accounting
- Cost center accounting—Determines where costs occurred in the enterprise, allocates costs to the departments of the enterprise in which they can be affected
- Internal activity allocation—Allows activities produced by the cost center to be used as reference amounts for the costs
- Overhead cost orders and projects—Uses order system for activity-based cost monitoring; is subdivided in profitability analysis for valuation of sold products on the basis of marginal or full costing

(according to cost of sales accounting); uses cost splitting into fixed and proportional components, which allows real contribution margins to be identified on the basis of marginal costs in profitability analysis

Overhead cost management can be displayed in process-view in the Business Blueprint by means of the Business Engineer. These process views provide examples for typical cost accounting procedures and their conversion into the R/3™ system. They include:

- Assessment procedure—A procedure that represents planned/actual accounting, which operates on the basis of full costing. Cost splitting into fixed and proportional components does not take place. Indirect costs are allocated to the cost recipient or products by the assessment procedure according to certain keys.
- Overhead surcharge calculation—Cost splitting into fixed and proportional components does not occur in this case. Only the labor costs are determined—using the planned hourly rate specified in cost center planning—for valuation of the activity quantity structure. The remaining indirect costs are circulated over overhead calculation to the cost recipients or products.
- Static standard costing—In contrast to the two procedures described above, static standard costing begins with division of the cost center structure into allocation bases or activity types and activity allocation. Cost splitting into fixed and proportional components does not take place in this case, either. The calculated (full) activity prices are transferred from the work plan into the calculation for valuation of the activity quantity structure. The costs of goods manufactured calculated by using product costing can be used in profitability analysis for valuation of sold products on the basis of full costing (according to cost of sales accounting).
- Flexible standard costing based on marginal costs—In contrast to static standard costing, this procedure begins by splitting costs into fixed and proportional components (based on a division of the cost center structure into activity types). The planned activity prices calculated using activity price calculation are transferred from the work plan into the calculation for valuation of the activity quantity structure. Analytical cost planning and the proportional costs calculated by it improve decision making based on marginal costs, for example, in the area of determination of short-term price floors. At the same time, cost object controlling determines the costs of goods manufactured on the basis of full costs.

The costs of goods manufactured calculated by using product costing can be used for additional charging. Using these, indirect costs can be charged according to their origin. Artificial overhead costs can be charged to cost objects with minimal effort and can thus be changed into direct costs. At the end of the accounting period, after all allocations have been made, the planned costs (target costs), adjusted to the operating rate, are compared to the corresponding actual costs. The target/actual differences can be analyzed as to their causes and then become the object of continued control measures within controlling.

10.5 *R/3™ BUSINESS PLANNING AND CONTROLLING SUMMARY*

The following tables provide an overview to the main scenarios, core processes, business objects, and organizational units that make up R/3 Business Planning and Controlling.

Scenarios

▶ Flexible standard costing/Contribution margin accounting in process manufacturing
▶ Planned costs/Contribution margin accounting in production by lot size
▶ Planned costs/Contribution margin accounting in repetitive manufacturing

Core Processes

▶ Cost /revenue element processing
▶ Cost center processing
▶ Activity type processing
▶ Internal order processing
▶ Sales planning
▶ Activity type planning
▶ Material cost estimate
▶ Profit planning
▶ Manufacturing order preliminary costing Production order preliminary costing
▶ Simultaneous costing
▶ Direct activity allocation
▶ Transfer of sales and distribution documents to profitability analysis
▶ Cost assessment
▶ Price calculation

Core Processes (continued)

▶ Process cost allocation

▶ Overhead calculation

▶ Internal order settlement

▶ Determination of work in process (WIP)

▶ Variance calculation of product costs

▶ Settlement of product costs

▶ Profit and contribution margin analysis

▶ Cost center analysis

Business Objects

▶ Cost element

▶ Activity type

▶ Revenue element

▶ Internal order

▶ Controlling document

▶ Cost object

▶ Costing estimate

▶ Profitability segment

Organizational Units

▶ Logical system

▶ Operating concern

▶ Controlling area

▶ Cost center

▶ Profit center

Real-World Example:
Convex Computer Corporation, Richardson, Texas

Convex Computer Corporation is an international concern, with manufacturing based in Texas and direct sales offices and a distribution network distributed through 48 countries worldwide. The company has about 1,000 employees and is a leading global supplier of computer servers, data management systems, and software products to a variety of scientific, engineering, and technical industries.

Convex Computer Corporation was looking for a business information system that could tie together all of its operations and employees around the world, especially in the areas of financial accounting and controlling.

Doyle Baker, director of information resources, says, "With international time differences and formatting variations of our various systems, we previously had to spend a lot of time sending and receiving data, reformatting it so we could put it into our system, then consolidating it for internal and external reporting purposes."

The company's marketing strategy sought to improve the performance/cost ratio of its products and to deliver better service to customers. Convex began with a hard look at how it did business and used IT. "We developed a 400-page document— written by end users as well as MIS staff—that defined the processes used by each functional area of the company to run their business. In that document, we put forth a plan to improve, reengineer, and, in some cases, do away with those processes." That vision and plan led Convex to SAP™ and, in particular, its R/3™ client/server applications for financial accounting and purchasing and controlling.

"Our European subsidiaries were either running their own individual software or using outside service bureaus, and we were having problems trying to consolidate the financial data," Doyle says. Financials, as well as general business data, flow regularly between Convex's Texas headquarters and its worldwide subsidiaries. The SAP™ system gave the company the desired integration. Convex is now flexible enough to change its business processes and organizational structures to meet internal or external market needs. The company is now evolving from a function-driven organization to one organized around processes and product lines.

"We wanted a business system that we could change as the business changed, without having to make any coding changes to the software. We can decide that a process needs to be changed, and the system is flexible enough to accomplish that without creating a backlog of high-end programming work," Doyle says.

Convex is already seeing benefits. Employees already exceeded the 10 percent improvement goal set for mastering the system, and gains in productivity have allowed Convex to reduce its staff in payables by 33 percent. A financial accountant who spent eight hours on one monthly task now does it in just five minutes. Another task has been reduced from twelve hours to five.

Adds Doyle, "During a typical month, each subsidiary used to spend up to a full day preparing its local ledger and sending it to corporate for consolidation. That time has been reduced to zero. All the subsidiaries have to do now is manage their local ledgers. Since we're all on the same, fully integrated system, we have immediate access to the subsidiaries' information. That means we don't have to waste valuable time when we're trying to analyze the results of a particular month or quarter."

11

Capital Asset Management

Today's increasing mechanization is leading to high fixed costs in the asset management area. Consequently, capital asset management—which encompasses all tasks relating to the project planning, provision, administration, and plant maintenance of operating facilities (assets)—is an important contributing factor to the success of a company. A high availability of production systems is essential for the cost-effective distribution of fixed costs.

A number of factors have heightened the need for effective plant maintenance. New demands for quality assurance, environmental protection, and system safety have underscored the importance of the regular maintenance of production systems. Regular plant maintenance of technical systems typically encompasses the following areas:

- Inspection (all measures that confirm the actual condition of an operational system)
- Maintenance (all measures that maintain the ideal condition of an operational system)
- Repair (all measures that restore the ideal condition of an operational system)

During implementation, new technologies and modern production systems must be targeted toward meeting the demands of these three task areas. This goal can be achieved through transparent, computer-based asset management.

The R/3™ plant management business scenario is a capital asset management process that provides the required support for the inspection, maintenance, and repair of an operational system. This process facilitates fast and meaningful information acquisition, improved planning, reduced maintenance costs, less-frequent machine downtimes, and so on. It is an integral component of the R/3™ system and works without an interface in conjunction with the logistics and accounting functions. The ongoing exchange of information with other user departments of the R/3™ system ensures current data and optimization of business processes through integrated workflow management.

Plant management represents an overall solution for tasks relating to the administration and maintenance of technical systems in all branches of industry. It supports the administration of company-internal systems (e.g., production, provision, disposal, and transport systems) as well as external systems (e.g., customer systems).

The capital asset management business processes, scenarios, business objects, and organizations are shown in Figure 11-1.

The basic scenarios are now described, using planned plant maintenance as an illustrative example.

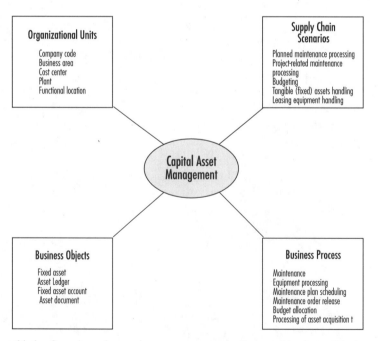

▶ **Figure 11–1**   Overview of scenarios, process, organizations, and business objects

11.1 PLANNED PLANT MAINTENANCE

Increasing automation combined with decreasing direct labor have resulted in higher fixed costs of operational systems. As this trend continues, plants and related equipment will need to be continuously available at or above specified performance levels, which will guarantee a cost-effective distribution of fixed costs and return on assets.

In addition, as companies reduce working capital and engage in other inventory-reduction programs, responsiveness to customers will be guaranteed only if a company can rely on the availability of its production facilities. Thus, an optimal plant and equipment maintenance program is crucial in these environments.

For maintenance operations to become more responsive, they will need to rely on other support functions within the organization. For example, a planned maintenance task or emergency repair operation might require spare parts, repair equipment, plant personnel, and external services, all brought together at the same place and time. To be effective, maintenance functions must be tightly integrated with purchasing, scheduling, human resource, and inventory control activities.

The value chain in Figure 11-2 describes how regular maintenance tasks are planned and processed.

Here we see the planning and processing of regular maintenance tasks for technical objects. The process begins with the use of a particular type of maintenance plan, such as single cycle plan, preventive maintenance, or multiple counter plan. Scheduling is used to create a timeframe for the maintenance orders and all maintenance items. Maintenance planning is followed by the processing of planned maintenance order. Processing typically involves release and implementation of the order, completion and confirmation, completion and settlement. Evaluations are available via the Logistics Information System (LIS).

An EPC diagram of this business-process scenario is detailed in this section and illustrated in Figures 11-3 and 11-4, which describe how preventive maintenance is planned and controlled.

The scenario begins with maintenance planning, which defines, schedules, and organizes a preventive maintenance plan. Maintenance planning is responsi-

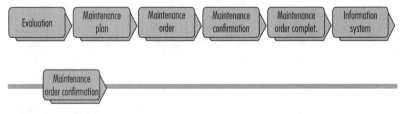

▶ **Figure 11–2**   Value chain: Planned plant maintenance describes how regular maintenance tasks are planned and processed

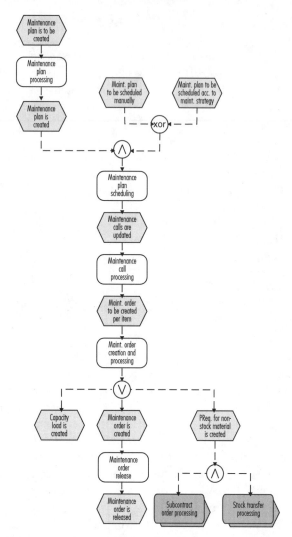

▶ **Figure 11–3**   Maintenance plan processing

ble for maintenance tasks repeated at regular intervals. As preventive maintenance is the primary function of this scenario, the most important task of maintenance planning is to keep a production plant permanently available in the long term.

Once a plan is in place, a maintenance order can be created. In the plant management system, maintenance orders are used to monitor the performance and progress of maintenance tasks and to collate and settle the resultant costs. Main-

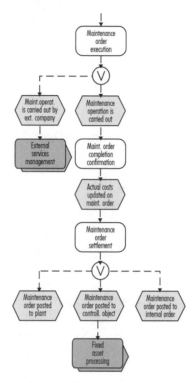

▶ **Figure 11–4** Maintenance order execution

tenance task lists and preventive maintenance plans form the basis of efficient preparation and planning of plant maintenance.

Finally, after the order has been confirmed, it can then be settled as a part of cost accounting. By integrating a maintenance plan with cost accounting, the system ensures that a technical system not only remains operational but also reduces unnecessary costs arising from repairs, system repairs, system replacement, or lost output.

Maintenance Plan Processing

Preventive maintenance plan processing specifies the time, place, and order in which certain maintenance tasks need to be carried out.

The scheduling rules for regular maintenance tasks are stored as preventive maintenance strategies. Within these preventive maintenance strategies, preventive maintenance packages are defined. These packages can be used to determine the intervals at which maintenance should be performed; for example, every 10,000 km or every 500 operating hours. Then, maintenance items are created that determine which tasks are performed, at what frequency, and at what objects (functional locations, equipment, assemblies, etc.).

Preventive maintenance plans combine the information from strategies and maintenance items. They result in the initiation of regular maintenance orders through scheduling.

Maintenance Plan Scheduling

A preventive maintenance plan consists of one or more maintenance items and a maintenance schedule, which combines maintenance items for the purposes of collective scheduling.

The maintenance schedule contains scheduling information from each preventive maintenance strategy assigned to the preventive maintenance plan, as well as maintenance plan-specific scheduling parameters that apply to this preventive maintenance plan in particular. In the plant management system, there are four scheduling options: time-based, time-based with key date, time-based account to factor calendar, and performance-based.

When the user schedules a preventive maintenance plan in the plant management system, the information mentioned is used especially to calculate due dates for the maintenance operations, which are then performed at the assigned technical objects.

When a preventive maintenance package becomes due, regular maintenance orders are created automatically for all affected maintenance items on the basis of maintenance plan scheduling. Continuous planning makes it possible, for example, that the orders for the next periods are always called, so that an appropriate order supply is always available.

Regular maintenance orders contain only those operations for maintenance items that are contained in the preventive maintenance package. In this way, scheduling automatically determines both the date and the extent of the required maintenance work.

Maintenance Call Processing

After maintenance plan scheduling, the preventive maintenance plan call is released either manually or automatically, depending on the item in the preventive maintenance plan. If preventive maintenance plan calls-on-hold still exist, these are either processed in advance, skipped, or canceled before manual release.

Once the preventive maintenance plan call has been released, a maintenance order is created for each maintenance item, which can then be created and subsequently processed.

Maintenance Order Creation and Processing

If maintenance tasks have to be performed, these are requested with a maintenance notification. They are planned in detail within the maintenance order, and their performance is monitored. The maintenance order also contains details of specific repair tasks.

A maintenance order can be created on the basis of one or more maintenance notifications. In the same way, a maintenance notification can be created for a directly entered maintenance order at a later time; for example, to enter data on machine breakdown or system availability with regard to the work performed at particular objects. Maintenance notifications and orders are completed after the requested repair tasks have been carried out (see Figure 11-2).

In the plant management system, maintenance task lists are used for regular and nonregular maintenance. Maintenance task lists describe the individual steps that must be carried out during inspection, repair, and maintenance. They also list the spare parts and tools needed to perform the tasks and specify the time needed for performance.

Managers can include all this information in a maintenance item by assigning a maintenance task list to the item. The operations described in the maintenance task list are performed at all technical objects that were assigned to the maintenance item.

Maintenance Order Release

Once the planning of the maintenance order and all required information have been completed, the order can be released for execution. Only then can the maintenance personnel at the customer company start to perform the tasks described in the order.

When a maintenance order is released, the system checks the availability of material and production resources/tools and required permits. These machine and production resources/tools data initiate maintenance tasks. When the order is released, material reservations (applicable to MRP and withdrawal) are created along with the purchase requisition.

Maintenance order release must occur before the order can be carried out.

Maintenance Order Execution

Maintenance tasks are performed according to maintenance orders. The order describes the type, extent, dates, and resources for performance and defines the rules for account assignment and settlement.

There are two variants for the performance of a maintenance order. A maintenance order can be performed by an internal business unit (e.g., a maintenance department) or by an external company.

The decision whether to perform certain tasks internally or externally depends on the costs of the alternatives and on certain internal and external factors.

Maintenance Order Completion Confirmation

Once a maintenance order has been released and maintenance work has begun, the personnel involved can enter confirmations in the system.

There are two types of maintenance confirmation: partial confirmation and final confirmation. Partial confirmation is made during the performance of the task; confirmations are made until the task is complete. Final confirmation is made after the task is complete. When final confirmation is made, the maintenance order is given the status "finally confirmed."

Confirmations supplement maintenance notifications. The data they contain are written to the maintenance history. A final confirmation can cause a new open notification to be created.

Maintenance Order Settlement

Maintenance order settlement is by definition part of cost accounting and therefore requires in advance rules for account assignment and settlement, which are copied to the maintenance order when the order is created.

The structure of a production order, as formed in materials management, corresponds to that of a maintenance order. Consequently, for source-related and period-based costing, maintenance order settlement requires the costs arising from the maintenance tasks. For this reason, in the context of maintenance planning, the following must all be determined: the calculated requirements, the replacement materials used in a maintenance task, the personnel involved in the task, and the consumption and usage of the required auxiliary resources.

On the basis of maintenance order settlement and the data included in the maintenance history, an unbroken analysis of all life phases of a technical system is provided by means of specific multiperiod comparisons as well as by temporal comparisons of system costs and performance.

A weak-point analysis building on this history within the framework of asset controlling ensures that the aims of capital asset management are achieved.

BUSINESS OBJECT

▶ *Equipment*

In R/3 ™, equipment is defined as any individual, physical object that is to be maintained as an autonomous unit. A piece of equipment can be installed at a functional location or in a piece of equipment for a certain period of time. In the course of its life cycle, it can be used at different installation locations. Pieces of equipment can be structured hierarchically so that the structure of complex pieces of equipment may be represented. They may also be linked to one another, enabling the global network structure of a technical system and the dependencies between the pieces of equipment to be represented.

The Equipment business object is used as a source of information for the following types of business analysis:

- Change Equipment
- Equipment List (Multilevel)
- Functional Location Structure
- Reference Location Structure
- Equipment Structure
- Material Structure
- Functional Location
- Reference Location
- Equipment List
- Material List
- Measuring Points
- Change Measuring Points
- Display Measurement Documents
- Change Measurement Documents
- Change Functional Location
- Change Reference Location
- Change Object Network
- Display Object Network
- Change material serial number
- Display material serial number
- Agreement of quantity data for inventory management and serial data

11.2   *DAMAGE-RELATED MAINTENANCE PROCESSING*

The R/3 ™ plant maintenance system integrates the activities required to maintain plants, equipment, transportation vehicles, or other technical or production systems. These systems may consist of plant equipment used by the company, company-owned equipment installed at customer locations, or customer-owned or supplier-owned equipment.

Maintenance consists of the following major tasks:

- Inspection—Determining the real-time conditions of a system
- Planned maintenance—Maintaining equipment on a scheduled basis
- Repair—Restoring the equipment to an appropriate level of performance

The equipment master file defines all maintenance activities that are performed on equipment. Individual pieces of equipment can be combined to form larger systems. For instance, an electronic device assembly line may consist of three pieces of equipment: an automated tester, an insertion machine, and a conveyer. The process of linking equipment together is described in the "functional-system information system" scenario.

Maintenance orders—the R/3™ mechanism for managing maintenance activities and collecting costs—are created and processed as a result of a notification process indicating that equipment is damaged or in need of repair.

The maintenance order places material reservations for stocked material or generates purchase requisitions for consumable nonstocked material and external services to be performed. A capacity load of all maintenance orders is generated to help balance supply and demand of required resources.

The detailed operations on the maintenance order are used to dispatch work. Completed tasks and material usage are posted to the maintenance order as well as technical data recorded during the maintenance work. Required technical recordings can be preplanned so that maintenance personnel can be told what data to record. When all operations are completed, the maintenance order is confirmed and the costs settled.

11.3   *PROJECT-BASED MAINTENANCE PROCESSING*

In this scenario, the full functionality of the maintenance system is available in the context of managing long-term capital projects.

All maintenance activities are performed on equipment that is defined in the equipment master file. Individual pieces of equipment can be combined to form larger systems. For instance, an electronic device assembly line may consist of three pieces of equipment: an automated tester, an insertion machine, and a conveyer.

This business scenario begins by defining a maintenance strategy, the rules, and sequences for planned maintenance operations. It defines the frequency with which the individual jobs are to be carried out—for example, every 2 months, every 5,000 km, every 500 operating hours—and the overall length of the maintenance cycle.

The maintenance strategy produces specific items to be planned and scheduled. When a maintenance plan is prepared, the system generates maintenance calls for all the maintenance items. At the appropriate time, these calls are converted into maintenance orders, the R/3™ mechanism for managing maintenance activities and collecting costs. Maintenance orders are also created as a result of a notification process indicating that equipment is damaged or in need of repair. In this scenario, every maintenance order is referenced to a work breakdown structure (WBS) element in the R/3™ project system.

The maintenance order places material reservations for stocked material or generates purchase requisitions for consumable, nonstocked material and external services to be performed. A capacity load of all maintenance orders is generated to help balance supply and demand of required resources.

The detailed operations on the maintenance order are used to dispatch work. Completed tasks and material usage, as well as technical data recorded during the maintenance work, are posted to the maintenance order. Required technical recordings can be preplanned so that maintenance personnel can be told what data to record. When all operations are completed, the maintenance order is confirmed and the costs settled to the work breakdown structure element in the project system.

11.4   CASH MANAGEMENT

The cash management business-process scenario manages liquidity to support company operations while providing information to put excess cash to the best possible use. Comprehensive cash management must support electronic banking, function alongside operations, and provide dynamic foreign currency handling. In addition, it must be able to handle such modern, global-economy challenges as:

- The emergence of electronic commerce
- Automated payment routines that optimize money market transactions and short-term interest income opportunities
- Shrinking cash transaction cycle times
- Growing global operations that require multicurrency cash management capabilities

The cash management scenario describes how cash transactions are planned and processed within R/3 ™. Current and future cash positions are dynamically updated and presented to the user. Cash management is extensively linked to electronic banking and integrated with the core financial accounting system and demand/supply chain activities. This provides extended cash liquidity forecasting capabilities.

The cash management processes handle all cash-related transaction and reporting activities. Cash management distinguishes between cash accounts (actual money) and clearing accounts (payments in transit). Cash management is integrated with the general ledger, accounts receivable/payable systems, as well as sales and procurement processing to provide extended cash liquidity forecasting capabilities.

The scenario provides for the processing of the following:

- Bank account statements (electronically or manually)
- Manually deposited checks
- Electronically deposited checks (lockbox processing in the United States, POR procedure in Switzerland)
- Bills of exchange that are "presented" by the bank or a vendor for payment
- Cashed checks
- Payment advice from customers and banks
- Planned items, such as tax payments, to account for anticipated cash flows

Data are posted simultaneously to the general ledger, accounts receivable/payable, and cash management systems. Using payment advice comparison, actual payments are matched to payment advice and then archived.

Cash positions and the liquidity forecasts are based on three integrated information sources within R/3 ™:

- Current bank account balances, payment advice, and planned items
- Accounts receivable and payable open items
- Sales and purchase orders

Based on the company's investment strategy and financial market information, short- and long-term investments and borrowings are planned and executed. Cash concentration (sweeping money into one account) and cash flow (expenditure and revenue) planning can be executed.

Period-end processing includes managing and accruing interest on short-term instruments (time and overnight deposits, and loans), calculating interest on account balances, and maintaining exchange rates.

11.5 BUDGETING

Integrated business systems are usually based on accrual accounting principles. This approach provides a solid foundation for financial accounting. For both public and private companies, however, accounting for outside entities requires careful management of funds as do controls for safeguarding liquidity and managing long-term capital investments.

For large organizations, this requirement presents a number of challenges. For one, data in traditional, general-ledger-based accounting systems are oriented to an accrual basis rather than an available funds basis.

For another, the enterprise might use different accounting structures in different legal entities or business units. Since budgetary control spans multiple business areas, a complex data integration effort is required to pull the data together into a useful and usable format.

Finally, global control of the budget, especially online monitoring of funds availability, requires tight integration of all business transactions across the enterprise, such as cash receipts, down payments, vendor invoice processing, and purchasing. Furthermore, these transactions might occur in a different currency than the one used for budgetary purposes. This complication requires additional control and monitoring.

R/3™'s budget control features are based on the R/3™ integration model and its multicurrency capabilities. The budget structures are related to, but independent from, the general ledger accounts, which allows them to be maintained and controlled independently from general ledger accounting.

The budgeting scenarios provide enterprisewide control of funds used in operations and capital investments. A budget integrates cash requirements for both operations and capital investments with planned cash receipts. This scenario begins, therefore, with identifying funds.

Organizational and functional hierarchies of the enterprise, which represent the areas to which the budget will be allocated, are defined to the system. Budget control, navigation, and user-security parameters are provided to help automate and secure the budgeting processes.

In the next step, these funds are combined into the total budget and then divided into individual plans for administrative and capital budgets. If applications of funds exceed sources of funds, the requirement to balance the budget can be identified. Different versions of the budget in alternate plans are recorded until the final budget is approved and released.

The budgeting scenarios differ in how budgeting tasks are delegated through the organizational hierarchy. In the "central budgeting" scenario, budgets for all business segments are created and maintained within a centralized control area of the enterprise. In local budgeting, budgets are created and maintained within the responsible business segment, and the enterprise budget is rolled up from these segment budgets. In central/local budgeting these approaches are combined.

The budgeting process also incorporates:

- Amendments and supplements to the budget
- Budget reductions and returns
- Transfer of funds between budget items
- Commitment authorizations
- Unexpected balances and shortfalls
- Anticipated expenditures

Receipts and expenditures based on ongoing business transactions are recorded and allocated to the appropriate budget item. With the budget and system control parameters in place, the budget verification process provides an active availability check of committed funds. This availability check is accomplished through purchase order integration to ensure that expenditures do not exceed the funds available. Vendor invoices are subject to review by those responsible for the budget. After the posting of each invoice, the system updates the actual data to be compared with the budget.

The reporting stages provide periodic and ad hoc reports that compare targets, expenses, and receipts in accordance with the budget system. Reports using other data, such as down payments, invoice amounts, and final payments, can also be prepared. A detailed audit trail of all transactions related to each budgetary item is available online.

11.6   FIXED ASSET PROCESSING

Traditional fixed asset systems provide depreciation calculations for taxes and financial statements. However, in addition to pure accounting and balance sheet preparation, there are extensive requirements for controlling and maintenance monitoring. In this environment, accounting is integrated with managing the asset's physical life cycle, which includes activities in purchasing, production, construction, maintenance, and sales.

A modern asset management system must facilitate decision making by providing depreciation simulation and forecasting and seamless integration to companywide budgeting, cost planning, and financial consolidation. Moreover, the complex requirements for group accounting on national and international levels also must be satisfied.

The fixed asset processing business scenario describes the financial, accounting, and controlling aspects of managing fixed assets. Together with the R/3™ procurement, plant maintenance, and investment measures business processes, fixed asset accounting is integrated into the company's operational, investment, and financial planning activities.

The first activity described in these scenarios is the acquisition of assets. Acquisition can occur in one of three ways:

- Asset acquisition preceded by an R/3™ purchase order and followed by the receipt of goods and the corresponding invoice
- Asset acquisition without a purchase order and based on a vendor invoice
- Asset acquisition through in-house production of a capital investment project or order

In R/3™, investment measures (investment projects and/or orders) are tools to manage and control the in-house production and construction of fixed assets. These activities are described in the project-related and individual investment measure processing scenarios (see Section 11.3).

Governments often provide support to encourage capital investment. The asset handling scenarios describe the processing of these investment subsidies and grants. They can be applied for, posted automatically, and adjusted manually if necessary. The accounting is handled either as a reduction to the asset value or as an adjustment to a liability on the balance sheet.

The next step is the calculation of depreciation. Planned depreciation is calculated automatically but can also be recalculated or changed manually should rules and policies change. Both planned and actual depreciation are calculated in multiple depreciation areas, using a parallel valuation technique. These calculations are based on different rules to meet the unique requirements of local legal and tax reporting, cost accounting, and corporate group consolidation. Depreciation values are transferred as planned, and actual costs are allocated to cost centers in overhead cost management. Depreciation simulation and forecasting for current and future accounting periods are available for an individual asset, a group of assets, or the entire portfolio. Asset and depreciation values can be adjusted during the life of the asset by processing "post-capitalizations" and "write-ups," respectively.

Several factors can lead to changes in the rules that determine asset valuation. R/3™ supports the following:

- Future replacement and insurable values are determined by using an index series.
- Revaluation can adjust for the impact of high inflation.
- New investment support rules and valuation methods (depreciation rules) can always be defined.

As assets are moved and reassigned to new company locations and business units, these changes are recorded and the related accounting is handled automatically. A mass change function facilitates large-scale changes. Stocktaking for fixed assets can be performed periodically, and adjustments entered as required. Moreover, as fixed assets are often insured because of their large value, insurance contract data are entered in the asset master file.

Removal of an asset from the asset portfolio is processed as a retirement. Assets can be sold or scrapped individually or in a group. Asset sales are fully integrated with the sales and accounts receivable functions and also include the calculation of reserves. A reserve is created when an asset is sold for more than its book value.

Year-end closing, archiving, and reporting complete the scenario.

11.7 *LEASED ASSET PROCESSING*

With ever-increasing technological advancements, companies are replacing and updating their assets more frequently to keep their plants, equipment, and offices up-to-date. From a finance perspective, leasing is often more advantageous than purchasing fixed assets. Although leased assets remain the property of the lessor, the lessee is usually responsible for asset maintenance. Specific tax and accounting principles have evolved to accommodate these business requirements. There are two methods for handling leased assets, depending on the terms of the lease and local tax conditions:

- Capital lease—Assets are capitalized and depreciated
- Operating lease—Lease payments are treated as an on-going periodic expense

Beyond specialized financial and accounting aspects of handling leases, management of the actual physical status of each asset and insurance requirements dictate that leased assets be treated in an integrated and comprehensive manner along with standard fixed assets.

The leased asset processing business scenario describes asset management and accounting functions for both operating and capital leases. It is integrated with other functions within the R/3™ financial, procurement, and plant maintenance systems.

Operating leases, although not part of the lessee's fixed asset portfolio, require tracking of individual asset records. These are maintained in the asset master file for management and insurance handling. Capital leases require the calculation of depreciation schedules, using the same features and functions described in the fixed assets scenarios (see Section 11.6).

Acquisition of leased assets triggers the following tasks:

- Maintaining the lease agreement
- Receiving the asset and the invoice
- Determining if it is an operating or capital lease
- Setting up the payment plan
- Posting to the fixed assets, accounts payable, and general ledger business processes

Periodic lease payments are calculated and posted to the accounts payable system for payment processing. The same set of depreciation simulation and forecasting features as described in the fixed assets scenarios are available here. Future replacement and insurable values are determined by using an index series. Modifications to the lease agreement are entered into the asset master record.

As assets are moved and reassigned to new company units, the changes are recorded. A mass change function facilitates large-scale changes. Stocktaking for fixed assets can be performed periodically, and the necessary adjustments are entered as necessary. Insurance contract information is entered in each asset master record.

Removal of a leased asset from the asset portfolio is processed as a retirement. Leased assets are retired in one of three ways: they are scrapped, returned to the lessor, or bought by the lessee and transferred into a standard fixed asset. Year-end closing, archiving, and reporting complete the scenario.

11.8   R/3™ CAPITAL ASSET MANAGEMENT SUMMARY

The following tables provide an overview to the main scenarios, core processes, business objects, and organizational units that make up R/3™ Capital Asset Management.

Scenarios

▶ Planned maintenance processing

▶ Damage-driven maintenance processing

▶ Project-related maintenance processing

▶ Budgeting

▶ Tangible (fixed) assets handling

▶ Leasing equipment handling

Core Processes

▶ Maintenance

  – Functional location processing

  – Equipment processing

  – Maintenance strategy processing

  – Maintenance plan processing

  – Maintenance item processing

  – Maintenance plan scheduling

  – Maintenance call processing

  – Maintenance notification creation and processing

  – Maintenance order creation and processing

  – Maintenance order release

  – Maintenance order completion confirmation

  – Maintenance order settlement

  – Maintenance order completion

▶ Investment management

  – Creation of asset master record

  – Project management

  – Budget allocation

  – Direct activity allocation

Core Processes (continued)

- Investment settlement
- Settlement account assignment
- Order planning
- Release of order
- Processing of internal orders
- Processing of asset acquisition
- Fixed asset retirement
- Preparations for year-end closing

Business Objects

▶ Fixed assets
- Fixed asset
- Asset ledger
- Fixed asset account
- Asset document

▶ Investment
- Capital investment measure
- Investment program

▶ Maintenance
- Equipment
- Maintenance plan
- Maintenance task list
- Maintenance notification
- Maintenance order
- Measurement

Organizational Units

▶ Company code
▶ Business area
▶ Cost center
▶ Plant
▶ Functional location

Real-World Example:
Seraya Chemicals Singapore Ltd., Singapore

Seraya Chemicals Singapore Ltd is poised to meet the high demands for petrochemical products in the thriving Asia-Pacific markets. Demand for petrochemical products in the fast developing Asia-Pacific region is expected to grow continuously at a higher rate than the world average. This strong and growing demand provides many opportunities for the establishment of the Second Petrochemical Complex on Pulau Ayer Merbau and Pulau Seraya, which strengthens its regional market presence strategically through the expansion of existing capacities and development of new high value-added products.

Seraya Chemicals Singapore Ltd is an integral part of the Second Petrochemical Complex. A joint venture between Shell and Mitsubishi, Seraya Chemicals operates a Styrene Monomer (SM) and Propylene (PO) plant, a Polyols plant and a Monopropylene Glycol (MPG) plant. These plants bring to the existing petrochemical complex new technologies and product lines.

The company started their implementation of SAP™R/3™ in May 1997 on the R6000 AIX Unix platform. The company first looked into Baan and J.D. Edwards before deciding on SAP™. One of the key factors in the decision-making process was that the company wanted to have access to the business supply chain models so that they could understand how to apply different products to their implementation.

Said Dr. Timothy Ng, Finance Manager, Seraya Chemicals: "As part of the infrastructure, we evaluated SAP™ from a zero base with other systems based on four criteria: the level of integration, both internally and with other systems; its scalability and expandability; cost effectiveness, and long-term vendor support and relationship. Overall, SAP™ came out tops."

Having open systems was very important to Seraya. That SAP introduced Business Application Programming Interfaces (BAPIs) into its product and enabled third parties to communicate with the R/3™ system was critical in their decision-making process. Seraya Chemicals does not have its own sales channel. It works exclusively through its parent companies. Seraya does provide a part of the sales process to these larger parent companies, as they do considerable work internally on sales and distribution services.

"One of the most exciting features of SAP™ is its ability in interfacing with other systems. While we have outstanding plant process applications, the systems needs to be integrated with business processes to eliminate unnecessary information processing and translation of data for meaningful analysis by management."

The company has been able to integrate on their implementation based on different supply chain models with different customized components. One is the distribution control systems (DCS) which integrates into the sales and business processes. Other interfaces have been built such as the planned supervisory system (PSS), which interfaces into the plant maintenance model of the SAP™ system, and others that interface between SAP™ and plant machinery.

"SAP™'s scalability and versatility with the ABAP/4 Development Workbench allowed us to customize and extend the PM module and fine-tune our requirements. This includes our Conditioning Base Monitoring module which allows for performance monitoring. Equipment usage can be optimized without affecting plant reliability as a result of extensive runtime analyses and evaluation for performance optimization."

Critical to Seraya's success is the ability to run operations virtually without break. In other words, the software importance of choosing SAP™ was not only to have the business models available but also to have a way that let them understand the impact of decisions in a very high performing environment. Supply chain optimization—which is a deciding factor for companies embarking upon the second generation ERP—is very important for them because they do optimization and load balancing, and they need immediate feedback about stock and stock management. They have, in essence, a supply chain in which 80% of the cost is directly related to how they manage inventory in their stocks.

Synchronous office integration is also a major demand for the SAP™ system. The company requires that they have immediate feedback from third-party products that provide material deliveries to people in the plant. In the future, the company would like to see products that deliver immediate information along the supply chain. The company would like to be able to use one of the supply chains—the stock material supply chain, for example—to identify participants along that supply chain and provide them with immediate feedback within their role in the company. Information delivery continues to be part of the company's on-going engineering effort to implement SAP™ R/3™.

With the implementation of SAP™ R/3™ applications, Seraya Chemicals has not only benefited in terms of integration and business optimization, it has also laid the foundation for long-term growth. Seraya chemicals is poised to meet the rigorous demands of the booming Asia-Pacific petrochemical markets.

12

Finance Management

In an environment of increasingly cutthroat competition, today's companies, regardless of size, have found that crucial to their survival are the efficient management of short-term, medium-term, and long-term payment flows and the appropriate handling of the resulting risks. Effective finance management is based on the integration of different areas of the company, especially the complete integration of all cash flow information. This integration affects everything, from short-term control and clearing of the bank account balances created, to medium-range planning and forecasting of the incoming and outgoing payments of customers and vendors, to long-term monitoring of operational areas such as purchasing and sales. Moreover, a company's success depends on how this information flows into already established or planned financial investment activities and financial borrowing activities in treasury.

The strategic establishment of financial objectives in a company are tied to revenue and risk goals. In this context, one can imagine, for example, making a decision about which accounts should always be available for cash concentration or generally determining the minimum balance to keep in each account. The financial concept must also incorporate legal requirements and regulations as well as establish guidelines for investment and risk, such as determining the types of financial products relevant to the company.

In order to cover fully all company-specific objectives, SAP™'s treasury system provides special methods and tools for looking at processes in an integrated fashion. These methods and tools are divided among three different components, according to their content:

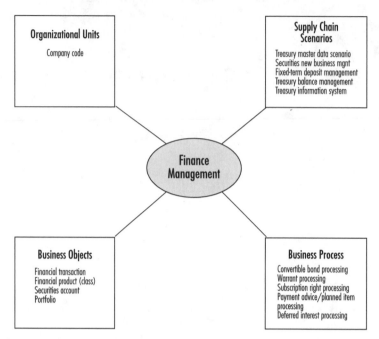

▶ **Figure 12–1** Overview of scenarios, process, organizations, and business objects

- Functions for efficient liquidity management are supported by the cash management component
- The market risk management component provides methods and procedures for evaluating risk positions
- Management of financial transactions and positions is supported by treasury management

These three components are described in more detail in the sections that follow, but the emphasis here is on the treasury management component. Figure 12-1 illustrates the full range of financial management in R/3™.

12.1 TREASURY MANAGEMENT

Building on the current liquidity and risk analyses, the treasurer makes decisions about the company's future financial investments or borrowing and implements these as financial transactions in treasury management. The purpose of treasury management is to manage financial transactions and funds balances, from negotiations all the way to the transfer into financial accounting. It should also provide flexible reporting and evaluation structures for analyzing financial transactions, funds balances, and portfolios.

In accordance with the division standard in the marketplace into short-term, medium-term, and long-term financial transactions, R/3™ treasury management supports the control of risk and liquidity items through money market and foreign exchange transactions in the short-term area and through securities and loans in the medium- and long-term areas. It also allows active management of interest and currency risks through trading of derivatives.

Moreover, treasury management in R/3™ supports efficient management of financial transactions through an organizational division (implemented in the process flows) into different areas, such as trade, back-office processing, and posting approval, as well as the subsequent transfer into financial accounting.

R/3™ treasury management consists of the following five scenario modules:

- Money Market/Foreign Exchange/Derivatives Trading
- Treasury Master Data scenario
- New Security Management
- Treasury Position Management
- Treasury Information System

The sections that follow present and explain in more detail, as an example and as reality, both the organizational requirements and the scope of functions of SAP™ treasury management. For the area of money market/foreign exchange/derivatives trading, we use the fixed-term deposit processing scenario as an illustrative example.

Fixed-Term Deposit Processing (Money Market/Foreign Exchange/Derivatives Trading)

Financial transactions involving fixed-term deposits are used for short- to medium-term investment or borrowing of liquid funds. Using the surpluses and deficits calculated in cash management as a basis, a company can implement planning decisions in fixed-term deposit processing (see Figure 12-2).

One prerequisite for running fixed-term deposit processing is that the master data required for trading fixed-term deposits has already been created as part of the money market trading master data scenario that has been run previously. The integrations presented here also show both of the possible entry points into the fixed-term deposit processing scenario.

Product Type Selection

When you enter any Money market/foreign exchange/derivatives trading scenario, you must first decide how any surplus should be used for liquidity that may have been calculated after running cash management and forecast as part of cash management. In the example presented here, the treasurer decides to invest the available liquid funds in the form of a fixed-term deposit. This decision-making process is purely manual and is based on the conditions and determining factors with which the treasurer is faced.

Fixed-Term Deposit Processing

Fixed-term deposit processing includes investment or borrowing of fixed-term deposits (see Figure 12-3). Investment or borrowing of fixed-term deposits (including overnight money and Euro funds) consists of transactions with a

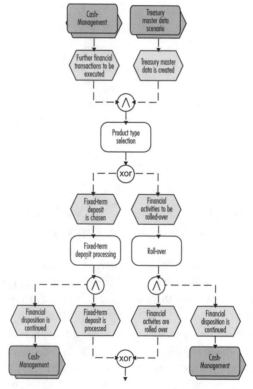

▶ **Figure 12–2**   Treasury manager

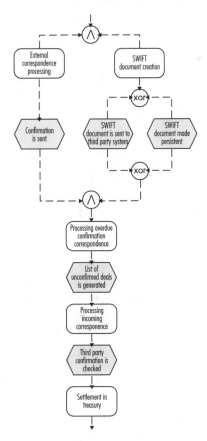

▶ **Figure 12–3**   Fixed-term deposit processing

fixed interest rate and an end of term that is agreed on up front. If the authorized business partners and their corresponding payment details have already been recorded, the only input required is the structure of the bond issues.

Rollover

As an alternative to a new investment or borrowing of a fixed-term deposit, you can roll over an existing fixed-term deposit transaction. It is possible to roll over a fixed-term deposit—with different conditions, if necessary—while keeping the original transaction number. The rollover adds a new activity to the transaction, which is handled according to the outsorting of the transaction and position management process. The end of term for a fixed-term deposit can be changed anytime until repayment, as long as (if the life of the deposit is shortened), this does not affect any interest transaction that has already been released, posted, or manually changed.

The effects on liquidity of the concluded transactions are, in turn, immediately available for display in cash management.

Correspondence

It is possible to use correspondence management or confirmation management immediately after the actual fixed-term deposit transaction. In this process, the transaction data (e.g., procedures, flows) is prepared for further processing as confirmations. You have the option of printing the data created or sending it directly from the system via telefax. Alternatively, you can create S.W.I.F.T. files for foreign exchange transactions. With the help of a user exit, this allows you to use matching systems like FX-Match for outbound document confirmation. When determining the correspondence, you can also specify that a counterconfirmation must be received from the business partner before the transaction can be processed further. The processing functions also include the ability to check whether any counterconfirmations are overdue.

Settlement in Treasury

As in trading, it is possible to call up information about recorded transactions and to perform corrections. The settlement function handles the checking and inspection of transaction processes. Missing information, such as payment instructions or posting settings, can be added. When the settlement transaction is saved, the system changes the transaction's activity category, in order to document its checking and editing processes. Figure 12-4 illustrates the entire settlement process discussed in the subsequent sections.

Netting Processing

Before transactions are transferred into Financial Accounting, it is still possible to net the financial transactions. With the help of Netting, you can combine transactions from the money market, foreign exchange, and derivatives areas and pay them together. One prerequisite for this is that the transactions were created in the same company code, with the same business partner, in the same currency, and with identical payment conditions.

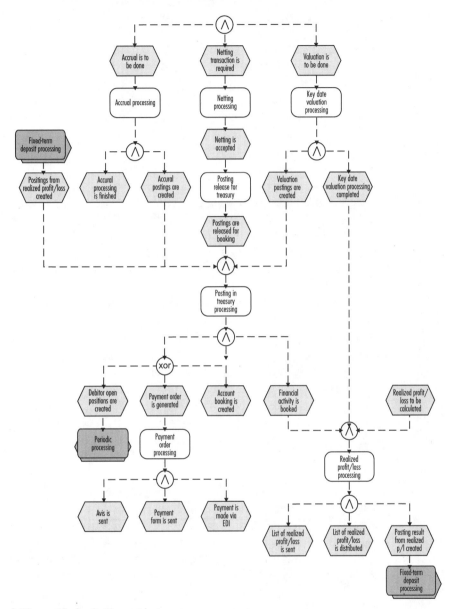

▶ **Figure 12–4**   Settlement in treasury

Posting Approval in Treasury

After the transactions have been recorded in trading and have been checked and completed in processing, account-based processing takes place. Before this can happen, the financial transaction must be released for posting. The user can choose any release principle desired, which includes determining for every product/transaction type whether specific posting approval is required.

Posting in Treasury

Before posting takes place, the flows of the transactions or positions to be posted are selected. The user can have the system perform a test run to check the correctness of the posting settings in the audit trail of posted records. When posting runs, the flows and the posting information are transferred to Financial Accounting, which creates the corresponding documents. Depending on the posting routine, this may trigger startup of the expanded payment program and the associated debit position and balancing in Financial Accounting or startup of payment request processing in Treasury. If the posting routine specifies immediate posting to G/L accounts, posting documents are created.

Beyond this, closing work must guarantee correct consideration of financial transactions and positions. So Financial Accounting also includes tasks such as accrual of expenditures and revenues related to a certain time period and valuation procedures. In money market trading, in addition to the accrual related to a certain time period, key date valuation is available, as is proof of profits and losses incurred.

Accrual

By using accrual, revenues and expenditures related to a certain time period are assigned to the time period in which they were first created, from a business standpoint. This is done using accrual on a particular accrual date (e.g., fiscal year end). The accrual is based on the transactions of the selected business processes that are relevant to the accrual. The accrual method describes how the amount to be accrued is to be calculated (pro rata temporis or pro rata temporis with linear accrual), whereas the accrual procedure describes the type of update made to the expense and revenue accounts used. A distinction is made between the difference procedure and the reset or accumulation procedure. When the accrual is carried out, the accrual amounts are calculated for any desired transactions/positions and time periods. For every relevant transaction, the accrual amount and the corresponding accrual flows are created. These can be posted immediately in Financial Accounting or processed at a later point in an update run.

Key Date Valuation

Key date valuation is account-based valuation using exchange rates or market values on a certain key date, and the resulting creation/cancellation of provisions, unrealized profits/losses, and write-ups and write-offs. The underlying exchange rate indicators or market values are dependent on the company code and the valuated product/transaction type. For example, in the case of foreign currency valuation, this means the use of spot transaction rates or calculated forward rates. The valuation run can also be executed as a simulation.

Realized Profits/Losses

As a prerequisite for the calculation of realized profits and losses, the transactions must be finished and posted. This function calculates the profit/loss that results from the difference between the book value and the price agreed on when the business deal was made. The calculation of realized profits and losses may also create transactions that must, in turn, be posted.

12.2   *TREASURY MASTER DATA SCENARIO*

Before financial transactions can be carried out as part of the operational scenarios, the master data necessary for this must be created. The goal of the master data business process scenario is to support this task in a sensible order. When this scenario runs, master data for the following objects is created:

- Business partners
- Traders
- House banks
- Partner banks
- Authorizations
- Payment details
- Correspondence
- Derived flows
- Master agreements
- Reference interest rates
- Indexes
- Security prices
- Securities accounts
- Classes
- Position indicators

12.3   NEW SECURITY MANAGEMENT

The new security management business process scenario describes the processing of a security transaction based on the different processing types and status changes. These describe which processing steps must be taken in each of the business areas, from recording in trading, to processing, and on to transfer into Financial Accounting. The result is a maximum of four different orders for processing, which have been named one-step, two-step (without order), two-step (without posting), and three-step new business processing. This determines the company-specific chain of activities that must be followed for an actual transaction for a product type. For each product type, there are alternative processing types available to the user. The procedure or status that the transaction is currently executing is displayed along with the transaction data.

BUSINESS OBJECTS

▶ *Financial Transaction*

The financial transaction business object is a treasury management component that acts as one of the control parameters in a commitment item master record. In R/3 ™, financial transaction is the technical name for a business transaction.

It is central to the recording of actual and commitment values in cash budget management and funds management. This leads to the following types of business analysis:

Cash Budget Management:

Master data indexes

> Commitment Items
> Commitment Item Hierarchy
> Index of Commitment Items
> Assign Commitment Items to G/L Accounts

Summary recs.

> Plan/actual comparison
> Commitment/actual/inventory

Journal Entries Reports

> Commitment/Actual Line Items by Document Number

> Commitment/Actual Line Items by Commitment Item

Funds Management:
    Commitment Items
        Commitment Item Hierarchy
        Index of Commitment Items
        Assign Commitment Items to G/L Accounts
        Assign Commitment Items to Cost Elements
    Line items
        Commitments/Actuals
        CO bookings
        Commitment/Actual Line Items by Document Number
        Commitment/act. for assgd bdgt
        Commitment/Actual Line Items for Assigned Overall Budget
        Commitment/Actual Line Items for Assigned Annual Budget

12.4 TREASURY

The treasury position management business process scenario contains the entire range of position actions in R/3™ Treasury, divided according to product category. In addition to position actions that span product categories, such as balance sheet transfers and securities account transfers, treasury position management also allows you to perform product-specific position actions; for example, processing of interest rate adjustments for derivative OTC interest rate instruments. The list that follows provides a complete overview of the position actions available:

- Securities account transfer
- Balance sheet transfer
- Processing of corporate action
- Processing of incoming payments
- Processing of securities rights
- Restraints on disposal
- Interest rate adjustment
- Calculation of the variation margin
- Periodic closing operations

12.5 TREASURY INFORMATION SYSTEM

You can display and analyze the financial transactions employed as part of the operational scenarios, as well as the resulting financial data, at any point in time using the Treasury Information System. So, for example, you can use the journal to select transactions for a certain time period that were closed by particular traders or with certain business partners. Furthermore, using the position list, you can perform position analyses with reference to traders or business partners by displaying transactions sorted by conditions. With the help of the payment schedule, you can call up incoming and outgoing payments related to funds transactions within a period of time of your choosing. Finally, a link to the SAP™ research tools allows you to access reporting and processing capabilities for noncumulative and cumulative values of money market trading.

As a standard, the R/3™ Treasury Information System provides reporting and analysis capabilities for the following report items:

- Financial transactions
- Positions
- Financial accounting
- Risk control
- Master data
- Regulatory reporting

12.6   CASH MANAGEMENT

The cash management business process scenario controls liquidity to support operational processes, while at the same time providing information to help funnel surplus funds to their best possible use. To be comprehensive, cash management must support electronic banking, shadow processes, and offer dynamic handling of foreign currencies. It must also be able to tackle modern, global-economy challenges, for example:

- The emergence of electronic banking transactions
- Automated payment methods that optimize money market transactions as well as the chances for short-term interest markdown
- Shorter cash flow cycles
- Increasing number of global transactions, which require the potential of multicurrency cash management

The cash management scenario describes how R/3™ plans and processes cash transactions. The current and the future cash position are continually being updated and presented to the user. Cash management is tightly linked to electronic banking and is integrated with the core Financial Accounting system as well as with the requirements/logistics supply chain. This provides greater opportunities for cash forecasting. Figure 12-5 describes the value chain for R/3™ cash management.

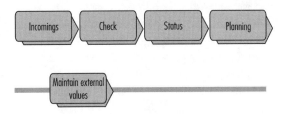

▶ **Figure 12–5** Value chain: Cash management handles cash transactions

In these processes, cash management handles all money-related transactions and reports. In cash management, a distinction is made between cash accounts and clearing accounts. Thus accounts that exchange money (actual money) as distinguished from transmitted payments (transmitted payments). Cash management is integrated with the systems of general ledger, accounts receivable/payable accounting, as well as sales and procurement, to create greater opportunities for forecasting cash.

This scenario handles the processing for the following tasks:

- Account statements (created electronically or manually)
- Checks remitted manually
- Checks remitted electronically (lockbox processing in the USA, ESR procedure in Switzerland)
- Bills of exchange that are "submitted" by the bank or a vendor for payment
- Cashed checks
- Payment advice notes from customers and banks
- Planned items such as tax payments, for taking anticipated cash flows into account

The data is posted simultaneously into the general ledger system, the accounts receivable/payable accounting system, and the cash management system. Payment advice comparison compares the actual payments to the payment advice notes and subsequently archives them.

The cash position and liquidity forecasts are based on three integrated information sources in R/3™:

- Current account balance, payment advice notes, and planned items
- Open items in accounts receivable/payable accounting
- Sales orders and purchase orders

Short-term and long-term investments and borrowing are planned and carried out on the basis of the company's investment strategy and information about the financial market. Planning for cash concentration (money transfer into an account) and cash flow (expenditures and revenues) may follow.

End-of-period processing includes management of and interest accrued on short-term instruments (time deposits and overnight money, as well as loans), account balance interest calculation, and maintenance of exchange rates.

12.7 MARKET RISK MANAGEMENT

The process of market risk control is a complex control cycle of data collection, risk measurement, analysis and simulation, and active planning of financial instruments. Due to its decisive role in the competitiveness of a company, this process must be integrated with other Treasury and business functions.

Due to the complexity of control and decision-making functions, SAP™'s market risk management scenario provides a multitude of support tools. Based on all of the payment flows of a company that feed into cash management, it accesses current and future cash flows as well as all concluded financial transactions. Consequently, SAP™'s market risk management also allows you to take into consideration all of the cash flows resulting from the position management of the concluded financial transactions in the context of operational cash flows.

Numerous key figures are available for analyzing and evaluating interest and currency risks of financial transactions or funds balances. An online interface (data feed) can access the market data or conditions current at that time to calculate so-called market-to-market values or effective rates and interest. Based on this, using SAP™'s market risk management with its extensive simulation capabilities, you can calculate the current risk profile for selected funds balances or individual financial transactions. You can calculate the potential change of a current market value either through simulation of a worst case scenario or through simulation using any number of selected market parameters (e.g., value-at-risk), and you can analyze the subsequent effects on the risk structure (what-if analyses).

The integration of SAP™'s market risk management with both treasury management and the operational procedures of accounting and logistics make active risk management possible. This integration allows you to support a multitude of financial transactions, including spot exchange transactions, forward exchange transactions, and the creation of hedging items.

The following methods and analyses are available:

- Position valuation
- Market-to-market valuation of all current financial instruments

- Future values for any horizons
- Key performance figures
- Effective rate
- Internal rate of return
- Key risk figures
- Currency exposures (market values or delta equivalents)
- Interest exposures (measured in base point values)
- Sensitivities (changes in interest, volatility, and exchange rate)
- Key value-at-risk figures
- Key liquidity figures
- Cash flows of variable and optional instruments

12.8 *R/3™ Finance Management Summary*

The following tables provide an overview to the main scenarios, core processes, business objects, and organizational units that make up R/3™ Finance Management.

- -
Scenarios

▶ Treasury master data scenario

▶ Securities new business management

▶ Fixed-term deposit management

▶ Treasury balance management

▶ Treasury information system

- -
Core processes

▶ Payment advice/planned item processing

▶ Cash concentration

▶ Bill of exchange presentation/check deposit transaction

▶ Incoming account statement (manual/automatic)

▶ Status analysis/Cash management and forecast

▶ Securities account transfer

▶ Corporate actions

▶ Convertible bond processing

▶ Warrant processing

▶ Subscription right processing

▶ Balance sheet transfer

Core processes (continued)

▶ Deferred interest processing

▶ Interest capitalization

▶ Edit spot exchange/forward exchange transaction

▶ Edit forex swap

▶ Edit standard currency option

▶ Edit exotic currency option

▶ Edit fixed-term deposit

▶ Edit deposit at notice

▶ Edit commercial paper

▶ Edit interest rate adjustment

▶ Edit variation margin

Business objects

▶ Financial transaction

▶ Financial product (class)

▶ Securities account

▶ Portfolio

Organizational units

▶ Company code

Real-World Example: Chevron Products Company, U.S.A.

Chevron Products Company is the U.S. refining and marketing arm of the Chevron Corporation, headquartered in San Francisco. The Products Company represents about $16 billion of Chevron's $39 billion total revenue, employing some 8,500 people with responsibilities for more than 10,000 facilities—storage terminals and service stations—across the United States.

Chevron implemented R/3™ primarily for refining its business processes. "Information systems are one of the critical areas we decided to focus on," says Paul Bennett, manager for the Advanced Financial Information Systems (AFIS) at the company. "We wanted to reduce the costs of our business processes and improve the quality of the outputs of those processes."

Chevron Products refines crude oil for sale as gasoline, jet fuel, and lubricants. The information systems supporting that activity had been based on some 120 disparate, mainframe-based applications. The R/3 ™ implementation targeted Chevron's financial processes and asset and project management.

"Each of the different parties had their own systems and, of course, different information in each of those systems," Bennett says. "There [were] considerable time lags in getting information, and frankly, a lot of bad information. Project managers and engineers just didn't have good information on where they stood, particularly if it was a large, complex project and there were a lot of people working on it. They would often track things in their own spreadsheet against their own budgets, but wouldn't see the items show up in their financial results for several months."

The company assembled a team of 30 people to analyze and reengineer its core financial processes to operate in the most efficient and value-added manner possible.

"We developed a vision of how all these financial processes should work by analyzing best-practices in a number of industries, says Jim Zell, AFIS project manager for the entire company.

The company is now currently using a number of R/3 ™ modules, including project system, materials management, service management, and plant maintenance. Plant maintenance has been an especially good area of improvement for the company, which uses the module to control and track maintenance activities for its 8,000 service stations across the United States for such things as constructions, repair, and landscaping.

"Our initial, and very successful, experience with plant maintenance is going to be closely looked at for possible application elsewhere within the company," Bennett says.

That success has been widespread throughout all areas of R/3 ™ implementation.

"The major benefits have come from reengineering our processes and supporting that reengineering with a highly integrated system with the right capabilities like R/3 ™," Bennett concludes. "Our project team thinks it's great. And key internal customers already see the value—they realize there will be tremendous improvements in the way we run our business because they have tools and processes that are much more powerful than what they had in the past."

13

Customer Service

Service is too often overlooked as a strategic weapon against the competition. In the marketplace today, a number of factors have converged to make service an even greater key to a company's competitive advantage:

- There is a growing complexity of supply products, leading to an increasing mechanization of living and working arenas.
- More and more, customers need comprehensive solutions, choosing to view primary services and customer services as a single unit that should meet their needs.
- The supply products are increasingly homogeneous and thus easier to compare. This trend impacts customer service because it can contribute effectively to the product and help provide differentiation, enabling a company to gain more maneuverability in its pricing policy for primary services.
- Revenue losses in primary services are increasing. Customer services can help compensate for these revenue losses and perhaps show the secondary services to be another cornerstone of the company.
- More and more environmental demands are being heaped on supply products. Customer services can provide effective relief with recycling that makes sense as well as environmentally friendly disposal of supply products.

Customer service organizations can use effective service to handle the relationship between customer and supplier breaking off once the sale of a supply product is concluded. Customers desire ongoing support from companies in the after-sales phase, especially if they have purchased complex, long-lived goods. The service area can help ensure that, even after the sale, customer satisfaction continues to grow and is assured over the long term.

These requirements place high demands on supporting systems, which must allow themselves to be measured not only by the extent to which they support individual service areas and subareas, but also by the extent to which they can offer a solution that meets all requirements from a speedily performed ad hoc implementation, to a long-term, planned expansion of installations with numerous parts deliveries and employment of many service technicians.

SAP™'s integrated customer service (in R/3™, the application Service Management component) offers a wide range of functions for handling all aspects of the service business, including:

- Management of customer products
- Warranty check
- Management of service contracts
- Service call logging
- Service order processing
- Replacement part deliveries
- Billing of service measures
- Evaluations

In this chapter, we will examine the implementation of these functions using the field service business process scenario. Figure 13-1 illustrates the main customer service scenarios discussed in this chapter. Also included are the core processes, business objects, and organizational units that are part of the customer service business process.

13.1   FIELD SERVICE

The field service business process scenario describes the processing of unplanned and planned (routine) services at the customer's site. Figure 13-2 illustrates the supply chain flow of the entire business process.

Service management begins by giving the company the opportunity to sign a service agreement with the customer during or after the sale of a product. Any number of different services can be included as contract items in this service agreement (for example, discounts on replacement parts, guaranteed response time, etc.).

When a need for service arises, it is recorded in a service notification, along with all of the relevant data (customer data, product data, breakdown data). If the

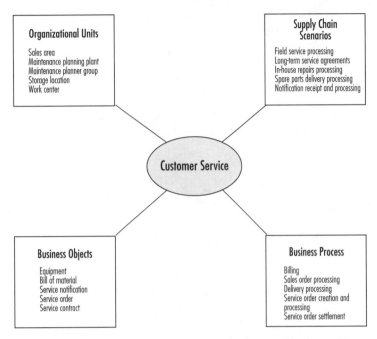

▶ **Figure 13–1**   Overview of scenarios, process, organizations, and business objects

link between the customer and the technical product has already been entered in the master data area during equipment processing and assignment, the number of entries necessary for recording the service notification is reduced to a minimum.

Likewise, there is a great deal of information to be gleaned from the service notification for the service incident (such as the warranty, the service agreement dates, and notifications recorded in the past).

The actual device repair can be handled using a service order, which allows materials and resources to be included in the planning. Confirmations allow monitoring of the progress of the order. A planned/actual comparison at the cost

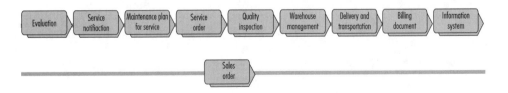

▶ **Figure 13–2**   Value chain: Field service processes

level is also possible. The actual costs incurred for the order, in turn, provide a basis for expense-related billing, which enables charging the customer for the actual costs incurred.

Figure 13-3 details how field service is handled in the R/3™ system.

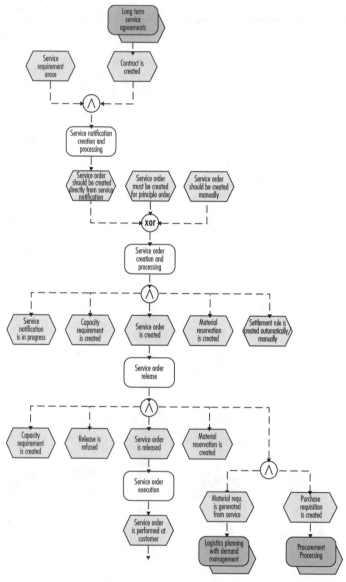

▶ **Figure 13–3**   Field service processing

Recording and Processing Service Notifications

The customer service process generally begins when the customer identifies a problem situation. The next step in the process is to record all of the relevant data for this problem within a service notification. It is worth mentioning here that it is also possible to give customers the opportunity to create service notifications themselves over the Internet.

The service notification functions can be used individually (e.g., to support a call center) or combined with other elements of service management (e.g., a service order, or a customer order).

It begins by identifying the customer and the technical product (functional location, equipment, material serial number, assembly). Once these data have been recorded in the notification, the notification processor can pull up more detailed data both about the product (reference to the agreement, warranty, past data) and about the customer (sales summary), in an effort to gain additional insight that may be helpful in finding a solution to a given problem.

The notification also helps record problems in a variety of ways. One can enter the problem as text or reference catalogs in the notification (e.g., by including damages in code form). These functions provide the basis for later evaluations in the Logistics Information System.

There are several alternatives for processing the notification from this point forward:

- Measures for the service notification can be created that seem most appropriate for eliminating a problem. For every measure, detailed schedule data and information about the effectiveness of that measure may be stored. The notification processor can also have the system come up with the measures. When doing so, the system includes applicable completion confirmations for an assigned service agreement, taking into consideration the priority of the notification. Service notification was designed, with the help of interfaces, to be open to enable links to non-SAP™ systems. It is possible, for example, to tie in solution identification functions in the form of a case-based reasoning system.

- Another possible solution to a problem may be to deliver replacement parts. For this reason, you can branch directly from service notification into sales order entry, and relevant data (e.g., ordering party, purchase order number) is automatically transferred from the notification.

- If an on-site visit by a technician is needed to solve a problem, a service order can be used. You can create this, too, directly from within service notification. It provides extensive planning functions, and it can include routings and maintenance BOMs, if necessary.

BUSINESS OBJECT

▶ *Service Order*

The service order business object represents a request for a customer service activity for a maintenance object. It is used to document service and customer service activities. Service orders may be used to:

- Plan specific tasks related to usage of materials and resources
- Allocate personnel to the service task
- Monitor the performance of service tasks
- Enter and settle costs related to service items

Data from the service ordered is stored in the system and can be used for evaluation and planning purposes. The business object service order is used as information for the following types of business analysis:

Service Order
> Display Service Order
> (Multilevel) Order List
> Change Service Order
> Change PM Orders by Operation List
> Follow-Up Editing of PDC Error Recs
> Confirmation using operation list
> Display PM Order Operations
> Actual Settlement: Order
> Display Order Group
> Set Status "Closed"
> Document flow list
> Material Where-Used List

Service Planning
> Package Order
> Where-Used List by Strategy
> Change Maintenance Plan
> Display Maintenance Plan
> Change Maintenance Item
> Display Maintenance Item
> Graphical scheduling overview
> MaintSchedule Date Monitoring
> PM Confirmations: Display confirmations list

List of activities
Material where-used list
Display document flow
Scheduling: Maintenance Scheduling Overview

Service Plans
Change PM Task Lists
Display PM Task Lists
Display Task Lists (Multilevel)
PM Task List Original Change Docs
Cost Maintenance Task Lists
Print Maintenance Task Lists
Evaluate PM Task List Change Docs

Opening and Processing Service Orders

Using a service order, one can plan and control the activities necessary for performing inspection, maintenance, and repair on a functional customer system. This includes restrictions on personnel (capacity planning, qualifications) and restrictions on material (availability of replacement parts and production resources). When selecting components, the user can access the object list that was created for the technical product. The inclusion of routings that have already been created, which describe exactly what is to be done, is also a noted benefit, especially for inspections.

As with a production order, individual order activities can be assigned to different work centers. If materials kept in stock are assigned to the activities, material reservations are created in the background. It is conceivable, however, that a service provider may contract out certain activities from the order. These activities can be specially marked in the order. This identification automatically starts the order process in the R/3™ system's materials management component, just as it does for material not kept in stock. What's more, in the case of external assignment, existing service specifications may be used to describe the activities to be carried out. For cost controlling, the order processor can at any time obtain a detailed overview over the planned-cost situation for the order.

Service Order Release

Service order release ends the planning phase and enables the employees, after printing out the work papers, to start the service work. Only now can the material reserved for the order be withdrawn and confirmations for the order be carried out.

Service Order Completion Confirmation

During and after execution of the order, the order processor has the ability to update the order with current data. Updating may include, for example, withdrawal documents or completion time confirmations. Thus, one can monitor the progress of the order continually at order level as well as monitor the costs at any time with a planned/actual comparison and intervene with corrective action if necessary. Services that have been performed by an outside contractor are confirmed as part of the order. When the services performed are accepted and the invoice is verified, the recorded values are passed on to accounting, and the service order is debited with the costs of the external service.

Technical Results Recording

Because only the technician who repaired the damage to the technical product can ascertain the cause of a defect, the notification (into which one can jump directly from the completion confirmation) has not only the damage catalog, but

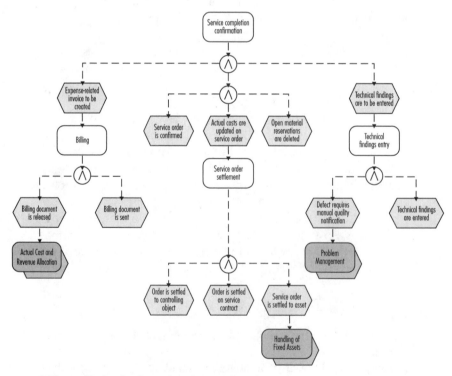

▶ **Figure 13–4** Service order release and settlement

also a catalog for damage causes and actions. Choosing from a series of codes, the technician can record the causes of the damage and the actions taken to repair the damage. This information, too, is available for further analysis in the Logistics Information System.

Resource-Related Billing and Invoice Processing

In order to be able to charge the customer for the actual costs incurred on the service order, the costs must be transferred into a sales and distribution document. This is done with the help of resource-related billing, in which all of the services and materials posted to the order are transformed into a sales and distribution document and can be processed further using the billing functions in the R/3™ sales component.

Debit memo processing also allows the user to update certain items in the debit memo, for example, to take a grace period into consideration. Once billing is complete, the revenues are visible in the planned/actual cost comparison for the order.

Service Order Settlement

Due to the material staging services and on-call services that it requires, a company's service area creates a high percentage of fixed costs. The service order functions enable the tracking of costs at order level, both for planned costs and for actual costs.

In order to further allocate the costs incurred as well as the targeted revenues, the service order must be settled. Settlement will also make costs transparent at higher levels of the organization. Depending on the need, different settlement receivers are available from Controlling for this purpose (for example, profitability segment or G/L account).

For controlling with respect to aggregate values, SAP™ provides the integrated financial statement CO-PA (Controlling - Profitability Analysis). This allows you to configure the results analysis freely, using company-specific definitions of characteristics and evaluations. This function makes it possible, for example, to answer such questions as: "How high is the profit margin for the repair services in the region *North* for the customer group large clients?"

13.2   LONG-TERM SERVICE AGREEMENTS

Service can create an additional revenue source for a company by offering new customer services as appropriate. In addition, long-term contracts provide added stability to customer relations. Moreover, given the complexity of many products and the growing interdependencies between companies and their customers, long-term service contracts are not only useful but necessary.

The sale of service agreements can be supported the same way as any other product is supported, with presales activities such as direct mailing campaigns. If the customer expresses interest in a service agreement, the interest can be recorded in a service agreement RFQ, from which a service agreement quotation can be created. If the customer decides to take the service agreement, all of the relevant data from the service agreement quotation that may have preceded it can be copied, and data specific to the agreement, such as the period of validity and cancellation data, can be recorded.

For each service agreement item, it is necessary to specify to which technical product that item applies.

Service agreements can consist of various types of service items. A service item may consist of:

- Material (a particular product, such as a replacement part)
- Time (e.g., hourly wage of the technician employed)
- Response time (period of time within which one is obligated to react to a problem notification)

Often, agreement services are billed periodically. When customizing the R/3™ system, you can specify at which intervals invoices should be sent to the customer. A likely example would be a monthly invoice produced with a billing plan.

If a malfunction occurs in the product, the system checks whether there is an agreement for the technical product specified. If this is the case, the agreement number is displayed in the service notification. In addition, the notification processor can use the product information to obtain an overview of the elements of the agreement. Response times and service windows guaranteed in the agreement are also taken into consideration. Any subsequent handling of the malfunction can then be done with a reference to the service agreement. For example, price agreements from the service agreement are taken into consideration in the order-related billing document, and the costs of the order are, if applicable, settled to the service agreement item. This process makes it possible to check the cost efficiency of service agreements.

Furthermore, it is possible to link a service agreement to a maintenance plan in order to plan recurring activities. One could use this function, for example, to work out a service agreement with the customer that covers regular maintenance for a particular product over the long term. At the same time, one could open a maintenance plan for a product and link it to the service agreement. The maintenance plan would then automatically generate either time-based or count-based service orders (depending on the system settings), and these would be settled to the service agreement.

13.3   IN-HOUSE REPAIR PROCESSING

Service activities are often not performed on site but in special service work centers in the company. The in-house repair processing flow involves essentially the same elements as described in the field service scenario, although in this scenario the focus is on controlling the internal processing of the device by means of the service work centers.

13.4   REPLACEMENT PART DELIVERY PROCESSING

Often, all that is necessary to resolve a malfunction is to sell a replacement part, which the customer then installs in the product. Because this fact is not always clear at the time the malfunction is reported, service notifications may at first be used to document the malfunction and made available in the system for further analysis.

The replacement part delivery processing scenario enables the user to go directly from service notification into customer order entry within sales and distribution processing. He or she can then record the required replacement parts in a sales document (SD). The entire functionality of the SD module is available for this purpose. So, for example, it is possible to make statements about the availability of the required parts immediately from within order entry. Likewise, after order entry, deliveries can be created and picked, shipping documents can be printed, and the withdrawal of goods from the warehouse can be posted. There is a seamless connection to the process of bill creation and processing. The document flow, which begins with service notification and ends with billing, provides comprehensive information about the process flow and the documents created in the process.

13.5   NOTIFICATION RECEIPT AND PROCESSING

The notification receipt and processing business process scenario is often used by companies whose customers have an intense need for skilled telephone consulting and therefore implement something called a *call center*. In most cases, it is sufficient to implement a service notification, several unique features of which are described below.

Generally, for this kind processing, it is necessary to support receipt of notifications by telephone. This support, which is generally known as CTI (Computer/Telephone Integration) is included in the R/3™ system's capabilities under the term SAPPHONE. With SAPPHONE, a link is established between the telephone system and the R/3™ application. The notification processor can be supported by the system in such a way that when calls come in, the system selects certain data related to the telephone number in question (e.g., customer number or the technical products the customer has installed). The results are stored in the service notification. Where outgoing calls are concerned, the notification processor can be relieved of tiresome dialing, because the dialing function can be stored in the service notification.

Because knowledge necessary for solving a problem is often distributed among many organizational units in a company, fast and efficient conveyance of the notification information between those units is essential. By implementing SAP™ Business Workflow, one can control both the operational flow and the management of the notification process.

Imagine, for example, that a problem notification is received by the notification receipt department. The notification processor records the problem data in the notification and draws the conclusion that an employee in the sales division is best suited to solve this problem. He or she can now store and save the name of a particular employee or, alternatively, an organizational unit, as the notification processor within the notification itself. SAP™ Business Workflow ensures that the employee in question is informed; for example, through receipt of a message in the mail system. The sales employee can branch from this message directly into the notification, process it, and forward it if necessary. Parallel to this workflow, a second workflow might monitor the amount of time the notification spends in processing and inform a supervisor; for example, if the notification is not given the status "finished" within 20 hours.

13.6   EVALUATIONS

The service area contains a wealth of information that is pertinent to many areas of a company. Most of this information can be divided into the following categories:

- *Technical Information*: Information about the causes of device breakdowns. This information can be sorted by various characteristics (e.g., breakdowns per customer, breakdowns per equipment, breakdowns per time period). It is especially relevant for departments such as Research and Development, because it can provide insight into product adjustments that might be necessary.

- *Process Flow Information*: Information about average times for processing a breakdown. This information affects for those responsible for the process, because it can highlight potential areas for improving the process flow (for example, a better division of the areas in which technicians are employed).
- *Controlling Information*: Includes, for example, information about average costs per order and information about the total cost and revenue situation in the service area. This information is especially important for calculating settlement prices.
- *Sales Information*: A company's service area acquires information on the after-sales phase that is of interest to Sales, but is often underrated by the same. Targeted evaluation of this information could lend insight into the customer's current situation. For example, information about the ages of the customer's devices could be used to propose a replacement investment.

The higher-level functions of the Logistics Information (LIS) help perform evaluations in the area of customer service. As in material management or in sales, the LIS enables decision support for statistical analysis and information delivery. The statistical information gathered can then be scanned with analysis tools for items that stand out and be prepared for display. One other function that is worth mentioning is Early Warning System (EWS), which, on its own and, of course, at an early stage, warns of noticeable data patterns that the user specifies.

13.7   *R/3™ Customer Service Summary*

The following tables provide an overview to the main scenarios, core processes, business objects, and organizational units that make up R/3™ Customer Service.

- -
Scenarios

- ▶ Field service processing
- ▶ Long-term service agreements
- ▶ In-house repairs processing
- ▶ Spare parts delivery processing
- ▶ Notification receipt and processing

Core processes

▶ Processing of debit memo request

▶ Service notification creation and processing

▶ Service order creation and processing

▶ Service order release

▶ Service order execution

▶ Service order completion confirmation

▶ Service order settlement

▶ Service order completion

▶ Technical findings entry (service)

▶ Billing

▶ Sales order processing

▶ Delivery processing

▶ Resource-related billing

▶ Evaluations: Logistics information system

▶ Catalog processing

▶ Functional locations processing

▶ Equipment processing

▶ Installation, dismantling, and modification of equipment

▶ Master warranty processing

Business objects

▶ Material

▶ Equipment

▶ Functional location

▶ Bill of material

▶ Routing

▶ Service notification

▶ Service order

▶ Service contract

▶ Customer inquiry

▶ Sales order

▶ Customer delivery

▶ Transport

▶ Customer billing document

Organizational units

▶ Sales organization

▶ Division

▶ Distribution channel

▶ Sales area

▶ Maintenance planning plant

▶ Maintenance planner group

▶ Storage location

▶ Work center

Customer Example:
Jet Aviation, Palm Beach, Florida, and Zurich, Switzerland

Founded 25 years ago in Switzerland, Jet Aviation began as a technical maintenance and aircraft repair service. Today, the company has more than 1,700
employees and is the largest charter flight airline in the world. Headquartered in
Florida, Jet Aviation's pilots touch down at 5,000 different airports. In addition
to its passenger and freight charter flight business, Jet Aviation offers a wide
range of maintenance services (originally its only service), overhauling, recon-
ditioning, and ground services. More than 26 international airlines use Jet Aviation's maintenance services, including Air France, American Airlines, British
Airways, United Airlines, Delta Airlines, and Lufthansa.

Before 1993, Jet Aviation had tried three times to modify its information system
to meet growing demands. Company management wasn't satisfied with the
results, mainly because of the lack of integration between different departments
and company locations and inadequate networking, all made worse by increasing volumes of information. The result: an information bottleneck.

"It was soon clear to us that we were not just talking about a reinterpretation of
information technology at Jet Aviation but about developing the right business
concept. Neither the existing business concept nor the internal systems had
been able to keep up with the company's growth," Eckart Meyer, a consultant to
the company, says.

Jet Aviation's maintenance services division is responsible for 130 different
kinds of aircraft, each of which has about 1,000 different parts with life histories of their own. Keeping track of all of this information, coupled with taking
on more and more new business, was a trouble spot for the company, as was the
inefficient way it sold its services.

"Service is the keystone of our business," Rolf Hohler, vice president at Jet Aviation, claims. "As a charter flight company, reacting quickly to customers' wishes is the basis of our business. Quick decisions and responses are required, whether the customer has a maintenance contract for us or wants to charter a flight. We must be available whenever we're needed."

A new business concept proposal recommended that Jet Aviation required the following implementations:

- An effective, thorough support of its main business processes—from customer order via materials management to work-order processing and customer invoicing
- Quantity flow processing integrated with the accounting department
- An information system spanning all locations and plants
- Indirect cost and production cost controlling for better management

To meet these goals, Jet Aviation took stock of its existing information technology and discovered that practically every department used different software and hardware. With SAP™'s R/3™ system, Jet Aviation was able to integrate all areas of the company. Today, Jet Aviation's accounting department is no longer responsible for just recording costs but also charged with delivering important management information.

PART 3

Architecture, Framework, and Tools

14
Architecture of the R/3™ System

Data processing systems must have a high degree of flexibility and integration to meet the needs of today's increasingly complex corporate structures. Areas formerly managed centrally are now frequently allocated to individual organizational units. As a result, processes such as inventory management, purchasing, or quality management differ from one department to another as well as from company to company. Moreover, market demands have caused changes in the domain of business processes, which now extend beyond the company itself to include customers and vendors. Because of this complexity, now, more than ever, companies must have fast, direct access to information and a high degree of communication between subareas.

Unfortunately, these needs are not being met by many companies' current data processing systems. Modern data processing systems require at least the following support:

- A high level of integration of business application systems to ensure optimal modeling of the business processes
- The uncoupling of application systems so that they can be implemented locally and regardless of the technology available
- Fluid communications between all corporate and personal information systems

Standard solutions to these requirements have previously met with only limited success. Centralized information technology systems rarely prove to be the answer. Excessively high response times during peak traffic periods, technical bottlenecks, different time zones for international corporations, and problems associated with system upgrading are just some of the challenges faced by business data processing. Data transport using the mechanism of distributed databases has failed to resolve these problems. The reasons for this failure include large overheads for communication, uneconomical data processing, and inadequate security measures.

Companies are moving from centralized computing to distributed computing in order to achieve the necessary flexibility and ease of communication. Major business software vendors such as SAP™, Oracle, BAAN, and PeopleSoft are embracing various approaches satisfying customers' demands for distributed application systems. These vendors are taking advantage of a pool of technologies that have recently materialized in the market as the basis for application distribution. These technologies—such as database replication, messaging, and remote procedures—are fundamental parts of "middleware."

Middleware, by definition, is the set of services that allow interoperability among vendors and enable development of applications that are portable across platforms. Middleware has evolved a secondary goal, which is to move as much of the programming logic and data access functionality to a centralized machine or group of machines. This "thin client" approach provides a much more robust mechanism for customer installations, maintenance, future enhancements and scalability. It has the capability of relegating the burden of most enhancements and maintenance to a few server machines rather than several hundred or thousand client machines. A good example of this is a web server. A web server can provide the logic and functionality to service thousands of clients and be the only physical link to an underlying source of data. Although the data are available to thousands of users, all maintenance and enhancements are performed in a centralized location. Middleware is generally the piece of software which defines a system's component programming model (COM, CORBA, etc.) Because middleware enables the development of more open applications, customers gain the freedom to hook up different applications with one another.

Middleware plays a pivotal role in current trends in business engineering solutions. Companies are beginning to unbundle middleware technologies as the driving force behind application distribution. Such an approach combines scalability with an independent, centralized database. Because vendors of enterprise architecture software rely on a centralized database, these vendors require the means to enable applications to communicate remotely so that the integrated applications can share data and transactions.

To meet the goal of creating a distributed environment, SAP™ developed a comprehensive middleware concept. This chapter looks in detail at this concept and examines SAP™'s approach to transaction management in distributed, process-driven businesses. It also explains the wave of new technologies and their impact on architecture.

14.1 R/3™ AND THE DISTRIBUTED ENVIRONMENT

Transaction management and mission-critical applications are inseparable for technology planners. As a leading provider of standard software in both traditional mainframe and open systems, SAP™ is an interesting case study in implementing an architecture for open transactions. R/3™ has a three-layer (see Section 14.2) client/server architecture that includes its own transaction management software. In this chapter, we examine SAP™'s client/server model and approach to transactions.

R/3™ is an integrated enterprise software system that runs primarily in open system environments such as UNIX and Windows NT. The applications use the Advanced Business Application Programming (ABAP/4) language and ABAP/4 Development Workbench, a toolset for building enterprise software. The three-tier architecture of R/3™ is supplemented by special services for printing, security, and communications. R/3™ allows the interplay and portability of applications, data, and user interface. This interactivity is achieved through the use of international standards for interfaces, services, and data formats. These are part of a longer industry framework for integrating applications.

R/3™ supports a large number of operating systems, database systems, and graphical presentation computers:

- Transmission Control Protocol/Internet Protocol (TCP/IP) as a network communications protocol
- Remote Function Call (RFC), which enables remote calling to application functions on other systems
- CPI-C for program-to-program communications across multiple systems
- Structured Query Language (SQL) and Open Database Connectivity (ODBC) to enable outside systems to access data stored in numerous databases
- Object Linking and Embedding (OLE)—now referred to as COM—for integration of Windows applications
- X.400/500 Messaging Application Programming Interface (MAPI) and Electronic Data Interchange (EDI) for external communication
- Business Application Programming Interfaces (BAPI) and specialized open interfaces to specialized applications, such as CAD systems, optical archiving, and data collection

In R/3™, dedicated, task-oriented servers—which are linked in communication networks—integrate data and processes. An R/3™ installation can take one of the following forms:

- Homogeneous—The same operating system is used on one or more platforms.

- Heterogeneous—A variety of different systems and platforms are used for presentation servers (e.g., Windows), application servers (e.g., UNIX or Windows NT), and a single database server (usually UNIX with Oracle®, Informix®, DB2/6000™, or Software AG databases).

In the latter instance, which is the most common, purchasers of R/3™ must accommodate a distributed environment of the most complex form. Heterogeneous installation may contain several operating systems, platforms, and combinations that have little in common except for the R/3™ application suite. One of the major attractions of R/3™ is that it can solve the distributed, heterogeneous, technical challenges found in most organizations today.

The high performance levels of R/3™ are due to the "configurability" of the system. This extensive flexibility of R/3™ is largely a result of SAP™'s implementation of middleware and the use of multiple application servers. These provide the following benefits:

- If one application server is unavailable, an alternate server is selected automatically.

- Load balancing is achieved by assigning a client to the least busy application server.

- Application servers provide consistent caching of data related to a client request. Caching reduces the load on the database server and provides better response times for the customer.

- Additional application servers can be added as needed to provide application server scalability.

The R/3™ Repository contains descriptions of all data tables as well as the software modules, including screen forms, business rules, and locations of the application servers. All applications are extracted from the R/3™ Repository (held on the single database) to the application server and from there to the presentation server when necessary. Consequently, updates to applications are automatically delivered to all R/3™ participants in a reliable manner with a minimum of systems effort. In a distributed, heterogeneous environment, this ability is a significant operational plus.

14.2   THE THREE-TIER CLIENT/SERVER R/3™ ARCHITECTURE

R/3™ transaction management should be understood within the context of the following possible scenarios for client/server system configuration:

- Centralized—A central host computer performs all processing tasks involving a single database, applications, and presentation (the latter via X terminals).
- Two-tier (often referred to as the "thick client/thin server" variation)— Powerful desktop systems take care of both presentation and execution of applications, with the single database server being wholly separate.
- Three-tier—Separate systems are used for presentation (for example, PCs, Macs®, etc.), application, and single database servers.
- Many-tier—The three tier extended with Internet application servers.

The application layer is a microcosm of middleware in R/3™. Whereas the presentation layer and database layer could run on different platforms, the application layer is tuned for transaction management, scalability, performance, and ease of maintenance/upgrades. SAP™ advocates the three-tier scenario, because this is where the R/3™ system strengths are most fully exploited. Also, the three-tier system optimizes platform flexibility for the customer. Figure 14-1 illustrates possible client/server system configurations.

End users can take advantage of the different cost structures of front-end and back-end computers. End users, in fact, are as much a focus of R/3™ as system resources usage or managers of IT departments. This focus is apparent in R/3™ architecture, which is highly portable by design. The SAP™ GUI, for example, permits presentation on a wide range of front-end computers. This capability is a software engineering luxury, especially since most desktops are MS-Windows. The industry has long been infatuated with broad teaching technologies that span different systems and greatly minimize the risks of being locked into a single platform.

The R/3™ architecture allows the application tier to be uncoupled from the presentation and database tiers. This separation is a prerequisite for distributing tasks in client/server configurations. To achieve the goal of portability in the R/3™ system, SAP™ had to make a decision about middleware in the early stages of the system's development. Because there was nothing on the market that suited SAP™'s needs, the company was obliged to devise its own middleware solutions, conforming wherever possible to appropriate standards.

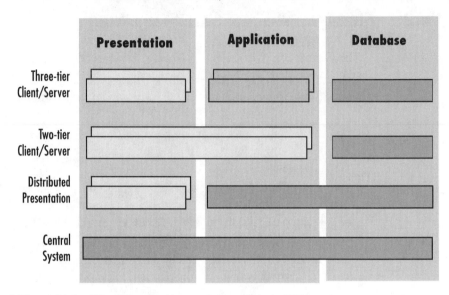

▶ **Figure 14–1**   Client/server architectural alternatives for ERP vendors

When considering middleware development in R/3™, the first question one faces is: How do transactions proceed through R/3™? With the exception of batch transactions, the transfer protocol of R/3™ middleware consists of two categories:

- Presentation protocol for exchanging data between presentation and application servers
- A database interface, using SAP™ structured query language (SQL), for transferring data between application and database servers (this is usually implemented over a LAN because large volumes of data are passed)

The presentation tier or front end of the R/3™ system is portable. R/3™ applications offer consistent appearance and functionality on presentation computers running Windows NT, OS/2®, OSF/Motif®, and Apple® Macintosh®. The R/3™ presentation software running on individual presentation computers implements the GUI by using the functions and resources provided by the operating system environment. The result is a very compact flow of data between the R/3™ presentation computer and the application server. The two computers do not pass entire screens back and forth, but rather they exchange logical information about control elements and user inputs. Typically, only one to two kilobytes of data need be transferred for each screen change. It is therefore also an easy matter to connect presentation computers over wide-area networks (WANs) as well as across local area networks (LANs).

The database interface isolates the mechanisms for transporting and managing data between applications and the database. It also has the key task of mediating between the logical structures of the data dictionary and the physical structures of the relational database itself.

The database interface handles data access through the use of SAP™ SQL, which is essentially a library of standard SQL calls available within the ABAP/4 environment. R/3™ architecture ensures that differences in the syntax and semantics of the SQL implementations of various database vendors remain hidden in just a few modules. This practice enables R/3™ to support all popular relational database systems whose performance is adequate.

Because relational database systems offer different subsets of the overall range of SQL functions, the ABAP/4 Development Workbench makes SQL available in two levels: SAP™ SQL and native SQL. The database interface translates SAP™ SQL into the native SQL of the database installed in the system. Native SQL is provided for by a second mechanism for database access that allows it to be embedded within an ABAP/4 program. ABAP/4 then passes the SQL directly to the database, bypassing the database interface completely.

14.3   BENEFITS OF THE R/3™ THREE-TIER CLIENT/SERVER

There are a number of benefits of the R/3™ three-tier client/server. They include portability, investment protection, multilevel implementation, optimum load distribution, and interoperability.

Portability—To implement business requirements through data processing, an infrastructure is required that makes the user independent of all aspects of the underlying technical system. R/3™ provides such a technology infrastructure largely by means of the multilevel client/server architecture of R/3™.

The basic construction principle of this architecture is the clear distinction made between the presentation, application, and database levels. This principle allows R/3™ to be transparently distributed over various computer systems (servers). For each of these levels, the R/3™ technology infrastructure offers corresponding services. These support the systems portability across heterogeneous presentation systems, application servers, and database servers. At the same time, they accept the system-specific characteristics of different servers and ensure optimal operation of the R/3™ system on each of these computers.

Regarding these three levels, R/3™ supports the following platforms:

- Presentation systems—SAP™ GUI is the graphical front end of R/3™. It is based on the Windows standard and can be executed in Windows 3.X, Windows 95, Windows NT, Mac OS™, OSF/Motif, and OS/2 Presentation Manager™.
- Application servers—The complete business logic of R/3™ applications can be executed without modifications on all major UNIX operations systems, AS/400® systems, and Windows NT. As clients, various application servers can obtain parallel access to data of a database server through Open SQL or Native SQL.
- Database servers—R/3™ can use different relational database management systems. These include IBM DB2™ (DB2/6000 for AIX® and DB2/400 for AS/400, Informix Online, Microsoft SQL Server, Oracle, and Software AG Adabas D.

Investment Protection—The operational benefit of R/3™ technology infrastructure results from the high system portability discussed above, the corresponding protection of investments in application software, and the business processes that are implemented based on this software.

The useful life of such critical software often exceeds ten years, whereas the innovation cycles of hardware and operating systems and databases are significantly shorter. The portability of the R/3™ system also guarantees adaptability to new base technologies such as object-oriented technologies (see Chapter 15). Moreover, portability permits companies a free choice among different system environments, which pays off over the entire life cycle of its data processing environments.

Multilevel Implementation—Distribution over all three system levels is often the best solution for large and distributed company structures. This solution not only applies to the presentation level where new PCs can simply be added if the number of users increase, but it also applies on the application level: Dedicated computers can be added for dialog-free background processing. They can also be added for specific operational application areas, such as sales quantity planning, sales, or financial accounting. Businesses are provided with complete transparency regarding how many application servers have been newly installed and where a given R/3™ application is currently running. Finally, on the database level, it is easy to change from single processor to multiprocessor systems or to cluster configurations.

Optimum Load Distribution—This kind of scalability provides a company with great freedom from a cost perspective. It allows businesses to install the optimum computer capacity on each level and provide for optimum load distribution even in client/server configurations with several thousand users. Consequently, companies are not forced to install computers and operating systems from a single supplier but have the option to implement a heterogeneous system environment.

Interoperability— Interoperability is an important aspect of the R/3 ™ architecture, because process-based enterprise software must coexist and cooperate with other systems to achieve business goals. Process orientation across business areas and applications require interoperability between distributed R/3 ™ applications as well as between R/3 ™ and external systems.

14.4 *INTERPROGRAM COMMUNICATION*

In R/3 ™, program-to-program communications are implemented with CPI-C. CPI-C is a relic of IBM's move to standardize communications as part of its System Application Architecture (SAA) push in the late 1980s, when SAP ™ developed parts of R/3 ™. The CPI-C functions have been integrated into ABAP/4. An ABAP/4 program can initiate or accept CPI-C sessions, exchange data, and set up and terminate connections. Program-to-program communications are always performed via an internal gateway that takes care of converting CPI-C communications to the externally used transfer protocol, for example, TCP/IP or LU6.2.

When speaking of network communications, it is essential to make the distinction between *synchronous* and *asynchronous* data transfer. Many situations exist in which applications need a mechanism for asynchronous communications instead of synchronous CPI-C communications. For instance, a target computer may be temporarily unable to accept data. In such cases, the R/3 ™ system can buffer the data in special queues and transmit it later on. The mechanism used to manage such queues is called Queue Application Programming Interface (Q-API). It can be freely integrated into application programs.

The format used to store data in a queue can vary, but batch input format, Batch Data Communications (BDC), is defined for accepting external data records into R/3 ™. The batch input format allows data to flow directly from the queue into normal interactive transactions. However, queues can also manage data in a freely defined format interpreted by the receiving program.

Another aspect of interprogram communication is the Remote Function Call (RFC), which is SAP ™'s implementation of Remote Procedure Call (RPC) in ABAP/4. RFC is the main means to access R/3 ™ applications and is the programming interface of R/3 ™. RFC meets the distributed computing requirements associated with utilizing an external service by calling a subprogram. The R/3 ™ Automation Software Development Kit contains available RFC libraries and RFC Dynamic Link Libraries (DLLs), dialogs, error management functions and relevant documentation, and example programs. RFCs can be used to call a wide range of R/3™ functions, modules, and external applications; for example, MS Excel, Lotus 1-2-3®, PowerBuilder®, Entis™, Visual Basic, Java™, and C. Furthermore, SAP™ is closely aligned with Microsoft's COM architecture and thus, using Microsoft's OLE2 automation, RFC is also available. This middleware technology delivers the ability to connect and incorporate business objects across multiple programs or files. Other R/3™ systems or applications can call R/3™ function modules via RFC. RFC hides the layer of CPI-C calls, the communication standard used by SAP™. To access an R/3™ system, other users' programs have to log on via defined standard function modules and can then call the specific function modules they wish to communicate with.

Transactional integrity is a key concern in remote transactions. In the context of R/3™, where a complete system could reside in the application server, it is almost mandatory to post transactions via application servers. RFC ensures transactional integrity in the following ways:

- RFC calls are executed in the same order and within the same program context in the target system as in the calling system.
- Provisions are made to ensure that each RFC call is not executed more than once.
- The status of an RFC call can be queried at any time.

RFC calls are essentially synchronous, but they can also be made asynchronously when the target system is inactive. In this case, the call is placed in a local queue and not sent until a later time. For instance, the call can be transmitted at regular intervals or at precisely stipulated times. The calls can also be controlled by the availability of the target computer. This form of RFC is discussed later in the section that follows.

14.5 MIDDLEWARE TRANSACTION MANAGEMENT

Realizing that the three-tier client/server has limitations in geographically dispersed enterprises, SAP™ pioneered the Application Linking and Enabling (ALE) concept based on business processes. SAP™'s ALE concept successfully removes the constraints of a single database structure by distributing database availability among different sites. ALE makes distributed systems possible by allowing users to set up application modules and databases at different locations. Figure 14-2 shows how the middleware technology is being added over time to enterprise software architecture. As R/3™ adds Internet, workflow, and business object interfacing capabilities, the level of sophistication needed in middleware technology increases.

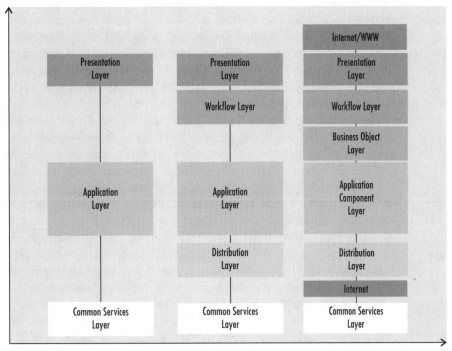

▶ **Figure 14–2** Middleware technology augments enterprise software architecture

Data are exchanged from a central system to a remote system, permitting applications to exchange information. ALE not only routes data, it also knows what data are needed in a given situation. In this respect, ALE is "intelligent middleware." ALE opens the way for efficient, secure communication of business information between different and technically independent systems. Also, ALE provides distribution models and technologies for application linking, plus tools for the design and operation of distributed applications.

The cornerstones of ALE technology are consistency of information, intermediate documents, and asynchronous RFC.

Consistency of Information—A conscious decision was made not to use a distributed database concept for ALE. From a technical standpoint, such a concept usually entails a high degree of administrative complexity and identical release status of all system components involved on all network nodes. This complexity runs counter to the idea of autonomy and often cannot be realized because of time and cost considerations, particularly if one considers a distributed scenario with economically independent units. From a business perspective, the database system cannot adequately represent a significant part of the application logic, such as security-related consistency checks. Implementing proprietary stored procedures is also not a valid solution for recovering business semantics, because this solution would come at the expense of portability. Most databases now support a concept of replication where identical databases can be written to in multiple physical locations as a singular atomic update. This technology is now widely used across WAN's, especially when the majority of users are reading and not writing data.

Intermediate Documents (IDOC)—ALE uses an operationally controlled asynchronous message exchange between autonomous, loosely coupled application systems. The pivotal center for a smooth and secure data exchange is the IDOC concept developed by SAP™. IDOC message types are characterized, in particular, by an expandable structure, compatible with new releases and suitable for complex data. After transfer is complete, IDOC triggers incoming processing in the target system. Data are processed according to the settings of the corresponding application, which can include posting. Besides other messaging systems, the Internet is also available as carrier in this business-object approach.

Asynchronous RFC—IDOCs have a neutral data structure that is independent of the specific application data. As a result, they can also be used by external systems as a standard interface for data transfer.

Figure 14-3 illustrates how SAP™ plans to enable application distribution across releases. The small bubbles represent business objects.

An application, configured to send data to another system, generates (in response to a corresponding event) a master IDOC. It contains both business data as well as the definition of the processing sequences to be triggered in the recipient application. The actual transfer takes place through the asynchronous RFC. Asynchronous technology, a cornerstone of ALE, is the key to messaging because it allows two or more systems to communicate without being synchronized. Consequently, communication is independent of momentary unavailability of the target computer. If the connection is not made, the ALE layer initiates and monitors transfer later.

14.6   *RATIONALE FOR DISTRIBUTED BUSINESS-PROCESS INTEGRATION*

Early in its development of R/3™, SAP™ understood that distributed databases were an inadequate means of processing complex business objects located in different systems. As a result, R/3™ was initially implemented with a single database in order to offer the necessary control and transaction separation. Although this single database decision is understandable in the context of the late 1980s, when R/3™ was first designed and built, it is no longer appropriate.

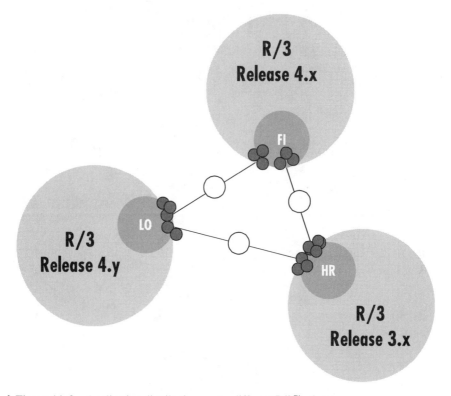

▶ **Figure 14–3**   Application distribution across different R/3 ™ releases

Organizations now have multiple database types on different systems. Under the conditions of current business realities, client/server technology must easily support more than one database (i.e., multiple databases which, when conjoined, constitute the entire R/3 ™ system).

In order to engineer business processes optimally, a business application system must be highly integrated. ALE is the mechanism that allows SAP ™ to integrate R/3 ™ data sources and databases (operational or data warehouse or other). The underlying principle of ALE enables an R/3 ™ installation to be distributed, yet integrated at the same time. ALE permits the implementation of loosely coupled clusters of applications. The applications run independently and have their own separate data in the distributed installations.

In order to install a distributed, integrated system, a logical model of the overall system must first be built.

Figure 14-4 illustrates possible distribution scenarios, to be discussed in this section.

One database, integrated R/3 system

ALE-integrated distributed R/3 systems

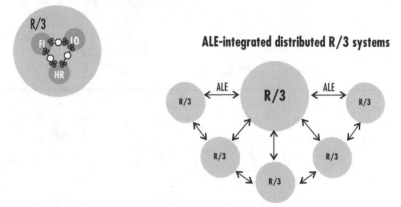

Central modular R/3 system

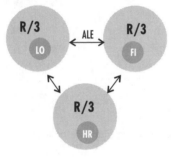

▶ **Figure 14–4**   Scenarios for application distribution

Within the framework of this configuration, the customer determines which applications are to run on which systems and how the applications exchange data. To assist in the development of distributed systems using ALE, the Business Blueprint contains predetermined scenarios for distribution. By referring to the Business Blueprint, customers can generate their own business models (see Chapters 2 and 3), and they can better understand the implication of changes to a business process as it affects the system organization in R/3™ (see Chapter 16).

From a design perspective, the inherent problem associated with the implementation of distribution scenarios is that databases do not have enough information about data stored inside those scenarios. Data dictionaries, such as the one provided in the R/3™ Repository, have information pertaining to the structure, but not the semantics, of data.

R/3™ operates in an online distribution environment, but the database administrator must define where the different data have to be stored. SAP™ has developed read-only replication services for R/3™ Executive Information Systems (EIS), but this is only a partial solution: In such updateable replicas for R/3™, most of the tables have to be completely available as replicas in all sites participating in a distributed database installation. This need implies substantial investment in hard disk space and network capacity, because all data have to be transported via a WAN. Heavy investment costs can only be avoided by imposing extensive restrictions on what is to be distributed and where. However, the administration tools that could perform this function are unavailable.

ALE is the basis for an alternative solution. ALE enables applications to know all the semantic facts about a particular set of data and to take control by using database distribution features. In other words, the application takes care of what data is distributed and where it is going. This control reduces the amount of data exchanged and therefore enables installations to be autonomous yet integrated. The reliable exchange of data from one installation to another can be performed by a database replication service. This combination of application and database technology offers the following benefits:

- High performance and reliable data replication
- Reasonable network price and performance
- Minimum hard disk requirements

As well as successfully overcoming the challenges presented by distribution scenarios, ALE is an essential component of the R/3™ system in other respects.

The ALE initiative began because many of SAP™'s existing (R/2™) mainframe customers didn't want—or were unable—to convert all of their existing applications to R/3™ in one step. Many customers wanted to run a piece of an R/2™ application in their existing host application environment, or different pieces of other applications (or the same application) in the new, distributed R/3™ environment. ALE was originally, therefore, designed to combine R/3™ systems with R/2™ systems.

With ALE, SAP™ further developed the multilevel client/server architecture of R/3™ for cooperative processing in an application interconnection of loosely coupled, technically autonomous SAP™ applications (R/2™ and R/3™) and non-SAP™ applications. This step was the first one taken in the direction of "Next Generation Enterprise" architecture (see Chapter 17), a milestone for modern application architecture.

ALE meets the requirement of many companies for distributed application systems that presuppose high business integration and have the potential to be completely decoupled for decentralized use. Possible distribution scenarios are centralized administration of purchasing contracts with decentralized procurement processing or linking centralized financial systems and decentralized logistics applications. The R/3™ Reference Model (particularly the process model) provides the basis for modeling these distributed ALE processes, using the Organizational Architect.

Business solutions that incorporated application linking provided the means for a smooth transition from R/2™ to R/3™. The demand for the benefits brought about by ALE primarily came from companies involved in business engineering. These companies required distributed application systems that would offer business-process integration while at the same time allowing the decoupling of systems so that they could be utilized at the local level.

In order to maximize both the integration and independence of these business functions, ALE was designed to do the following:

- Enable communication among different releases of SAP™ application systems
- Ensure that data exchanges continue to run without maintenance after system upgrade
- Allow enhancements to be carried out simply and, if necessary, by the customer
- Detach applications from communications
- Attach non-SAP™ applications without losing consistency between business functions and data
- Address connectivity between R/2™ and R/3™ systems and between distributed R/3™ systems
- Offer distribution across platforms

In the end, ALE must be understood as a concept and technology that dramatically altered the way SAP™'s R/3™ architecture looked in multisite deployments. ALE meets middleware challenges such as distribution, delivery of planning, installation, conformance to underlying business models, support, and delivery.

14.7   CAPABILITIES OF APPLICATION DISTRIBUTION IN R/3™

Application distribution is an essential technology requirement for supporting integrated business processes. As discussed previously, ALE is message-oriented middleware that enables SAP™ mainframe and client/server applications to share data. ALE is responsible for communications, protocols, translations, and store-and-forward issues (where appropriate) within the R/3™ system. To meet all these responsibilities, ALE defines what message is to be communicated, how applications behave, and when and how synchronization takes place within the system.

Synchronization of business processes takes place at the application level rather than the database level. Application integration is carried out not in a central database but rather via either synchronous or potentially asynchronous communication. R/3™ has a distributed applications strategy that enables users to run distributed business processes at various sites. ALE enables users to construct and operate distributed applications along with the controlled exchange of business (transactions) information. This functionality is achieved via applications (R/3™ and non-R/3™) that communicate with each other.

The following distribution scenarios are available in R/3™:

- Local sales and central dispatch
- Local and central profitability analysis
- Local and central sales and operations planning (SOP)
- Distribution of contracts from a central purchasing department to local purchasing departments
- Sales information system, stock information system, and purchasing information system available throughout the system
- Separation of accounting and logistics
- Attachment of external warehouse management systems and warehouse control

These distribution scenarios have the following implications for R/3™ users:

- Transactions can take place across application servers based on numerous data services.
- Data are replicated where required according to an underlying distribution model.
- Buying multiple applications from different vendors is made easier.
- ALE represents a pioneering norm.
- R/2's Achilles' heel—the single database constraint—is contained.

With the opening of R/3™ to distribution possibilities, SAP™ launched a much broader effort to enhance the way that applications are assembled or "manufactured" at the customer's site. Figure 14-5 illustrates how SAP™'s application manufacturing is designed to support numerous customer R/3™ systems with various application priorities.

In sum, the architecture of application distribution in R/3™ consists of three layers that support essential services: applications services, distribution services, and communication services.

One database, integrated R/3 system

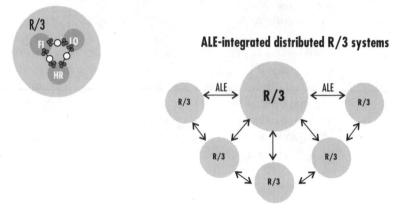

ALE-integrated distributed R/3 systems

Central modular R/3 system

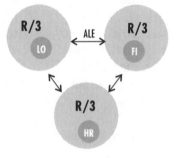

▶ **Figure 14–5**　Application manufacturing

Applications generate messages containing specific attributes; for example, parameters for determining the message recipient, the transfer mode, and the type of processing to be used on the item received. Applications support workflows for processing incoming messages. Business metadata (like that for defining the structure of master data) are available for purposes such as configuration and synchronization of messages. Events occurring at the data level—such as changes to data records—automatically generate messages to other systems in the network.

Distribution services implement the specific functions needed for the loose coupling of business applications. These functions include:

- Definition of messages and attributes independently of the system level (R/2™ or R/3™)
- Description and monitoring of dependencies of systems in the network with regard to the message used

- Stipulation of message recipients
- Filtering and conversion of messages
- Storage, relay, and adjustment of "reduced master data," for example, those subsets of master data required in connected systems

As a feature of distribution services, R/3™ compresses messages because certain applications would otherwise generate a very high volume of messages.

For communications within the system network, messaging middleware opens up the possibility of employing different solutions and/or products for "transactional electronic mail," including linking with different EDI subsystems. In this context, R/3™ supports:

- X.400 and MAPI as the e-mail standard
- X.435 as the application to application extension of X.400
- Deployment tools
- General messaging infrastructure with proximity to mail systems, for example, messaging support for software such as Microsoft Exchange and Novell® applications.

14.8   *TOOLS FOR APPLICATION DISTRIBUTION*

In response to the demands of R/3™ users, ALE reduces the degree of rigid integration in the R/3™ system. However, it's hardly a simple task to split up such a tightly integrated application suite as R/3™ into geographically separate units. Numerous aspects of this procedure must be defined and then customized. For example, organizational roles—such as purchasing, payment processing, or inventory management—must be defined at specific locations. In one scenario, for example, a central purchasing function can coexist with local payments functions.

ALE permits the splitting up of data and functions among network sites, providing three tools within the R/3™ system:

- Model-based application distribution
- Distribution Reference Model
- Business Blueprint (R/3™ Reference Model)

Each of these tools is explained in greater detail in Chapter 16 as part of the R/3™ Business Engineer; a general overview of the three is now presented.

Model-Based Application Distribution

The concept that process and organizational models are interrelated was described in detail as part of the event-driven process chain. The modeling tool is a complete workstation that supports a Windows GUI. This tool draws on data from the Distribution Reference Model. It graphically depicts the structure of a distributed R/3™ system. Data and graphical objects can then be manipulated to allow planners to "place" the model elements where they choose. When creating a conceptual design for distribution, customers should consider the following important questions:

- At which locations are the distributed R/3™ systems to be installed?
- Which applications are to run on which systems?
- What master data and what transaction data are the applications to exchange with each other?
- What control data must be included within the distributed systems?

Distribution Reference Model

To support the distribution of the R/3™ system, SAP™ has included a Distribution Reference Model in the R/3™ toolset. In this model, the scenarios for companywide distribution are predetermined and stored. These scenarios are designed to facilitate initial ALE implementation and planning. In addition, they show the scope of distribution possibilities within the R/3™ system (although R/3™ users should note that not all business applications can be distributed).

Using the Distribution Reference Model, customers can develop and realize their own distribution configuration. The R/3™ distribution models represent distribution scenarios of business processes and provide a proven basis for customized business engineering solutions. For example, ALE supports business processes for the distribution of accounting and logistics, sales, invoicing and shipping, local and central profitability analyses, and also central and local sales and operation planning.

A typical distribution scenario involves communication among three ALE application systems. For instance, a company's headquarters runs R/3™ as an enterprisewide reference system for master data and control tables and uses the system for such applications as accounting, human resources management, central purchasing, sales planning, or as a cross-application information system for logistics.

In the manufacturing plants, R/3™ is installed as a local SOP system for production planning and control, and it also handles local purchasing and inventory management. In the sales offices, R/3™ takes care of sales, shipping, inventory management, and the purchasing of trading goods.

ALE links these distributed application systems together via a configurable distribution model, ensuring the exchange of business information messages, updates of master data, and coordination of control information. During both the setup and operational phases of distributed application systems, transparency and ease of handling are preserved no matter how comprehensive the scenarios. Distributable process units (such as inventory management) guarantee data uniformity throughout the distributed system.

One main advantage to the implementation of the Distribution Reference Model is that its data are stored in the R/3™ Repository. In other words, the data are directly tied to the system as business objects. The Distribution Reference Model and Organizational Architect gives organizations precisely the functionality, flexibility, and utility they want.

Using the Business Blueprint for Application Integration

Business distribution scenarios are linked to the SAP™ R/3™ Reference Model (the Business Blueprint). R/3™ makes this link possible by allowing the rapid customization of business processes to take place. Perhaps the most important single fact about ALE is that it conforms to underlying business models, as contained in the R/3™ Business Blueprint (see Chapter 2).

Two basic client/server mechanisms implement distributed coupled integration. First, the exchange of messages that contain application data comes from standardized IDOCs, which can be communicated using the standard extended markup language (XML). The R/3™ EDI interface also uses IDOCs. Second, primary data can be replicated. These two mechanisms have several advantages. For instance, they enable support for the integration of non-SAP™ applications. Also, they introduce standardized routines for exchanging messages between the applications of different systems. Finally, technically independent systems and the integration of business processes in different systems become real possibilities.

In its current form, the architecture of R/3™ ensures integration in two ways: by completely modeling each business process along with its data within the R/3™ system and by performing each database update for business transactions in a so-called logical unit of work (SAP™-LUW). As a result, the contents of the central database are always logically consistent with regard to business criteria.

Ultimately, ALE makes the task of business engineering with the R/3™ Reference Model easier in the following respects:

- ALE enhances the knowledge transacted to the database systems.
- Business logic can be split up and allocated at an early stage of business engineering.
- ALE minimizes conflicting situations resulting from purely synchronous communications functions.

ALE delivers these benefits by featuring a communication capability that is not restricted to the R/3™ system. Efficient business-process integration between technically independent systems, the use of standardized communication procedures, and the incorporation of other applications are all possible. ALE allows applications to be implemented both locally and in parallel. Also, SAP™'s approach to application distribution avoids bottlenecks in processing large data sets.

14.9   CONCLUSION

SAP™ has proven to be a pragmatic adapter of open systems standards (remote procedure, EDI, MAPI, CPI-C, etc.). In creating R/3™, SAP™ had the responsibility to assure that simple and complex business transactions could be executed in a wide variety of system constellations. Although they opted to use a novel approach in some areas (such as RFC), SAP™ still maintains a large degree of openness to external applications mapping transactions in the SAP™ world. SAP™ not only delivers a finished set of applications, but it also provides the development tools and middleware. Although developing external applications that interface to R/3™ may require a considerable amount of internal R/3™ knowledge and resources, this strategy will further strengthen SAP™'s position in the application market because it allows almost any application to be developed.

R/3™ is the open transaction processing model for a long and impressive (and growing) list of world companies. SAP™ is therefore in a particularly strong position as the industry forerunner in determining how and where middleware will connect its own applications and those from other companies. As a sign of R/3™ success, SAP™ has offered ALE to the Open Application Group, a consortium of client/server vendors that has agreed to cooperate on developing interapplication interfaces. SAP™ also publishes application programming interfaces so users can rely on ALE to link SAP™ and non-SAP™ applications (see Chapter 15).

Many of SAP™'s current initiatives seek to find complementary software partners who see R/3™ technology as an essential component of their future plans. Many companies are looking for a client/server system combined with multiple-platform capability. This trend means that the future development of applications resembling R/3™ is highly likely. However, such projects will become a reality only if they are linked with R/3™.

The fundamental purpose of application distribution is to allow the R/3™ architecture to evolve so as to facilitate the addition of R/2™ and R/3™ connections and to expand into application networks comprising loosely coupled SAP™ and non-SAP™ applications. To meet its goals, R/3™ uses messages exchanged by the distributed applications on the basis of predetermined business rules and objects stored in R/3™'s Reference Model. Also, R/3™ makes extensive use of asynchronous links in order to avoid the previously rigid ties to a central database. By enabling R/3™ to evolve in these ways, its ALE concept allows almost any application to be developed as a supplement to R/3™.

The major challenge and ultimate goal for enterprise software vendors is making it possible for systems to interact seamlessly with one another. The R/3™ architecture is one half of the seamless integration equation. The next chapter, R/3™ Framework and Infrastructure, completes this discussion with an examination of the R/3™ framework for business system interaction.

15

R/3™ Framework
and Infrastructure

As part of an ongoing effort to apply leading technologies to the infrastructural challenges of enterprise computing, SAP™ has created a sophisticated platform for interacting with enterprise application software systems. With the business framework, companies can build a technological platform that supports continuous process change and not just one-time efforts. The connection between business and technology was not always so strong. In the past, information technology was used to help companies automate existing business processes. Now, the goal is not automation but the use of technology in new ways to completely change how businesses operate. The ability of client/server technology to integrate applications and the new emphasis on integrated business-processes redesign in business engineering have brought management and IT professionals closer together.

IT-supported business engineering and design are the result of 1) a trend toward increasing the productivity of software development projects and 2) more general movements taking place in the business world, such as quality, total quality management, business-process reengineering, and lean management. Management philosophies have changed from managing all parts of a particular business transaction to optimizing the transaction itself. This fundamental shift has paved the way for businesses to use technology to describe, simulate, and model organizations, as well as for seeing how changes made to the organization affect processes.

It is a mistake, however, to use technology simply as a one-time vehicle in business change. A fundamental question for implementing any software system is whether the underlying architecture of the new software system will support ongoing change. For example, every company wants to shape its processes to best suit the market segment, customer group, or product line in question. But if those processes should ever need to change—and had already been individually and indelibly programmed into the system—companies would find themselves straightjacketed by their own routines. The details of many processes must be able to respond to changing market requirements. The essential feature of standard software, then, is not just quick implementation but the ability to adapt and change within a live system as well.

Business engineering is a second-generation approach in which models of business processes are used as reference sets for a change in process. BE involves not only revamping or changing an organization but doing it continuously over time. SAP™'s new paradigm, called "configure to order," aims to tackle the problems associated with managing change by providing a complete infrastructure for assembling applications at the customer's site.

The Business Framework is the conceptual basis for the Business Engineer, application development, the Repository, and third-party integration. SAP™ initiatives in software development and management have made it possible to provide such a framework and infrastructure. These initiatives include the R/3™ Repository (including business processes, business objects, data, interfaces, and business components) and the ABAP/4 Development Workbench. These products provide the basic framework for the Business Engineer (to be examined in full in Chapter 16).

15.1 BACKGROUND OF BUSINESS INTEGRATION

The historical stimulus for enterprise data processing (EDP) concepts originated with hardware and software manufacturers, who provided new possibilities for efficient use of EDP. Companies found EDP useful because its requirements were derived and specified from the real commercial world. In the 1970s, data processing suppliers tried to optimally support the requirements of the various individual functional areas but failed to consider the interdependencies between previous and subsequent areas. Closed hardware architectures allowed only the development of software solutions that were closely linked to the operating systems. Incompatibilities between the data processing systems of various suppliers led to so-called island solutions. The existing, proprietary systems were counterproductive to integration and could only partially satisfy the functional requirements.

In the 1980s, the situation described often led to projects ending up as Computer Integrated Manufacturing (CIM) "ruins." Traditional functional organization structures—which were dominant in most companies—reflected the implementation of primarily "functionally conceived" information systems. The results of this development were fragmented enterprise process chains, too many organizational interfaces, and a plethora of data processing system interfaces.

The increasing independence of software from hardware undermined the dominance of proprietary systems. The integration problems of the 1970s were to be solved by the arrival of integrated database systems and networks. The access to the same databases by various functional areas was intended to make data created in one area immediately available to all other areas. A low-redundancy, easy-access structure was intended to do the following:

- Provide complete and correct data
- Provide up-to-date data for all areas of the company
- Avoid data redundancy
- Avoid data transfer errors
- Reduce change effort
- Increase information transfer speed

The widespread enterprise problems of data redundancy and inconsistency were to be resolved by the development of conceptual data models. Armies of theorists and practitioners modeled company data by using Chen's Entity-relationship approach. As a result, the commercial application data models were able to increase the awareness of suppliers and users for data structure and integration aspects of interfaces, but they did not achieve a decisive breakthrough in software selection. Also, because of their complex notation, data models remained largely the preserve of a small circle of informatics and were only able to partially satisfy user requirements.

The inadequacies of the data models led some scientists to investigate the fundamental questions of model or enterprise architecture construction (e.g., CIM-OSA). A group of tools suppliers began to develop computer-aided software (CASE) tools to overcome the functional inadequacies in the standard software of the 1980s. These tools included IT-oriented methods—for example, SA, SA/RT, SADT, PAP, Petri nets, functional trees—to describe functional and procedural aspects.

User-unfriendly interfaces, inadequate integration to the physical implementation, lack of consideration of organizational change, and clumsy handling limited the use of the CASE tools to a small number of IT-oriented users. Problems arose because of IT engineers' inadequate understanding of end-users' company requirements and commercial solutions.

The practitioner's approach—creating a user software solution from a detailed commercial requirements description using CASE tools—failed completely. The theorists approach, providing an architecture for integrated software development projects, bogged down at an early stage. Practical commercial solutions were also a weakness for theorists in their design of business processes, largely because they were only able to suggest unrealistic design recommendations.

The development of client/server commercial applications solutions, for example, the SAP™ R/3™ system, made new organizational design approaches possible for many companies. The new design possibilities, however, also increased the decision complexity in the creation of the data-processing-aided, information-processing concept. At the same time, the IT and management trend has seen a shift from department-oriented optimization to an integrated business process of the most important value chain. The design of business processes replaced the data-oriented approach of the 1980s as the focus of attention. "Process owners," who are responsible for the performance of complete processes, were often nominated. The focus of the requirements analysis discussion also shifted away from technical details to commercial problems. Technologies such as client/server systems, databases, and networks became accepted as quasi-standards.

Whereas data modeling was the preserve of a small group of experts, business-process design requires communication between IT suppliers, IT management, organization planners, and end users that spans across department boundaries. The representatives of various disciplines such as economics, engineering, informatics, and so on, also need to talk to each other. For all of these reasons, SAP™ brought a method discussion about the representation of business processes to an end in 1992 and began as quickly as possible the development of the R/3™ system process contents.

15.2　SAP™ BUSINESS FRAMEWORK

To aid in an understanding of the Business Framework, another brief history is in order. The strategic development of interfacing and integration of technology as well as the strong emphasis on easier-to-handle functional components led to the eventual Business Framework product. As mentioned in Chapter 14, SAP™ pioneered the three-tier client/server architecture that eventually turned out to be the foundation for high scalability at many R/3™ customer sites. With ALE, the foundation was laid for the interoperation of components across multiple, physically separated R/3™ sites. Workflow introduced the notion of flexible, customer-individual business processes on the basis of business objects. The SAP™ initiative made the Business Blueprint and business rules inherent in R/3™ accessible for the continuous reconfiguration of the live R/3™ system.

Recognizing the fact that no communication is possible without establishing widely adhered-to business content standards, enterprise vendors have sought to drive these standard initiatives forward. SAP™ began with many special-purpose interfaces, then integrated desktop applications using OLE. It moved on to complementary software, interenterprise communication via EDI, and then allowed for new ways of Internet computing. SAP™ finally decided to make the corresponding business application programming interfaces (BAPIs) public so that new business content standards could be set as quickly as possible.

All of these separate initiatives have converged and culminated in the Business Framework. The Business Framework is based on business objects, business components, and business processes. SAP™ business objects (compliant with Microsoft's Component Object Model and OMG's CORBA) are assembled business components that implement the business processes.

Configuration of Enterprise Applications

The entire commercial information-technology community is keenly interested in the ability to deploy enterprise business systems that allow for the following:

- Fast implementation of new functionality with low risk of stoppages
- Dynamic reconfiguration of implemented systems
- Guaranteed maintainability and upgradeability
- Centralized as well as decentralized deployment potential
- Reuseability of components from different manufacturers
- Easy collaboration of systems from multiple vendors
- Very high scalability (millions of users)
- End-to-end business processes beyond the enterprise
- Quality, reliability, availability, and security—without compromises

In addition, the IT community wants a greater pool of employees who are knowledgeable in the vast array of technologies, more and more an issue in recent years.

The Business Framework is an approach to implementing "Next Generation" enterprise technology, which is based on the foundation for R/3™'s original three-tier, client/server, open architecture. The virtue of the Business Framework is that new BAPIs appear continuously and mainly are geared, from a business standpoint, toward the Internet. Totally new applications complement R/3™ as satellite systems in the Internet. Moreover, dedicated functional servers— such as "availability to promise checking" and "price calculation"—are also introduced. The whole of R/3™ is further componentized, beginning with the separation of financials from logistics and human resources. Industry-specific solutions from SAP™ find their way to the market as separate components. On this basis, new industry and company templates enable faster initial configuration and dynamic continuous reconfiguration.

As such, SAP™ is realizing the goal of "object orientation," which allows for easy distribution of information processing. In object orientation, templates are encapsulated and communicate only by messages to each other. But rather than trying to assemble technical objects and attempting to build object-oriented business systems bottom-up, SAP™'s approach is top-down. SAP™ begins with the real business world and mirrors it in its business system, always keeping in mind the practical capabilities of today's IT technology. This strategy is reflected in the Business Framework as well: Business components from SAP™ or third parties can be combined to offer value-added solutions for the customer. In this way, the customer has top priority, and the underlying technology is available and open, free to be used for the creation of business solutions.

Rationale for the Business Framework

The idea of a business framework is not new. The concept of frameworks has been widely used in the programming community as a means of better integrating the work of independent application developers and providing for future changes in programming standards and practices. Many companies, such as IBM, Tivoli, Microsoft, and Sun Microsystems, have developed frameworks aimed at simplifying the ways in which different software products interact. SAP™'s idea to apply this to enterprise software, however, is novel.

SAP™'s Business Framework has its roots in the concept of application manufacturing. In essence, the framework enables customers and third-party software products to assemble applications with very few barriers. Key elements of the framework include the application components, application development tools, and the collective interfaces provided.

Components communicate with one another via interfaces. As such, interfaces represent a kind of contract between components. For two components to be integrated, their interfaces must fit—they have to negotiate a contract between themselves. That is to say, integration can only be accomplished if there exists a common business sense in which the individual contracts can be reliably negotiated and executed. The whole integration is more than the sum of its parts; integration involves the components and their interfaces.

The number of components must be high enough to achieve a considerable level of agility but low enough to manage the resulting system. The position of the resulting interfaces must be deep enough to gain a significant level of flexibility but high enough to enable easy reuse of SAP™ and third-party components. The integration must be tight enough to gain real-time business benefits but loose enough to avoid lock-in situations because of too many dependencies of the underlying components.

SAP™ seeks to provide a balanced solution with as many advantages as possible for all different purposes. The building blocks of the Business Framework are the Repository (the integration technology of distributed R/3™ architecture), the ABAP/4 Development Workbench and BAPIs, and the Business Engineer (discussed in Chapter 16).

15.3   *REPOSITORY AS INTEGRATING FACTOR*

The R/3™ Repository is the foundation of the Business Framework because it clearly captures all the business semantics of a business in the Business Blueprint processes, business objects, and the organization model. The R/3™ Business Blueprint, which describes and documents R/3™, is unique and is maintained in the (logically) single Repository of R/3™. This R/3™ Repository encompasses the business- and application-related metadata in a tightly integrated manner.

The R/3™ Repository is one of the core parts of the R/3™ system and a general container of business engineering information. The Repository contains a comprehensive description of the R/3™ application, including all metainformation about models, technical programming objects, and business objects. The R/3™ Repository is also the central container for all of R/3™'s application information, including new development, design, and maintenance of applications and other components. The R/3™ Repository is able to exchange information via an application programming interface (API) with graphics software, modeling tools, or business-process engineering tools.

The R/3™ Repository is the bridge between business engineering—which uses the R/3™ Business Engineer—and application development, which focuses on programming with the ABAP/4 Development Workbench, as shown in Figure 15-1. Process models, organization models, function models, data models, business objects, object models, and related data and connections are all stored in the R/3™ Repository. The R/3™ Repository also stores information such as data definitions, screens, and program objects used for developing or extending the R/3™ enterprise application suite.

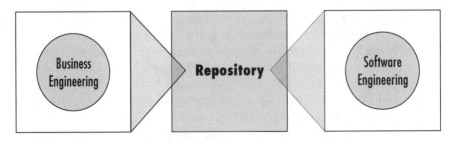

▶ **Figure 15–1**   Business and software engineering in R/3™ repository

Business engineering requires a broad level of information integration to achieve the desired effects in business design and change. Integration at the conceptual and functional level is heavily dependent on repository technology. SAP™'s goal is to integrate the functions of different areas and target groups, including workflow, application distribution, data model, programming, customizing, implementation, consulting, and organization.

The technical basis for the R/3™ Repository is the ABAP/4 Development Workbench. Repository objects need only be created once, and they are automatically available to all developers throughout the system. The "activeness" of a Repository object depends on whether it is defined as being either modeling or runtime. There is no redundancy of data. Changes made to objects cause programs to be automatically generated the next time they are used. Many companies are realizing that code generation makes a great deal of sense if they are maintaining large complex object models. The Repository Information System lets users search for R/3™ Repository objects and shows where they are used throughout the system. For example, a process model, as it relates to a certain part of the application, can be found in the repository.

The R/3™ Repository offers:

- Versioning of all development objects
- Security and access control mechanisms for all objects, allowing users to structure privileges for each programmer or team of programmers
- A utility for promoting objects from a development system into a test system and then on into a live system
- An elaborate cross-referencing utility for all objects
- An application programming interface for accessing different types of information

Storage is critical for permitting users to access the business objects and allowing them to better visualize the process. The R/3™ Repository can be "viewed" with the R/3™ Business Engineer's online graphical browser tool, which acts as an R/3™ business "road map." Because the Business Engineer reads directly from the Repository, it can access all the most current process information, application components, and objects. These include everything from sales and distribution and production planning to financial accounting and quality management. The R/3™ Repository is based on a sophisticated meta-model that describes the intricate interrelationships among information objects.

For companies that want to go beyond looking at the information stored in the Repository, the API has opened up the Repository to third-party companies. BE consultants might go into the R/3™ Repository to show customers the business-process models available in R/3™ and thereby dramatically shorten the time they need to understand and implement R/3™. Business modeling tool vendors can use the API to connect to the R/3™ Repository, take information out, and display it in graphical desktop tools such as Visio®·. Application tool developers might use SAP™'s Desktop Integration Software Development Kit, which has access technology to development objects stored in the Repository, to trigger satellite development projects or new applications that hook in with R/3™. Even desktop users can access the R/3™ Repository from other applications, such as MS Excel or MS Word, to see what's inside and how it works.

Another major development of the Repository was the inclusion of the Business Blueprint. The Business Blueprint is a valuable asset that is used in every type of SAP™ documentation; for example, rollout training and application documentation. The Blueprint is not only an integral part of the SAP system, it can also be integrated into multimedia demonstrations of SAP applications, making it a useful reference point for training courses and documentation. This integration is made possible with the Repository API and the object-oriented interface that works with market standards such as OLE (COM) from Microsoft.

Open interfaces make the exchange of information more fluid. Bearing in mind that most third-party consulting organizations have their own methods, even their own modeling tools in some cases, the provision of such an infrastructure depends on the flexibility of the Business Engineering Workbench. R/3™ has APIs and standardized interfaces so that non-SAP™ applications can communicate with the R/3™ Repository. SAP™ provides a complete infrastructure and a set of methods for the standardized operational integration third-party software products with the R/3™ Repository. In the future, the Repository will be accessed by graphics tools, dedicated CASE tools, and selected BPR tools, which should be able to store objects uniformly within the SAP system.

The key facets of Repository integration include business processes, business objects, business components, data models, and interfaces.

Business Processes

As discussed in Chapters 2 and 3, between 1990 and 1992, SAP™ developed the EPC method to specify a framework for the logical and graphical arrangement of business-process elements so that all participants could understand the processes better. It was particularly important to SAP™ that the process models could be read and analyzed by persons who were not involved in the modeling and that people from different professional qualifications and experiences would be able to communicate by using the Business Blueprint.

The EPC method represents business processes simply, comprehensibly, and at the same time unambiguously. The EPC describes the logical and chronological sequence of events and tasks (functions) or the events and processes. The

EPC method combines data, tasks, and organizations and thus is the central element in business-process engineering. For example, the task processing type and the transfer medium between consecutive tasks are significant in the business-process analysis. In particular, gaps in the business-process chain created by the change of media are often an indication of weak points in flow organization. Another important element in the EPC is the organizational assignment of tasks to the responsible parties or to the company organization units.

Department or position can be assigned to a process that enables either to be followed across several organizational units. Because organizational units are often created according to criteria other than the logical business-process structure for integrated task processing, counterproductive structures can be uncovered. Processes can be aggregated for analysis at different levels of detail.

The systematic specification of the process limits using "start" and "end" events allows processes to be documented as process components that have an internal and external structure. The internal structure shows the possible configurations of a process component. The user's functional requirements are identified by reduction and selection. SAP™ displays the functions that can be deactivated, while continuing to guarantee the performance of the process component. The external structure shows the possible combinations of available process components. Customer-oriented value chains (scenarios) are created by combining process components. The compatibility of the available process components is shown, thus providing a framework for the creation of commercially meaningful value chains.

SAP™ guarantees internal consistency and external compatibility with the process components in the Business Blueprint. The possible combinations are available in a process component library and are indicated by the start and end events that various process components have in common. In addition to navigation support, process paths provide graphical orientation. The 800-plus existing process components of the Business Blueprint have over 10,000 possible combinations. The customer chooses from among the available process components in the Process Library and arranges them in value chains according to his or her commercial requirements.

Business Objects

R/3™ contains more than 170 different SAP™ Business Objects documented in the Business Object Repository. BAPIs are provided by methods of SAP™ Business Objects and have various usages; for example, they also are the foundation of SAP™'s Internet strategy by providing high-level interfaces to R/3™'s mature functionality. In the future, BAPIs will contribute to the realization of component software by enabling object-oriented communication of R/3™ components.

An SAP™ Business Object consists of four layers. The first is a business object kernel, which contains the core business logic. The second layer contains constraints and business rules (responsible for integrity). The third layer contains the methods, attributes, input event control, and output events. The final layer is the access layer (COM/DCOM, CORBA, SAP™-RFC). SAP™ Business Objects implement standard object-oriented technology capabilities such as encapsulation, polymorphism, and inheritance.

SAP™ decided to introduce business objects in R/3™ that have key business meanings and that describe integrated business aspects of the system. Inherent complexity of the business is made manageable by introducing business encapsulation. Business Objects not only describe the business at a more abstract level but also introduce the behavior into the description. From the 4,000 data objects of the Enterprise Data Model, SAP™ identified the core SAP™ Business Objects that represent the central business logic of R/3™. Inasmuch as business objects should represent the world as the SAP™ user sees it, common Business Objects take the form of purchase orders, material, vendor, price condition, and so on.

There are a number of perceived benefits of business objects and object-orientation technology. They are as follows:

- Business objects promise to model the IT world in the terms and concepts of the real world.
- Business objects promise to increase the productivity of end users significantly because the culture clash between the "real" and IT worlds is supposed to vanish.
- Object orientation allows for plug-and-play with best-of-breed application components from diverse vendors because objects have well-defined (messaging) interfaces.
- Applications can be developed and maintained very efficiently with industry standard tools (Visual Basic (VB), for example).
- Object orientation allows for much higher scalability because the objects can easily be distributed and thus more computing power can be exploited.

SAP™'s primary objective of introducing business objects lies in representing business semantics. Based on experience and a thorough understanding of how the real business looks, the business can be modeled adequately in the IT world. The chosen approach, once again, is top-down. The real business world is the starting point, and the Business Objects are modeled and implemented as closely as possible to that world. Thus, solid and stable business objects can be used as building blocks for enterprise systems. Keeping the "artificial" IT world as close as possible to reality results in maximum flexibility and rapid adaptability to changes in the real business.

This approach contrasts to the common bottom-up approach of introducing object-orientation (OO) programming languages and trying to build business objects out of low-level technical objects. The introduction of OO programming languages must instead be the final step of applying OO technology in the area of enterprise business systems: the key and starting point is using "OO in the large" techniques—i.e., business objects—and from there on applying OO technologies down to the "OO in the small" level.

Data Models

Each business object has exactly one associated Data Model (the "Business Object Data Model") that describes the structure of the internal data of the business object. The purpose of this Data Model is to ease the understanding of the semantics of the business object.

Often, it is not easy to understand business objects just by looking at their description or interface (methods, attributes, events). Thus, a look at the internal data structures—which are at a more detailed level than the business objects themselves—can help in understanding the semantics of the related business object. Once at the detailed level of the Data Models, one can easily navigate to related entity types of the Enterprise Data Model and see the integration of the related business object data with other entity types, as described in Chapter 16.

In a data-oriented sense, business objects present an abstract level of information, whereas the Data Models describe the complete detailed integration information. The SAP™ Enterprise Data Model is a semantic data model describing the "real-world" data modeled in the R/3™ system in purely business terms. The real-world data is sorted into entity types and given unique definitions. Part of this activity is concerned with forming and reviewing concepts. There are relationships between the various entity types, and these relationships have business significance.

The basic modeling constructs are the entity type, the data model, the specialization type, and the relationship type.

Entity type—Entity types portray real-world objects (entities). They possess business significance and have characteristics that are defined by means of attributes. Entity types have counterparts in the R/3™ system. The correspondence may not necessarily be one-to-one, but usually it is. Several entity types can be grouped in one table.

Data model—Data models are used to structure entity relationship models, which can be highly complex. A data model groups other data models and/or a set of entity types to form a unity that is of practical business value. One example is the Purchasing data model, the content of which includes the Purchase Order data model and other entity types.

Specialization type—Generalization is the method of choice for grouping similar entity types that have common characteristics. The resultant entity type is then given a generalized name that is appropriate to its specialization (e.g., a purchase order is specialized as "vendor order" and "stock transport order").

Relationship type—Relationship types portray mutual relationships between entity types from the business perspective. Relationships are directional and lead from a start entity type (on the left) to a dependent entity type (to its right). Each entity type depends for existence on those to its left: the farther to the right it is, the greater its dependency.

Object-Oriented Interfaces

Object-oriented interfaces establish a new quality of interfacing between components. Up until now, a software module called another by its name and passed the parameters along. If the name of the to-be-called module or the interface parameter had to be changed because a slightly different function was applied, a reprogramming of all calling modules was unavoidable. Object-oriented interfacing tries to overcome this deficiency. All interface definitions are maintained in an "active" repository. The calling module consults the repository to negotiate the applicability of the desired interface (after having looked up an appropriate function). Then the calling module calls the to-be-called module with a surrogate name supplied by the repository. The repository then figures out the content and location of the function's actual implementation and calls it on behalf of the calling module. By means of this indirect calling sequence, a new level of exchangeability and flexibility is accomplished.

Standardized interfacing is the most important feature of the SAP™ Business Object architecture. Interface definitions can be pulled from the Business Object Repository. Then, standard object-oriented interfacing technologies such as COM/DCOM or CORBA can be deployed, even in a dynamic manner. This interoperability is bidirectional: external components can call R/3™ components and R/3™ components can call external components.

In combination with the interface inheritance and delegation support of the Business Object Repository, SAP™ Business Components can easily be enhanced or exchanged. If there is a need for a different custom-tailored behavior of an SAP™ Business Component that is not (yet) supported via R/3™'s customizing, a new component can be supplied by the customer and plugged in via the interface delegation mechanism of R/3™. With the help of the interface inheritance, SAP™ can supply new functionality without sacrificing support for the older functionality.

Business Components

In general, software components should have the following properties:

- Prefabrication—users should not be forced to change the coding of the component
- Preintegration—users should not be forced to develop (batch) bridge programs
- Ready-to-use—no technology obstacles should deter the immediate use of the component
- Customizable—components should be able to be customized to actual requirements
- Maintainable—components should be replaceable or upgradeable
- Scalable—components should be completely encapsulated (the user should have no indication that he is accessing a system external to R/3™ or vice versa).
- Use of published interfaces—components should have long-term, stable, public, standard interfaces
- Minimum infrastructure requirements—infrastructure requirements should be minimized to gain implementation and deployment speed

SAP™ Business Components are "good citizen" software components that have all of the above properties. These components make use of business objects and business processes as their elementary building blocks. Because they inherit all the interfacing capabilities of the business objects, they are as flexible as needed for businesses.

Business Components share a common design and have a common business understanding. They share a common business process, business object, and organizational model. They also have a common business infrastructure, which contains basic business rules such as factory calendar, multicurrency, and multi-country processing. They also share a common deployment and execution platform (based on industry standards), which enables the actual operation, including administration, management, and tuning, of the resulting business systems.

New levels of scalability and overall performance can be accomplished with the Business Components. Separated databases can better exploit high-end Symmetric Multiprocessing (SMP) as well as clustered medium-range SMP computers. A lower level of concurrency achieved via more asynchronous message-oriented communication allows for shorter response times. And overall additional performance improvements will enable larger R/3™ implementations than ever before.

SAP™ can deliver new functionality by adding new interfaces and keeping the old interfaces upward compatible. New functionality can be deployed without disruption of the executing business system. On the basis of the release-independent interface compatibility of SAP™ Business Components, R/3™ customers can deploy new functionality on an "as needed" basis by just exchanging the components they need.

Critical to SAP™ and its customers is the preservation of the integration of the separate SAP™ Business Components. In order to guarantee the all-time fit of its components, SAP™ develops the components internally and independently but integrates them already in the SAP™ software factory. Out of this integrated system, the separately deployable components will be tailored within SAP™'s Business Framework. Thus the levels of integration are guaranteed.

15.4   ENTERPRISE APPLICATION DEVELOPMENT

In 1994, SAP™ decided to package and market the technology behind the R/3™ business application as the ABAP/4 Development Workbench, a collection of programming tools designed to develop software. It was used either for extending and adding to R/3™ or for developing independent client/server applications.

The SAP™ software development environment is a collection of tools, components, facilities, and methods for creating software systems. These software engineering tools can be used to customize or extend the functionality of R/3™ or to develop completely new applications. The toolset supports the whole software development life cycle from specification to maintenance. Life-cycle spanning activities reflect organizational policies and procedures, such as quality management, project management, documentation, and prototyping. For a developer, that means a holistic solution for the complete software development life cycle.

Figure 15-2 illustrates how R/3™ has extended its functionality over the years and how it continues to expand.

ABAP/4 Development Workbench

The ABAP/4 Development Workbench includes the ABAP/4 4GL (SAP™'s own fourth-generation programming language—a cross-breed of COBOL and Pascal), editors, debuggers, function libraries, data dictionary, data models, process models, and a repository. The Development Workbench also has interfaces to CASE tools, business engineering tools, and other development systems. The product is designed to be used by programming teams—with a focus on UNIX and Windows NT—and has its own version control system and promotion system.

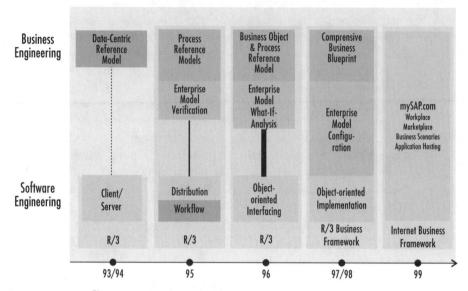

▶ Figure 15–2   SAP™ software development evolution

The Workbench allows users to focus on business problems, not on learning a new computing language. By means of these tools, an application can be built and run across a wide range of user interfaces, data managers, networks, operating systems, and machine platforms.

Users can select the modules they need from the wide range of products available, customize the functionality to meet their own specific requirements, and adapt it to new business procedures when required. The development tools include an extensive library of predefined business functions that can be easily inserted into new programs. This saves the programmer from having to reinvent the wheel, thus boosting both productivity and quality. Network communication also stays completely hidden from the application programmer's view.

The ABAP/4 DW's design promotes database-independent applications. It consists of a three-tier client/server architecture with a database server, application server, and a presentation server (see Chapter 14). Using ABAP/4, developers need not concern themselves with database access, GUI presentation, or splitting the application across dedicated servers. Thus, programs are source-code compatible across the platforms that are supported. The development environment creates multilanguage applications—including Japanese—making international applications possible.

The ABAP/4 Development Workbench can manage a large number of transactions as well as support environments with guaranteed data integrity, high availability, and transaction rates. It also takes advantage of specialized performance characteristics of different hardware platforms and operating systems. Without any substantial changes, an application can run under Windows, Macintosh, OSF/Motif, and Presentation Manager. Other major benefits of this three-tier architecture include:

- Splitting of applications across servers
- Specialized toolset for large development projects
- Open remote function calls from other systems
- Application portability across data managers
- Presentation on leading GUIs
- Reliable transaction management

Development Workbench Features

ABAP/4 DW is a comprehensive software system. Developers often prefer the integrated nature of its tools and the strength of its debugging and reporting. The Repository (see Table 15-1) is seamlessly linked with other components such as Screen Painter and Program Editor, making database access convenient. SAP™'s concept for life-cycle support of applications is implementation oriented. CASE facilities (data, function, and process modeling) are available through an interface to the Repository (in development). In addition, SAP™ has data models, function models, and business analysis software in the Business Engineer. SAP™ offers a graphical tool for data modeling, but it is hardly a complete CASE tool. SAP™ plans to support some type of standard CASE interchange format in the Repository API.

ABAP/4 DW consists of an application development environment and a run-time environment. The product features the following key areas:

- Programmer productivity
- Integrated development environment
- Reporting
- Maintainability
- Client/server development and deployment
- Interface building

ABAP/4 DW is a repository-based environment that facilitates application development and supports large teams. It has an interface-building tool for GUIs. GUI support is biased toward Windows and Motif. OS/2 Presentation Manager and Macintosh are supported, but not with the same level of functionality (e.g., graphics). Character mode is not supported. The Workbench contains strong debugging and testing tools, a version control system, performance analysis tools, a promotion system, and an integrated data model.

At the center of the development environment is the ABAP/4 Repository, which contains descriptive information—for example, formats and type—about the applications. The Screen Painter, a tool for creating GUIs, can access the Repository to get information about tables or groups of tables, regardless of their physical location. The Program Editor is also tightly integrated with the Repository. When a particular table name is used, developers can browse through it with a double-click from the editor. ABAP/4 DW has a powerful cross-reference facility for tracking usage of program and data objects.

ABAP/4's logical databases contain hierarchical, structured information about tables and control functions for manipulating data and processing reports. The 4GL ABAP/4 enables reporting and has many specialized language constructs. There is also an end-user tool (Query) that allows the user to make simple reports.

A testing tool features the ability to check the results of a run with predetermined input data against previous runs and/or user-supplied correct input data (including regression tests). This kind of test can be run with several sets of input data, and different functions of a function group can be run in a different sequence; for example, for testing the state of the function group.

For performance tuning, the user can analyze the resource consumption of his program, drilling down to a particular statement (e.g., SELECT), get the exact times spent in each part of the program at different levels of detail, trace database accesses, analyze cache hit rates, get a display of system activities, and so on.

The ABAP/4 DW provides not only a platform for developing client/server applications but also a development system that is itself a client/server application. Scalability is a key feature supported by the ABAP/4 DW. Also, assigning the correct size to an application presents little difficulty because applications written in ABAP/4 are portable to a wide range of machines.

Table 15-1 summarizes the main features of the Development Workbench.

Table 15–1   Features of the ABAP Development Workbench

Feature	Description
Application Debugger	Facilities for locating and correcting errors in application logic or data handling; tracking for flow of control in an application; easy means of checking program procedures; remote debugging
Database Access	Variety of database maintenance tasks; useful for initially building an application database

Table 15–1 Features of the ABAP Development Workbench (Continued)

Feature	Description
Data Modeler and Enterprise Data Model	Subdivided into models for individual R/3™ applications; models can be shown either as graphic symbols or as text; graphic models always depicted in same, standardized structure; easy for users; can be easily changed
Development Organizer	Meets all requirements for "team management"; development environment includes complete management of all releases and versions
4th Generation Language Code Generation	High-level application development language; basis for SAP™ applications; integrated architecture together with the ABAP/4 Dictionary and individual development tools; structured programming; portable compiling language; program development supported by prototyping
Function Library	Facility to develop and deploy an application rapidly in numerous languages; translation modules; business graphics
Online Help	Implemented for all features including language reference; portable; runs without modification across all environments; Windows help
Performance Monitors	Monitoring and measurement of user activity, resource usage, and database status
Report Builder	Graphical tool for designing production reports; report templates; ABAP/4 statements
Repository and Data Dictionary	Facilities to create and maintain definitions, application defaults, and business rules; centrally stored data definitions; support for analysis and design tools; objects (screens, menus, programs, tables, data definitions) maintained and stored in repository
Screen Painter/Menu Painter	GUIs created by allowing user to make menus and function key assignments for applications
User Interface Builder	Tool for screens, menus, and dialogs; control for user/application interaction; graphical development and deployment capabilities
Version Control, Promotion Model	Promotion of applications from development, testing to production; versioning of individual development objects; allows changes to be off-loaded and recaptured
Workbench	Ability to build, modify, and test all application components quickly; direct user activation of debugger; dictionary online help for integration of all applications; development objects in form of a structured list

15.5   CONCLUSION

A critical ingredient in business engineering is the ability to accommodate continuous change. Unlike geographical maps, which portray information that is relatively static and stable over time, the "maps" or IT models of businesses are in a constant state of flux and need to be continually reconfigured to respond to factors such as company growth, changing market conditions and customer demands, and pressures from competition.

Because business conditions continually change, it makes little sense for companies to use new information technology as a one-time vehicle in BE. For example, a company may choose to shape its processes to suit a particular market segment, customer group, or product line. But if these choices are irrevocably built into the system or cannot be easily changed, the company will find itself confined by its own processes and unable to adapt its information system to meet new needs. The solution to this problem is for IT software to be designed to accommodate the ongoing changes that occur within organizations.

Over the years, companies have found it necessary to customize R/3™ applications to suit their specific needs. The need for customization created a niche for the creation of new SAP™ applications, an increased market for third-party applications. What evolved from these developments is the R/3™ Business Engineer, a broad vision for application manufacturing, which we will examine further in the next chapter.

The combination of the programming capabilities of the ABAP/4 Development Workbench with the openness of the R/3™ Repository and the continuous BE potential of the Business Engineer provides a complete infrastructure and framework for assembling applications at the customer's site. This infrastructure grants the customers a large number of "configurations"—that is, the ability to change an application to meet specific deployment needs—to respond to changes in their business environment, such as a new global distribution channel, corporate structure, or personnel reorganization. By virtue of these software developments, SAP™'s application-manufacturing framework for configuring enterprise applications spans services, software development, and business engineering. SAP™ coined the phrase "configure to order" for describing this framework.

Ultimately, this chapter has revealed the underpinnings of SAP™'s Business Framework, a concept that attempts to serve as a basis for integration with other vendors' products. The next chapter looks at how the Business Framework and Business Engineer function together.

16

Business Engineering in R/3™

In BE, the focus of IT implementation expands from simply managing all of a company's transactions to fully optimizing the transactions themselves for the benefit of the company and its customers. Software is used to describe, simulate, and model organizations and to consider how changes made to the organizations affect processes. The organizational structures of the business processes—representing the actual business transactions and communications conducted by the company—are mapped into the architecture of the information system. The system thus includes a working description of how things are done in the company, including the flow of information and communication as well as information about the company's tasks and functional structure. A well-integrated information system not only improves overall business operations but also makes it easier for the company to identify areas for further improvement.

Although companies can gain much efficiency from optimizing their business processes, until recently, many found themselves in a predicament after embarking on BPR. After critically reviewing their existing business processes, many companies completely discarded them and then created new process designs. The costs inherent in reinventing processes were often miscalculated, and the risks of not finding a software solution to match the new process design were also very high. After expending a lot of capital implementing tools and systems, many companies had to throw out much of their process design work, primarily because their information system software could not adequately support the new design.

SAP™ recognized that the solution to this problem is model-driven configure-to-order. In configure-to-order, models of business processes offer predefined functionality as a foundation, and companies change the parameters of the models as needed to set up their customized information system. Because this approach eliminates the need to start from scratch in process design, it not only greatly simplifies and expedites IT implementation but also enables companies to rapidly adapt the information system in response to changing business conditions.

The R/3™ Business Engineer supports model-driven configuration of the R/3™ system by providing sample business objects and business processes that reflect the best-business practices in successful companies. These can either be used "as is" or extended and customized by a company to suit its individual needs. These predefined processes are supplied in the comprehensive Business Blueprint, which is provided in the Business Engineer.

With the Business Blueprint, companies can quickly map their business requirements into the information system, use processes already proven to work in the system, and then make modifications as needed. Thus, the underlying architecture of the software supports business modeling both in the initial process design or redesign stages and in phased implementations. This approach is the most effective way for companies to minimize their risks and optimize their results when undertaking business engineering.

16.1   R/3™ BUSINESS ENGINEER OVERVIEW

The Business Engineer is a new platform for planning and configuration applications. Business Engineer tools support initial implementation of integrated process chains and allow for ongoing postconfiguration as business needs change. These capabilities permit step-by-step enhancement and extension of the business application areas where R/3™ is used. The Business Engineer functions as a customer-specific business application repository that accompanies a customer's implementation of the R/3™ system throughout its life cycle.

A set of tools, technologies, and methodologies, the Business Engineer is designed to assist a company in changing from a traditionally structured organization to an information-oriented one. The main goal of this process is to streamline the implementation of enterprise application deployment. Figure 16-1 illustrates the Business Engineer elements discussed in this chapter.

The Business Engineer emphasizes those tasks related to planning, understanding, and implementing R/3™ in an organization. It is developed and used by SAP™ sites in consulting projects and implementation initiatives such as Accelerated SAP™ (ASAP) R/3™ implementation. The Business Engineer is an effective set of business-engineering tools supporting process analysis, design, and configuration. These tools have improved significantly SAP™'s implementation procedures and process optimization.

Having the ability to create models coincides with some of the traditional aims of CASE vendors (see Chapter 2). But more important is that SAP™ offers

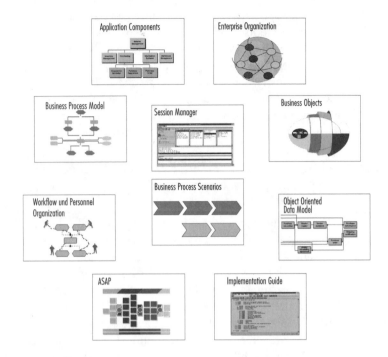

▶ **Figure 16–1**   Overview of the parts of the R/3™ Business Engineer

its blueprint as a descriptive—but not necessarily normative—solution for every customer. Customers can create or extend the blueprint with a number of different tools. The Business Engineer offers:

- A business tool in a client/server architecture that contains descriptive model information about the SAP™ application
- A family of browsers to help users understand the underlying application
- An impact analysis of certain models with other parts of the R/3™ implementation process
- An entry point into the application development process
- A comprehensive, live model of the enterprise that serves as a foundation for configuring R/3™
- Tools for navigating and configuring an R/3™ system
- Methodologies for modeling the enterprise and implementing R/3™
- A template model for starting R/3™ implementation projects
- An open R/3™ Repository API that enables R/3™ to be integrated easily with legacy, current, and future systems

As an open application with internationally accepted standards, the Business Engineer and its components can be used with third-party tools. The Blueprint's standards allow the distribution of SAP ™'s products with other partners and modeling with other vendors' products.

The Business Engineer supports the full range of BE activities by means of an integrated toolset that accesses the R/3 ™ Repository, which is the central container for R/3 ™'s application information, including the Business Blueprint.

16.2 BUSINESS ENGINEER AND STREAMLINED IMPLEMENTATIONS

The benefits of using the Business Engineer and ASAP include faster, streamlined implementations, primarily because customers can use the provided models and default settings as a foundation and then configure their requirements to order. New R/3 ™ users gain a head start on implementing R/3 ™ because the provided models are reliable, and they can quickly map their unique requirements into R/3 ™, performing only those customization activities that are needed at each phase of R/3 ™ implementation (see Chapter 3). Using the Business Engineer, R/3 ™ customers can achieve early and continual returns on their investments. In fact, a 1996 study by the Yankee Group in Boston, Massachusetts found that the Business Engineer reduced system configuration times by as much as 40 to 50 percent.

The Business Engineer enables corporate business analysts or system designers as well as consultants and specialized application developers to perform R/3 ™ implementation tasks. Figure 16-2 illustrates the online selection screen for the hierarchy of process models in the R/3 ™ Reference Model.

The Business Engineer also frees business consultants to spend more time on higher level business design issues rather than on implementation details. Implementation experts are then freed to leverage their business knowledge in a more efficient manner. With better access to R/3 ™ information and the ability to integrate the Business Blueprint with their own consulting methodologies, consultants can become more productive, thereby providing better value to customers and enhancing their position as advisors on BE with R/3 ™.

The Business Engineer is actively connected to the customer's R/3 ™ system; that is, users interact with the Business Engineer online rather than operating it in a standalone environment. Companies can set up the enterprise by configuring models, then test the design "live" within the R/3 ™ system to verify that it operates at all desired levels. Moreover, business objects, processes, organization, workflow, distribution, and the underlying data are all integrated in the Business Blueprint, and users can view, configure, and customize them with online tools. Users browse or navigate from one view of the Business Blueprint

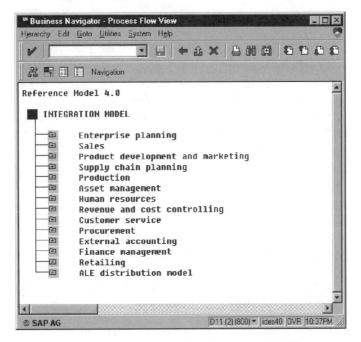

▶ **Figure 16–2**   Business process scenarios in the R/3 Reference Model

to another by using the GUI, configure the running R/3 ™ system by selecting parameters with a graphical implementation guide, and view running transactions to verify that the system operates according to the company's needs.

Users can navigate anywhere in the Business Blueprint. For example, they can proceed from a process model into a workflow and then into an organization. Users can even drill down through business objects and business processes to view underlying data structures. Finally, the Business Engineer also provides an open API to the central repository of R/3 ™ that greatly simplifies and speeds the building of interfaces that connect R/3 ™ to external systems.

Section 16.3 explains how the Business Engineer helps deploy an R/3 ™ system in the following areas: enterprise organization, blueprinting, and implementation support.

16.3   *MODELING THE DISTRIBUTED ENTERPRISE*

Using the Business Engineer, customers have access to the Business Blueprint and its set of predefined processes, which serve as the company's starting point for business engineering through model-driven configuration. A comprehensive design, the Business Blueprint is key to achieving efficient R/3™ deployments.

As we have seen, the blueprint contains views of the enterprise, including sample business objects and business processes that reflect the best-practices in successful companies (see Chapter 2). Included in the Business Blueprint as a foundation for the customer's application are more than 170 core business objects—purchase orders, sales orders, bills of materials, and so on—and over 800 process models. They are configured and populated with company data through the use of Business Engineer tools. The Business Blueprint is actively linked to the R/3™ application being installed. For example, a customer can use the Business Engineer to select a certain function within a purchasing model and see the associated transaction live.

As discussed earlier, the more than 800 predefined business processes in the Business Engineer were created using the EPC process description language, a unique methodology for graphically defining and displaying business systems. Users work in an understandable graphical environment to add their own company-specific details to the predefined processes. Graphical portrayal of business processes helps users understand how data flow through business areas and shows how various company functions interact with each other. Because any breaks in the chains of tasks and responsibilities are graphically illustrated, potential areas for optimizing the business become especially clear.

Other methodologies supported in the Business Engineer enable users to graphically perform object modeling, organization modeling (setting up both organizations and the distributed enterprise), and workflow modeling. These methodologies include data modeling, the Procedure Model, and the Organization Architect. Data modeling is supported through structured entity-relationship modeling. A graphical project management model provides a complete on-line solution for implementing R/3™. The Procedure Model is an active implementation system that helps users step-by-step through the selections of setting up R/3™, and it can export information about an implementation project to third-party tools, such as Microsoft Project or Word. The Organization Architect is a graphical modeling tool that sets up the division of tasks in a distributed enterprise. The Organization Architect uses Application Link Enabling (ALE) to link R/3™ applications in geographically separate locations and to facilitate communication between independent systems, such as between SAP™ R/2™ and R/3™ systems and between SAP™ and non-SAP™ systems.

Application Components

The Business Engineer centers on application components and broad business process "value chains," which consist of application areas or business modules.

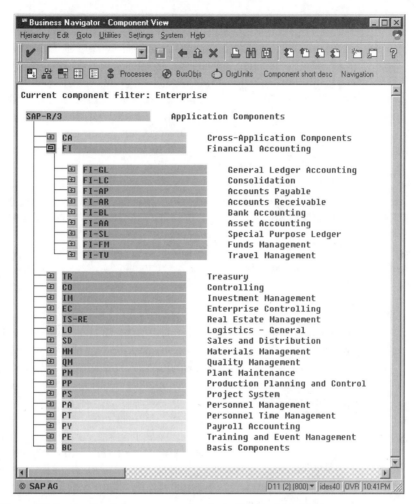

▶ **Figure 16–3**   Application component view in the R/3 Business Engineer

The application components act as a consistent aid to navigation, describing all logical parts with uniform terminology. Within the application components, multiple levels describe the complete R/3™ application, as shown in Figure 16-3. For example, the application components can permit navigation down to "purchase requisition creation" to see which processes, object models, and data models are involved in the procedure.

The key to understanding and designing processes is having an information base that shows the comprehensive conceptual structure of many business processes. The description of the process is important, as is the way the processes can be used by customers and consultants for business analysis, reengineering, and implementation projects. This information base contains the relationships among business events, business functions, business objects, and organizational units, all of which can be evaluated from different perspectives.

Business engineering tools require application components for a structural view of the enterprise application. A business engineer can find and isolate the part of the application that is related to his or her current scope of interest. For example, in the area of financial accounting, the decision maker can use the Legal Consolidation component to locate associated processes. From the process model, the decision maker can then see the organizational data and business object views available in Legal Consolidation.

Although most users do not want to change the underlying data, they can drill down directly from the object deeper into the system. Navigating from the business object view to the data model of that business object enables users to see and understand the underlying tables, fields, and data elements. From this point, a user can also navigate into the particular elements that use that data across the system.

Session Manager

The Session Manager is the part of the R/3 ™ Business Engineer that determines the actual presentation of R/3 ™ on the desktop. An innovative Windows application that manages work sessions with R/3 ™, the product makes it easier to work with R/3 ™ than having multiple windows open. Figure 16-4 illustrates the Session Manager user interface.

The main features of the Session Manager include:

- Icon or text display of the main menus in R/3 ™ (these relate to the application components)
- Display of submenus within multiple columns or subwindows (similar to File Manager)
- Three modes of component configuration: user specific, company specific, and global
- Interfaces to SAP ™'s R/3 ™ security profile
- A workbench that can contain shortcuts to R/3 ™ processes
- Internet browser compatibility in R/3 ™ Release 4.5

The main idea behind the Session Manager is that the brunt of R/3 ™ functionality is seldom borne by any one individual. Furthermore, the manageability of R/3 ™ sessions and multiple windows is at times difficult. With a tab-control window, essentially all information is clearly presented. By offering an alternative to the Windows-native GUI management, Session Manager simplifies the way

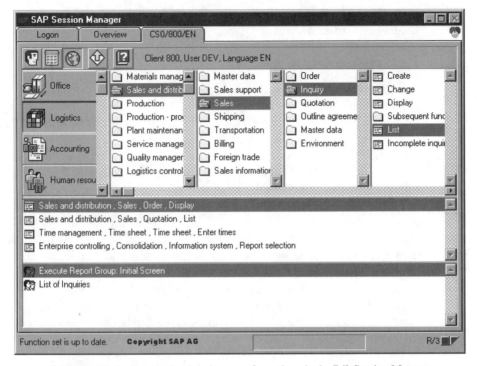

▶ **Figure 16–4**   Personalized desktop configuration via the R/3 Session Manager

in which end users will see their particular configuration. In many ways, Session Manager is the most obvious place to visualize the "configure to order."

Configurations are done with the application component. In the global mode, all components are offered and any transaction can be executed (permission and security checks applied). This feature is important for system administrators and developers. In the company-specific mode, only the configuration that is valid for the company exists. The information about the components is taken from the enterprise implementation guide (see Section 16.5), which publishes the information about the current configuration. Only business processes that were activated from the Business Blueprint can be transacted. Lastly, in the user mode, the parts of R/3™ available to the logged-in customer appear in the Session Manager. This mode greatly simplifies the way R/3™ works because the customer only has to deal with his or her own usage domain. Other business processes do not appear. The Session Manager knows how to read the information from R/3™ when the person logs in to the system.

Session Manager is a core part of the Business Engineer and SAP™'s Desktop ERP (see Chapter 17) initiative, because, for many, visualizing and simplifying is the first step toward streamlining and implementation, the overall goals of the Business Engineer.

Enterprise Organization

A key component of the Business Engineer is the enterprise organization. SAP™ has pioneered a highly graphical support tool for understanding underlying structures, such as purchasing organization, sales organization, or cost center in R/3™.

Now that the window of opportunity has been opened for distributed business processing, R/3™ Release 4.5 includes new functionality for modeling organizational units across R/3™ system boundaries. SAP™ addresses the logistics of distributed business processing by means of its ALE architecture, which heavily influences the modeling procedure. Organizational units can now be modeled and assigned to their respective geographic locations regardless of system boundaries. Customers can model their organizational structures with SAP™'s Distributed Architect, which shows a map of the world and the locations of the customer's plants, sales organizations, and SAP™ company codes. Customers can use the map to determine which functions should be included in which organizational units and how the functions can be integrated into a distributed environment using ALE. Figure 16-5 shows the relationship between the organizational system structure in R/3™ and the company or enterprise organization.

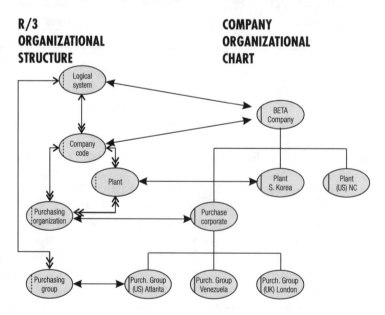

▶ **Figure 16–5**　Mapping the ERP structure to the business organization with the Business Engineer

Processes are an integral part of organizations. Once a company has determined what processes it uses and what steps are required to implement R/3™, these processes are transformed into the company's organizational structure. To meet process goals, a company must have the ability to model organizational structures and represent tasks, resources, qualifications, and so forth. These can be modeled with SAP™ organizational management, which illustrates a company's organizational units, positions, jobs, workplaces, and people.

16.4   USING THE R/3™ REFERENCE MODEL

As described previously, the Business Blueprint is a compilation of over 800 processes that represent vast business experience, especially in the areas of consulting and development. As SAP™ developed Release 3.0, two main goals served as a touchstone: first, to integrate the Reference Model with the data model (the data model having always been part of the SAP™ system) and second, to integrate the Reference Model with the data model with the R/3™ system itself so that they could be addressed by other tools in the ABAP/4 Development Workbench.

The Business Blueprint models clarify functions and processes and identify inconsistencies, redundancies, and areas requiring data processing support. By using the Blueprint, customers can compare and organize their requirements in a simple, standardized manner. These models are then used as the basis for further project work in R/3™.

The Business Engineer helps users work their way through R/3™ with clear business language, rather than with technical jargon. The Business Engineer also employs online graphics to map the processes, configurations, and variations in R/3™. The tool's versatility provides a key ingredient in customizing R/3™ into a powerful information technology system. By selecting and adjusting the model data, a user can determine the scope and content of the actions to be performed within a chosen process. The ability to navigate through the variety of model types and collect information about the process design are essential for understanding the business models behind R/3™.

Business Object Model

More and more information technology organizations are planning to spend increasing amounts of money on object technology. The four main reasons for the rising interest in object technology are increased productivity, faster development, better quality, and easier maintainability. An object model, in SAP™ terminology, shows the relationships among the business objects in a particular application component.

In addition to object modeling or classification, any object architecture should take into account business rules and methods for interobject communication within that architecture and should incorporate standard methods for accessing such objects from outside. SAP™ has designed its communication methods from the outset both for internal use within the SAP™ system and external access using OLE (COM) or Common ORB Architecture (CORBA).

Business objects themselves contain data models, one option for accessing them. There are also new data models that describe how business objects interact, providing a much more detailed level of data modeling than is possible with the current Entity Relationship Model. In other words, users can now navigate through the data models across several levels, starting with a business area—purchasing, for example—viewing the most important data objects used in that area and then expanding them to the finest detail permitted by the data models.

Business objects can be explained in terms of reference, process, and data models within the SAP™ system. One example of an SAP™ business object is a purchase order, which refers to other business objects from sales, such as purchasing, customer, and order type.

A business object view permits business engineers to locate particular areas where the focus of their analysis can be improved by capturing functionality and data in the Business Blueprint. Business objects provide not only a higher level of understanding of business process but also the ability to "specialize" business objects, making them reusable and productive parts of system planning.

Business objects operate on messages from other systems. The messages are then cataloged in the Business Object Repository (see Figure 16-6). Using the clearly structured, externally published data structure, the messages then flow into a type of workflow system within the SAP™ system, where they are either processed automatically, assigned to a work list, or channeled into a semiautomatic processing system with exception handling. The business objects are specially structured to allow for these types of workflow processes.

Object-Oriented Data Model

Early in the R/3™ development cycle, data models were used extensively to communicate the structure and business semantics of database tables. The first releases of R/3™ were shipped with SAP™'s enterprise data model. This model has become crucial to all subsequent enhancements: Each time an enhancement is made, careful consideration is given to whether the data models should be changed or whether enhancements should be implemented as add-ons. Customers can see whether the data model is technically capable of covering their specific requirements, and, if not, how it could be enhanced for such purposes.

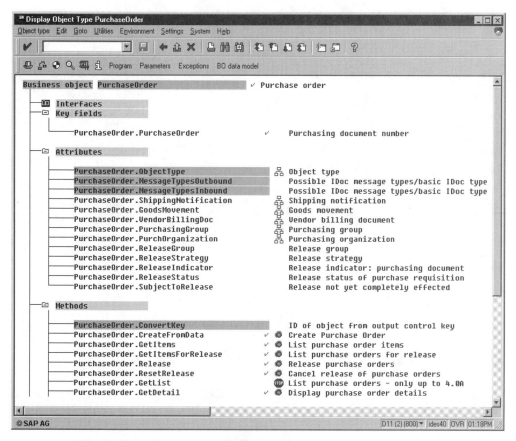

▶ **Figure 16–6**   The business object model via the Business Object Repository

The enterprise data model, however, is so detailed that only a handful of specialists know it really well. It can be said to resemble an expert system that represents information in abstract "chip form" without telling users how specific chips function or how they can be used. Data models are created with the aim of formally illustrating the data needed to perform business functions within a larger context that spans multiple functions. SAP™'s data model portrays relevant information objects and their relationships with one another from a business standpoint, doing so in the form of a structured entity-relationship model.

The entity types are representations of real-world objects that have significance in a business context and correspond to something within the R/3™ system. Relationships among the entity types are, like foreign-key relationships, classified on the basis of their type and cardinality. Entity types can also be broken down further into specialized subtypes. An extensive enterprise data model-

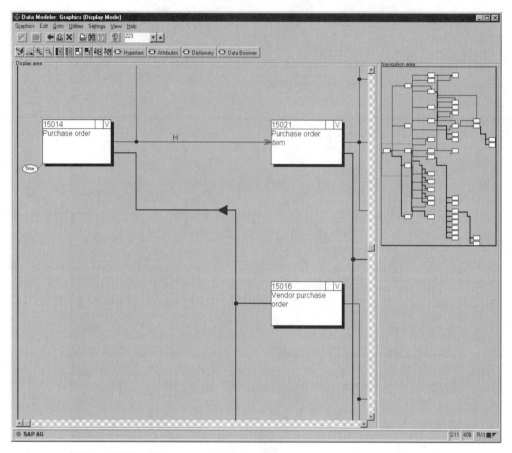

▶ **Figure 16–7**   Object oriented data model

ing tool helps define the objects that are central to a company's business processes and helps locate the dependencies and relationships between these objects. Take, for example, the Business Object purchase order. In order to understand the content of the object, an "object-oriented" data model shows the data relationship at a high level of abstraction, as illustrated in Figure 16-7.

Business Process Model

The language and methodology for describing business process modeling in the R/3 ™ system, EPCs depict business information systems for the benefit of users, managers, and consultants. When companies are faced with the complexities of planning a business information concept, however, different issues require different analyses of aspects of the business. To fill this need, the R/3™ system also produces EPCs that focus on various aspects of a business interaction. These include functional views, organizational views, information-flow views, and data views (see Chapter 2 for a more complete illustration of these views). Each view answers a distinct question about the interaction of business processes. The process view is the central view, which then incorporates each of their views.

Before a company begins the challenge of modeling new business processes, R/3™'s blueprints act as a guide to reassess current processes. By using the Business Blueprints, the company can compare customer requirements and organize them in a simple, standardized manner. These models then are used as the basis for further project work in R/3™.

Figure 16-8 shows how the R/3 Business Engineer has full access to the process models contained in R/3.

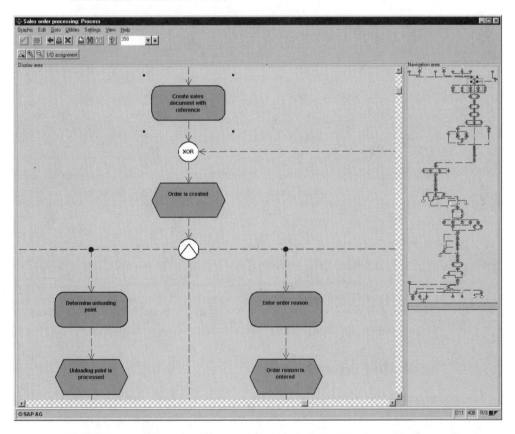

▶ **Figure 16–8**   Business process models, such as Sales Order Processing, are depicted as EPC diagrams in the R/3 Businenss Engineer

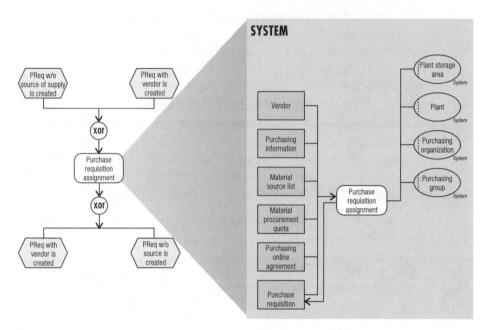

▶ **Figure 16–9** Process model view of different business internals

Process Models can also be useful in interactive prototyping since they are connected with a live system, as shown in Figure 16-9. The process model templates in the SAP R/3 system also have a link to the operational system (Figure 16-10).

The next view is that of a value chain. A value chain, illustrated in Figure 16-11, is made up of the most important, available process chains and shows how they flow through different parts of the company, connecting the process chains to one another. Value chains are deemed important by the value they bring to the company (more money, better customer service, more efficient employees, etc.). The more detailed view of the blueprint shows even more process chains and connections to different application components and departments.

Workflow Model

Workflow is just one way of tailoring the standard R/3 ™ system to customers' specific requirements. Each time the SAP ™ system is installed, the standard SAP ™ processes have to be adjusted to cover the customer's needs as effectively

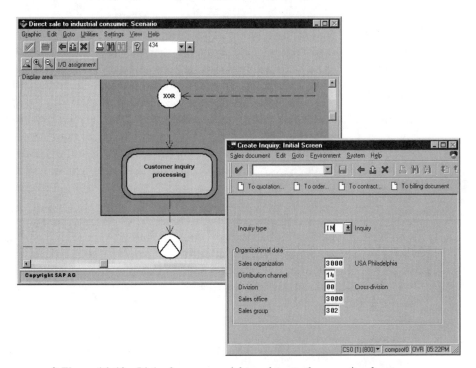

▶ **Figure 16–10** Link of process model templates to the operational system

▶ **Figure 16–11** The value chain shows how process integrate many aspects of a business, in this case, production by lot size

as possible. The system can also be configured—that is, the system parameters can be set with customizing objects. To a certain degree, customizing objects can be seen as a second type of object architecture that exists alongside the typical business objects and enables the customer to control the SAP ™ process chains. Figure 16-12 illustrates a workflow model for a requisition item release.

For example, the customizing objects specify how the process chains are viewed and contain default parameter settings. When creating customizing objects, it is important to specify the design of the GUI for maintaining customizing objects, identify any object relationships that have to be taken into account, and work out the ways in which customizing objects can be transported from test systems to production systems or from a template or master installation to distributed installations.

Associated with workflow is the dynamic model of the enterprise organization. The R/3 ™ approach is to interlace workflow and the personnel organization with tasks. These tasks map the organization and workflow so that a process can always be correctly executed in whatever organization exists at that time. Workflow and personnel use the same type of information basis and repository items to accomplish this.

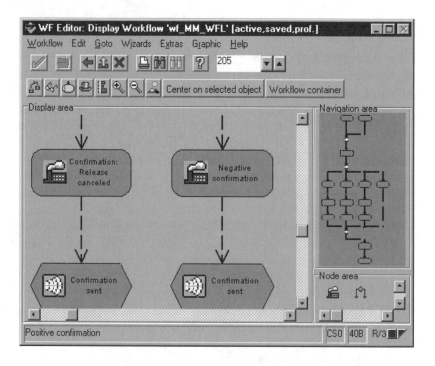

▶ **Figure 16–12**   Workflow model for requisition release in R/3 repository

16.5   GUIDELINE FOR IMPLEMENTING R/3[TM]

The implementation guide or Implementation Management Guide (IMG), a detailed, on-line method of customizing the R/3[TM] system, is used during the design and implementation phases. For each business application, the IMG explains all the steps in the implementation process, offers the SAP[TM] standard (factory) settings, describes system configuration work (activities), and opens the activities interactively.

Four levels of the IMG are available:

- SAP[TM] Reference IMG—Contains documentation on all the business application components supplied by SAP[TM]
- Enterprise IMG—A subset of the SAP[TM] Reference IMG that contains documentation only for the components selected for implementation
- Project IMGs—Enterprise IMG subsets that contain only the documentation for Enterprise IMG components selected for implementation for particular customizing projects
- Upgrade Customizing IMGs—based either on the Enterprise IMG or on a Project IMG; shows, for a given release upgrade, all the documents linked to a release note

Regardless of the view selected, the IMG lists all of the steps needed to implement R/3[TM], supports documentation and control during implementation, and provides users with a note function that will later maintain their project documentation in the IMG. The complete version of the IMG contains guidelines for all the business applications available in the system. The functional view of the IMG is created when users choose which functions they want to use from the different applications. The resulting function-specific implementation guide includes the exact steps involved in the selected functions. With this guide, users get a smaller, individually tailored version of the complete guide. Of note is the fact that the function view of the IMG exists only once in the system, although the project documentation will remain intact. When a new function guide for another application is created, it replaces the first function-specific IMG.

Customizing objects is the basis for the R/3[TM] configuration procedure. This procedure in turn is described in detail in the IMG. The IMG contains complete instructions for establishing every possible setting in the SAP[TM] system, so that it covers all imaginable processes and models. But the SAP[TM] system is so large—the functionality of Release 4.5 takes it much further than ever before—that in addition to describing each possible setting completely, SAP[TM] has also had to address a second problem: the need for a procedure to reduce to the absolute minimum the number of settings required by any one enterprise. SAP[TM] has designated this process as "filtering," a process that enables SAP™ to produce an individual configuration guide for each customer from the basic IMG.

16.6   *PROJECT MANAGEMENT PROCEDURE MODEL*

The implementation model is a tool for preliminary planning of R/3™ implementation or customizing projects. The model gives a comprehensive overview of how to implement R/3™, including steps for organizing the project, coming up with a target concept and a detailed design, preparing for production, and starting production.

SAP™ experience has shown that for most customers, the best way to implement R/3™ is gradually. There are two areas in which trade-offs are required: the complexity of the system and the speed of the implementation. It is vitally important for customers to perform procedure-based, phased implementations. Procedure-based implementations need to be carried out gradually. This process entails first identifying the most important business processes (with a view to production operation), refining them, and finally, activating other less important processes in one or two phases as necessary.

For each phase of the implementation, there is a set procedure. The goal of this procedure is supporting a lean implementation. In other words, companies should create a procedure that does not make too many demands initially yet still addresses all important considerations. For example, a procedure may entail taking into account the actual system environment, integrating legacy systems, and transferring data from such systems. Such a procedure is a big help for individual customers, who can then create the system environment independently. To a certain extent, the procedure is also a benchmark for the various methods offered by other consulting partners. In the future, consulting partners should be able to develop their own implementation methods, but they will still require a point of reference—the SAP™ Procedure Model—which customers will be able to use themselves to differentiate between essential and nonessential (or secondary) functions.

These steps are organized into four project phases: organization and design, detailed design and implementation, preparation for production startup, and production. The recommended phases describe which activities need to be carried out to implement R/3™. In recent versions of R/3™, the Procedure Model has been replaced by a more modern "roadmap" in ASAP (see Figure 16-7).

16.7   ACCELERATEDSAP™

AcceleratedSAP™ (ASAP) is SAP™'s comprehensive implementation solution for streamlining R/3™ projects. It is the process component of TeamSAP and was introduced in June 1996 and released for worldwide availability in June 1997. It is continuously being improved and updated by an international consulting team that collects very detailed feedback from SAP™ customers who already use it. ASAP optimizes time, quality, and efficient use of resources.

AcceleratedSAP™tackles the implementation and on-going optimization of R/3™. The similarity to the common abbreviation for "as soon as possible" is, of course, no coincidence. Offering comprehensive, front-to-back support with tools, recommendations, and checklists, it has all the answers to questions such as:

- How much will my project cost and how long will it take?
- How do I go about the implementation?
- How can I insure quality?
- What tools can I use?

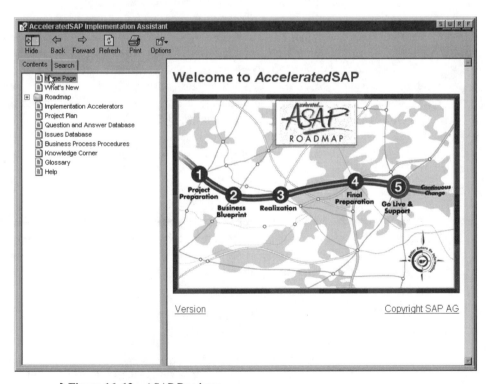

▶ **Figure 16–13**   ASAP Roadmap

ASAP bundles the expertise gleaned from R/3 implementation projects carried out over the past five years. ASAP offers the best from these experiences, process-orientation throughout, and a streamlined implementation procedure. In addition to the implementation tools contained in the R/3 Business Engineer, ASAP offers templates, checklists, and examples, which normally must be created from scratch for every project. It includes a project plan in Microsoft Project®, and templates in PowerPoint® or Word® that cover all the issues typically dealt with by the steering committee, for example. While experienced consultants have such documents in hand, first time R/3 implementators likely do not. ASAP focuses on the coordination of all elements that help make an implementation successful.

The Roadmap

The Roadmap is a project plan with detailed descriptions about what, why, and how certain activities are performed. It describes all activities in an implementation, makes sure that nothing is left out, and that project management plans well in advance for the execution of end-user training, for example. The Roadmap also includes the entire technical area to support technical project management and addresses things like interfaces, data conversions, and authorizations earlier than in most traditional implementations. It even includes printer setup that often proved to be difficult in the past. The Roadmap contains descriptions about what and why SAP™ does certain things (see Figure 16-13). Wherever possible, ASAP provides examples, checklists, or templates as samples; for example, for a cutover plan. These samples, called Accelerators, are used as a starting point to avoid "reinventing the wheel." They are used in any type of implementation, even when customers do not use all ASAP elements.

Tools

Tools include ASAP-specific tools to support project management, questionnaires for the business process consultants, and numerous technical guidebooks and checklists. The backbone in the R/3™ system is, of course, the Business Engineer with all of its configuration tools.

R/3™ Services and Training

R/3™ Services and Training includes all consulting, education, and support services, such as the hotline, EarlyWatch, remote upgrade, archiving, and so forth. These products help standardize certain consulting tasks so that they can be performed as quickly as possible.

AcceleratedSAP™ is divided into the following phases.

Phase 1: Project Preparation

The Project Preparation phase is concerned with organizing the executive kickoff meeting and making all the organizational arrangements for the project team. Once the team has been chosen, they are trained in the ASAP methodology, a rough project plan is drafted, and the hardware order is checked. The project starts officially with the kickoff meeting, which is attended by the project team, SAP™ consultants, and the customer's steering committee. Checklists and templates are available for all the activities in this phase to facilitate work and to ensure that nothing is overlooked. Based on an estimated project duration of 6 months, this phase would take between 1 and 2 weeks.

Phase 2: Business Blueprint

The aim of the Business Blueprint phase is to document your requirements. Interviews and workshops on the individual enterprise process areas, supported by questionnaires and graphical process chains from the R/3™ Business Engineer, help customers decide which R/3 business processes to use. Interfaces, legacy data, and other technical matters are also covered. The R/3™ processes are demonstrated using the International Demo and Education System (IDES), a version of the complete R/3™ system that SAP™ offers to all customers for hands-on experience of the software. Together with the consultants, customers create the Business Blueprint, a to-be business analysis that consists of written and pictorial representations of the company's structure and business processes. Once the blueprint has been approved, it becomes the central document in the project and is used as the basis for all further activities. At the end of this phase, the project managers use the Business Blueprint to plan resources, check hardware requirements, and clear up any open issues. Again, based on an estimated project duration of 6 months, this phase would take 3 to 4 weeks.

Phase 3: Realization

Based on the processes documented in the Business Blueprint, a baseline system is configured to match your company structure 100% and to cover 80% of your daily business processes. The system is configured and documented using the R/3™ Business Engineer tools. The technical team sets up the system administration and plans the interfaces and data transfer. SAP™ consultants work together with the project team, so that they can apply the skills they've learned in the training courses. At the end of the phase, the customer project team presents the central business processes to a larger group of end users and decision makers, to verify that the blueprint has been implemented correctly. The customer system is not configured during the Business Blueprint phase, so that the system produced here—known as the baseline system—is the basis for the production system. There is no prototype that's discarded. Fine-tuning takes place during the validation phase.

Phase 4: Final Preparation

The Final Preparation phase sees the consolidation of all the activities in the previous phases and is aimed at readying the R/3 ™ system and the company for production startup. This phase covers the final system tests, end-user training, and migration of data to the new system. The conversion and interface programs are all checked, volume and stress tests are run, and user-acceptance tests are carried out. The first EarlyWatch session, which is designed to actively tune the R/3 ™ System, often takes place at this point. To train end users, the project team utilizes a train-the-trainer method to train key users. The goals are to develop the expertise needed for day-to-day business and to promote end-user acceptance. Another purpose of this phase is to create a production-startup strategy. This plan specifically identifies the data-conversion strategy, internal audit procedures, and end-user support (internal help desk). The final step is to sign off the system, go live, and switch on. This phase takes 4 to 5 weeks.

Phase 5: Go Live and Support Continuous Change

Immediately after going live, the system is reviewed to ensure that the business environment is fully supported. This means checking the business processes and technical parameters and interviewing end users. In the last step, the business benefits of the new system are measured, to monitor the return on investment from the start. This can be followed by more phases aimed at further improving the processes.

Most of the project activities take place in the Blueprint phase. Iterative Process Prototyping is one analysis technique in this phase; its goal is to build customer-oriented net value-added chains on the basis of the R/3 ™ reference processes.

16.8   WORKFLOW AND PERSONNEL ORGANIZATION

Workflow constitutes a series of process models and templates that can be shaped to meet customer requirements. What distinguishes workflow processes from other business-process chains is that they must be mapped not only to the enterprise's organizational structure but also to individual message recipients—the people who are expected to process specific workflow tasks. This mapping involves a second modeling level that is based on the general process-modeling level.

The main tasks of SAP™'s workflow management are to support information flow, reduce the workload of system users, and offer services that simplify and speed up the completion of business processes.

SAP™ business workflow links information and business objects together with processes, making both of these available to users, as shown in Figure 16-14.

A built-in relationship exists between the object model and workflow. The registration of objects that participate in business workflow takes place by means of definitions of object classes in the R/3™ Business Object Repository. Here, the participating objects are accessed with the SAP™ Business Object Broker. A "broker" acts as a control mechanism for accessing business objects. Available objects in the repository can be divided into business objects and technical objects.

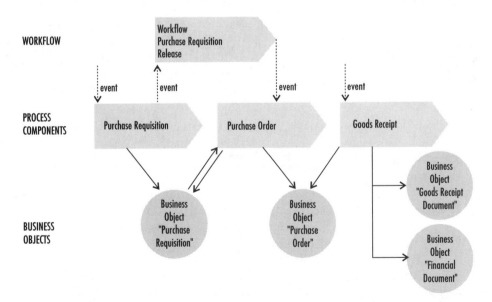

▶ **Figure 16–14**   Business Engineer integration of business process, business objects, and workflow

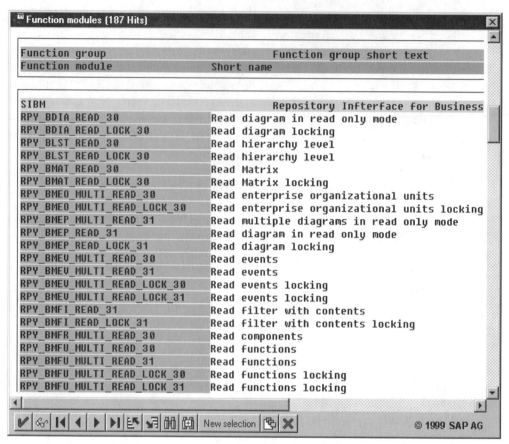

▶ **Figure 16–15** Open interface for third party software access in the R/3 Repository

16.9 *OPEN REPOSITORY INTERFACE*

As mentioned in Chapter 15, the R/3 ™ Repository forms the core of R/3 ™. It contains a comprehensive cross-section of the R/3 ™ application, including all meta information about programming objects, models, and business objects.

The central container for all of R/3 ™'s application information, the R/3 ™ Repository includes new development, design, and maintenance of applications and other components. The R/3 ™ Repository can export information via an API to graphics software, modeling tools, or business-process reengineering tools.

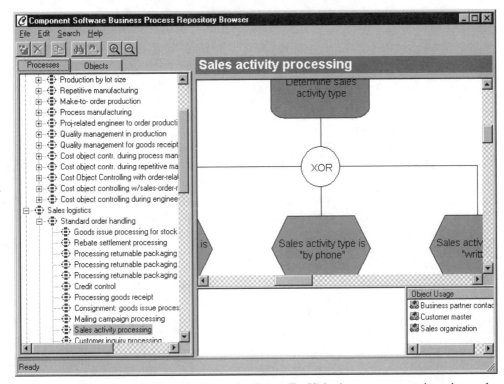

▶ **Figure 16–16**   Enterprise Integration Server (Ent IS) business process repository shows relationships between process models and business objects

Storage is critical to permit users to access the business objects and always be able to see what they are doing. The Repository can be viewed by using the Business Engineer. Because the Business Engineer reads directly from the Repository, it can access all the most current process information, application components, and objects. These include everything from sales, distribution, and planning to financial accounting and quality management.

For companies that want to go beyond looking at the information stored in repository, the API opens the Repository to third parties. Business consultants can go into the Repository to show customers the process models available in R/3 ™. Business-modeling tool vendors can also use the API to connect to the Repository, extract information, and display it in various tools. Application tool developers can use SAP ™'s R/3 ™ Automation Software Development Kit, which has access to development objects stored in the Repository, to trigger satellite development projects or new applications that hook in with R/3 ™. Figure 16-15 shows the API calls for accessing the Repository.

Several other third-party tool vendors are also currently codeveloping with SAP™ display tools for the Repository and Reference Model. IDS Professor Scheer AG has formed a partnership with SAP™ to integrate ARIS-Toolset™ into the R/3™ Repository by means of a client/server interface. The ARIS-Toolset 3.1 is intended to be the graphic-modeling front end for the Repository. Intellicorp (www.intellicorp.com) likewise has embarked on a joint venture with SAP™ to include the Business Blueprint in its LiveModel™ for R/3™ and R/Viewer software tools for R/3™ implementation. Micrografx (www.micrografx.com), a Dallas, Texas-based early desktop graphics pioneer, supports the R/3™ Reference Model with its Enterprise Charter iGrafx product. Component Software, Inc., a young Cambridge, Massachusetts-based start-up formed by a group of ex-SAP™ developers and authors of this book, released EntIS in 1998, which is a system configuration tool that uses business process and business object information to reveal configuration options in SAP™ R/3™ (see Figure 16-16). Finally, the Seattle-based Visio Corp., a leading supplier of enterprise-wide business diagramming and technical drawing software, is working with SAP™ to use Visio technology as a graphical tool to display process models in R/3™. Visio (www.visio.com) has so far produced The Visio Business Modeler™, a desktop tool to access process models in the Reference Model.

Finally, the inclusion of the Reference Model in every type of SAP™ documentation—for example, in rollout training and application documentation—enables the Business Blueprint to be exported for multimedia demonstrations of SAP™ applications. In this respect, it is a solid point of reference for training courses, documentation, and the actual R/3™ system.

The R/3™ Repository also provides the Open R/3™ Repository API, a programming interface that opens up the R/3™ Repository to customers as well as to third parties such as consultants, business modeling tool vendors, and application tools developers. Third-party developers can now link the R/3™ Repository—including the Business Blueprint—to such external applications as graphics software, modeling tools, or business process engineering tools. R/3™ information can be exported (and later imported as needed) for many purposes, including viewing enhanced graphical portrayals of the enterprise as well as creating demos, training programs, documentation, and so forth.

The open R/3™ Repository API integrates R/3™ with legacy and other systems, a process which in the past has been the most time-consuming and error-prone aspect of R/3™ implementation.

The API greatly simplifies and speeds the building of interfaces to connect R/3™ to external systems by giving implementers and third-party developers software access to core R/3™ application information using a high-level "meta language."

Using the meta language eliminates the need to perform low-level coding for each interface, reducing the need to create unique interfaces on a case-by-case basis for each customer. It also makes building interfaces faster and more reliable because implementers can more easily understand the system and what information is to be exchanged through the interface, which helps them develop well-defined, stable interfaces. Interface testing and verification are simpler and take less time.

As previously discussed, vendors in desktop software and other segments are planning to integrate the Business Blueprint into the systems they deliver to customers, thus giving R/3™ customers more choices and extending the reach and scope of R/3™. Many SAP™ consulting companies also will use the Business Engineer to integrate their toolsets with the Business Blueprint for improving the efficiency of their R/3™ implementation projects.

16.10 BUSINESS ENGINEER: FUTURE VISION

R/3™ Release 4.5 represents a step forward in BE and, in particular, the integration of reference models and a wide range of implementation tools such as ASAP. In addition to integrating the tools into a "workbench," SAP™ has shaped the object models and the R/3™ Reference Model to more closely correspond with R/3™. There have been a number of business-process-driven, customer-oriented implementations that achieve the goal of providing individual customer systems efficiently and in a cost-effective manner. Two prominent examples are INTERSOLV, a Maryland-based application enablement enterprise software company, and Marathon Cheese Company, the first U.S. customer for accelerated consumer products.

The R/3™ Business Engineer will evolve into a system for business configuration. This potential opens up the possibility; for instance, for SAP™ consulting to preconfigure the system before shipping or for R/3™ to be configured after installation. In this scenario, configuration is based on either the customer's specific requirements (e.g., corporate standards defined by a large, multinational firm before it embarks on configuring the individual systems) or on industry templates, which will also be provided by SAP™ partners. Thus, several approaches will be available for business configuration. It's important that such configuration last for the duration of the SAP™ implementation, so that the same framework is used throughout its life span.

Business configuration allows processes to be configured individually. One important feature is the direct link between the processes in the implemented system and the business configuration. For example, users will view models of business processes in the actual system, so that users working with one specific transaction can see how the transaction fits into the whole process of the enterprise. Because SAP™ provides quality-management procedures in the implemented processes, customers who have made their own modifications to the SAP™ system, for example, can verify that they have been implemented correctly. After release upgrades, or even release changeovers, customers will check that all the settings have been preserved and also to verify automatically that the applications have been upgraded successfully.

The R/3™ Business Engineer, ASAP, and the Business Blueprint are included in the standard R/3™ system Release 4.5. They support the same navigation concept. In keeping with the philosophy of BE, it will be possible to tailor these models to individual customer requirements, superimposing a layer of customer-specific modifications or enhancements onto the components, which can be stored together in the R/3™ Repository.

Another option is the use of templates, many of which are already available. An example of a template is a set of configurations for the SAP™ system designed for a specific industry. With them, enterprises do not have to start customizing from scratch; rather, they have a preconfigured base. A large, multinational company, for example, with several dozen international installations, will be able to implement a core system that it can use as a basis for its individual installations. The Business Engineer can be used for these purposes as well.

Finally, SAP™ plans to offer a process-monitoring system that will make it possible to tell how often specific processes are used and how much it costs to include them in the SAP™ system. SAP™ wants to be able to monitor how frequently each process is used and feed this information back to the Business Blueprint, which is currently used for configuration. This will enable SAP™ to compare different systems, with a view to identifying the most efficient configurations. SAP™ believes that in Release 4.5 it has laid the foundations for such developments to take place in the near future.

Early on, SAP™ recognized the need for both representative business models to ease initial implementation and a set of tools and methodologies to support continuous change. SAP™ embarked on a mission to aid customers in their continuous engineering efforts by providing a long-lasting platform for managing change. The Business Engineer brings many advantages to companies and their implementation teams. It provides the complete business blueprint, tools, methodologies, and interfaces that enable implementation teams to perform business process analysis, design, and configuration both initially and on a continuing basis.

17

Next Generation Enterprise

The Internet and World Wide Web have had such a profound impact on enterprise computing that we use the term "Next Generation Enterprise" to describe the dramatic and fundamental shift in the way application software works. The Internet combined with the culmination of the core elements of client/server—such as scalability, messaging, application partitioning, and distribution—and the technological possibilities now available to facilitate large-scale application components are fueling a forthcoming revolution in the way business and technology interact.

17.1   WHAT IS INTERNET ERP?

The three-tier client/server technology has gained wide acceptance because of the success of products such as R/3™. In the early '90s, SAP™'s chief architect and cofounder Hasso Plattner entered the modern client/server enterprise software race with a new processing concept divided into three key areas: database management and storage, application logic, and presentation logic. Plattner's design and thinking were on the mark, as the price of high-performance hardware needed to host powerful enterprise software (application servers) continued to decrease, making it easier for large international companies to scale their operations. As we have seen, scalability and flexibility are the real hallmarks of the three-tier architecture.

But in the early '90s, the commercial arguments for three-tier (or "n" tier) were somewhat unclear. Spawned in a time when there were at least four major contenders for becoming the enterprise GUI of choice—Windows, OS/2, Motif, and Macintosh—the presentation server quickly became the Achilles' heel in Plattner's corporate offensive. The idea behind the presentation server is that enterprises need to have a minimum functionality on a maximum number of GUI platforms. Some competitors, including the California-based Oracle and PeopleSoft, had started with a two-tier or "fat client," where application and presentation logic are bonded in one platform. These played on the lack of GUI functionality and subsequently pinned SAP™ to the wall. Clearly, the strategy of being everything for everybody's desktop was a feat that required too much effort. Then came the Web.

The technological foundations of the Next Generation Enterprise are heavily influenced by the Internet. The Web user interface or browser has already become the dominant user interface in corporate enterprise computing. This success has ramifications for the transaction-based computing model popularized by SAP™ and others. For instance, users want to easily navigate between slabs of text pages, set bookmarks, and move back and forth. Sequential, unidirectional movement between transaction screens is a remnant of the early design days in R/3™.

The Internet has made it very easy to find any information at any time. This ease is especially relevant to technologies such as messaging, replication, application partitioning, communication protocols—all of which are commonplace to three-tier. Security, another strength of three-tier client/servers, will remain a key concern due to the need to have information that is both widely accessible and stored centrally. New kinds of enterprise "firewalls" will deal with a new era of open intraenterprise computing. The combination of the Web and three-tier spells radical change.

In the Next Generation Enterprise, the vendor will need to learn that content communication is as important to the enterprise software application architecture as are the technological foundations. In general, vendors are concerned about Web enablement, which simply means that an enterprise software can exchange information and data with the Internet. The dominating factor for business applications, however, is the ability to map content such as that contained in the business blueprint into business transactions inside and outside the organization (Figure 17-1). With a new focus on process orientations, companies once again will have to redesign their infrastructure. Some important areas where content and technology will coalesce to make a difference include:

- Electronic commerce
- Business intelligence
- Decision support
- Data warehouse
- Information access

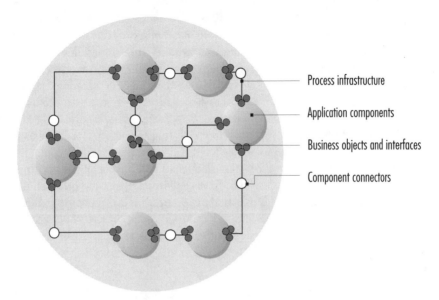

Process infrastructure

Application components

Business objects and interfaces

Component connectors

▶ **Figure 17–1**   Next Generation Enterprise architecture

- Knowledge management and collaboration
- Data mining for relationship management

These areas will emerge in very important ways with such context-aware technologies as workflow, procedure wizards, and process agents, all of which are able to act as guides in the process environment. That blueprints will be widely available to more parts of the enterprise application will make them infinitely easier to use.

Ultimately, technology that was a weakness in three-tier, such as SAP™'s R/3™ presentation server, turns out to be exactly what is fundamental to the Next Generation Enterprise—that is, having thin and ultrathin browsers or layers that facilitate using the enterprise software. These thin clients will have one major impact, however, on the enterprise desktop ownership strategy as practiced by vendors: Customers will want to use the browser as the access mechanism for enterprise applications. In other words, instead of just tabbing and clicking through screens in a business transaction, customers will want to get addresses, go to bookmarks, and access comprehensive help. The enterprise vendor thus is relieved of having to engineer interfaces. Whereas the interface was a weakness, R/3™ and other products will have bolt-on possibilities for browsers and utilize the capability to add new components written in Java or provided as an ActiveX™.

Using software components will require comprehensive transaction management and distribution functionality. These are the strengths of systems such as R/3™. Furthermore, the business context of information used in a component will need to be derived from context-rich monitors that work together with business content such as in the Business Blueprint. For example, consider the way in which reports are created in many of today's software systems. The sales report may provide information about how many products are sold and where, but they tell little about order processing. Using an Internet browser and process model for order processing on one hand and a component for data manipulation and presentation on the other, process owners will have a new way of making a content-rich interaction. They will have the simplicity of the browser, the content of the data, and the map of the business process on their desktop, all in one. To make all of this happen, vendors will need to hook all these technologies together, a complex issue that is the main subject of the remainder of this chapter.

17.2 *NEXT GENERATION APPLICATION COMPONENTS*

In the Next Generation Enterprise, what once dominated the past 25 years of enterprise software development will abruptly end. Mammoth software integration, or packaging all functionality into software modules, simply cannot work without a common memory and data storage space. Storage was one of SAP™'s advantages in the R/3™ development because it included the mainframe product architecture embodied in R/2™. The integration became a monster, however, as R/3™ swelled into a 10-GB complex system. Component products solve some of the integration problems, but there is no all-encompassing product concept. Even SAP™ admits that this development is important for its future. For the Next Generation Enterprise, companies will face a number of new challenges, namely the combinatorics of software components and the ownership and maintenance issues related to application assembly via components.

SAP™ is attempting to make its technical infrastructure better integrated with the Internet and third-party application components or "applets." Application components are self-sufficient, independent, CORBA- and MS-COM-compliant software products that understand how to interoperate with enterprise software systems. These fall into three categories:

• Utility or technical components

• Generic business objects

• Specialized business applications

In Release 4.0, SAP™ is including more than 25 Internet application scenarios that can access R/3™ business logic through BAPIs, which enable external access to business processes and objects in the R/3™ system. R/3™ Release 4.0 contains more than 180 open BAPIs across all R/3™ business applications areas.

BAPIs define an open business standard for direct communication between business applications from different suppliers. BAPIs provide a standard, multi-vendor interface for common business content, such as "Order," "Customer," or "PartNumber." BAPIs allow business systems to exchange transactions directly across enterprise boundaries. For example, one company's order requisition can be sent directly to and processed by another company's order-entry system without human intervention (the order-entry clerk) or a predefined point-to-point transaction (EDI).

Because the R/3™ Internet application scenarios themselves run on the R/3™ Internet Transaction Server, the core R/3™ system has to be extended only with respect to interfaces. All BAPIs are implemented as methods of business objects in the R/3™ Business Object Repository, thus not only providing access to Internet applications but interfacing as well; for example, on the basis of Common Object Model (COM), Distributed Common Object Model (DCOM), and CORBA. Higher-level interfaces make it easier to make changes and modifications later on.

By relying more on third-party software developers, SAP™ is attempting to deliver the functionality, integration, and requirements that many of its customers desire. SAP™ will enable third-party software developers to interact better with SAP™ infrastructure and interfaces through add-ons and the like. This "market enlargement" will not only help achieve the goal of a more seamless integration with the Internet, but it will also encourage more tools and software developers and more BAPIs for building Internet applications. The seamless integration of SAP™'s technical infrastructure with the Internet is, however, just one step. The next and perhaps more intriguing step concerns how SAP™ and its third parties plan to put this infrastructure into practice.

Application components are the keystone in Next Generation Enterprise architecture. As vendors such as SAP™ extend today's enterprise platforms by adding interfaces and third-party applications, they continue another trend that has dominated the enterprise market for the past 20 years: responsibility outsourcing. This trend is seldom discussed by industry pundits but nonetheless is critical for the coming radical change. With the decision to go to any of the leading standard enterprise software vendors, Chief Information Officers often outsource their responsibility for technology decision making. This approach is crisis driven, impacted by issues such as Year 2000. The CIO feels obligated to give up responsibility because the mammoth application completely dominates the enterprise, transforming the enterprise application into the computing infrastructure. In answer to end users seeking to use their Internet browser for a corporate computing project, the CIO throws his hands up and proclaims: "Our enterprise vendor does not provide this functionality yet, but they have promised it in the next release." Application components will end this charade, and the Next Generation Enterprise will offer the infrastructure that takes advantage of a battery of technologies outside the proprietary domain of any particular software vendor. The Internet will replace the vendors' infrastructure that they collectively fought so hard to attain in the past decade, and CIOs will take charge of the computing landscape.

17.3 *THE INDUSTRY REFERENCE MODEL, PROCESS CONFIGURATION, AND VERTICAL MARKETS*

In the mid 1990s the enterprise software market began to shift away from general purpose solutions and toward industry-specific solutions. Having a generic Business Blueprint no longer fits with the product development and implementation strategy. SAP™ changed its entire sales organization in 1997 from regional to industry focus, dividing the company into business units such as:

- Aerospace & Defense
- Automotive
- Banking
- Chemicals
- Consumer Products
- Engineering & Construction
- Healthcare
- High Tech Electronics
- Insurance
- Media
- Oil, Gas
- Pharmaceuticals
- Public Sector
- Retail
- Service Provider
- Telecommunications
- Transportation
- Utilities

For the Next Generation Enterprise, SAP™ and other ERP vendors will base their sales, marketing, and production around the aspects of a particular industry. This focus mandates a specialized model for each industry. Hence, industry-specific reference models and new technologies that work with these models have emerged to improve system usage. Because of its broad appeal, simplicity, and large installed base of browsers, the Internet is one of the most obvious ways to communicate the content of specialized models.

SAP™ is also planning to make the Business Blueprint more integrated with the Internet and with Internet scenarios. The goal is to show more processes and scenarios that could run outside R/3™, such as obtaining order confirmations through Internet mail or ordering from product catalogs on the Internet. With the heightened emphasis on the Internet and market enlargement through third-party software development, SAP™ realizes that more and more it will have to map processes that are essentially outside of R/3™. While one could argue that toolsets such as ARIS Studio, iGrafx, and Live Model already fulfill such a role, SAP™ wants to supply more of a standard. SAP™ is also looking to improve the structure of the Business Blueprint so that the models can be better understood by people outside the data processing community, such as finance professionals and front-line managers who not only know the business better but are closer to the processes themselves. Improvements in the Business Blueprint's notational structure are currently underway.

Even though SAP™ is a pioneer in the creation and publication of business blueprints, others in the software industry have banded together to work on a larger, more generic business-process model. Called the "Supply Chain Operations Reference Model" (SCOR), this model is backed by the Supply Chain Council, which is a nonprofit corporate special interest group based in Cambridge, Massachusetts. This group is devoted to improving supply chain process descriptions and mapping the results into its software purchasing decisions. SCOR has the potential to become the industry blueprint of choice, because it is not specific to any one vendor. For the Next Generation Enterprise, this multivendor approach will be required for intrabusiness as well as extra-business collaboration.

The next important area of Reference Model developments involves software construction from the models. The goal for process model configuration and automated customization is to enable users to work mainly from the business-process models. The consultant, for example, needs to be able to do the customization right from the models. This goal should be realized once these models are formed on specific industries, that is, industry-specific templates. This leads us to the last area of development, the creation of vertical market blueprints or templates.

Although the Reference Model has been very good at improving the understanding of organizational structures, the process models now cover enough areas to tackle entire industries. Special applications for specific industries will help business engineers start with an industry template and build from there. For example, someone in the publishing business can draw from the Reference

Models for their business and configure them accordingly. SAP™ has been strong in petrochemicals for 25 years, and it anticipates expanding in other areas and countries. In the United States, for example, SAP™ wants to have more development in high-tech, chemicals, and consumer package industries. For this development, R/3™ needs to be configured more with specific industries. Vertical markets will be used more in Release 4.0, where a large set of new functionality will be built around retail markets.

17.4   *SUPPLY CHAIN OPTIMIZATION, PLANNING, AND EXECUTION*

The R/3™ Business Blueprint and ERP industry initiatives such as SCOR both help to establish a common descriptive language for business logic and a framework for understanding how business processes, objects, and organizational units relate to each other. Even though this is a boon for SAP™ and an advantage for R/3™ customers, clear descriptions of the business process inside R/3™ help third-party software suppliers and some SAP™ competitors better understand and contend with SAP™ on the basis of open process integration. In the late 90s business engineering shifted its focus from process improvement within an organization to process integration across different organizations. Supply chains represent cross-functional integration of activities that span the borders of organizations and companies—for example, ordering raw materials through manufacturing or the planning of products through distribution and delivery. The main principles of supply chain integration are:

- Extending the enterprise to embrace all aspects of a product or service
- Integrating business systems of customers, suppliers, and partners to create a common information basis
- Providing real-time decision support to increase responsiveness
- Striving for execution excellence by fully automating and optimizing business practices

Process integration across the supply chain is the new challenge for the ERP industry in general and SAP™ in particular. To that end, SAP™'s Business Framework is designed to help companies integrate their respective data processing products. After business process improvement, companies will strive to leverage their specialized know-how and partner with companies that work in tandem to deliver a comprehensive supply chain solution. Business solutions (such as sales force automation, interactive reporting and decision support, and supply chain optimization) need to be tightly integrated with R/3™ in order to permit real-time data exchange and processing. Companies want to extend beyond SAP™'s R/3™ system and integrate all systems of parts suppliers and finished goods distributors.

To provide a comprehensive enterprise solution, SAP™ plans to deliver an integrated set of capabilities including:

- The SAP™ Business Warehouse—A special purpose application that summarizes data from R/3™ applications and external data sources and supports retrieval and analysis of enterprise business data. This new application aims to improve R/3™'s lack of OLAP reporting capabilities, and signifies a major shift from transaction processing to business analytic.
- The SAP™ Advanced Planner and Optimizer—A decision support product that works with R/3™ data to provide improved forecasting and optimization about different parts of the supply chain
- The SAP™ Sales Force Automation—A special-purpose application that helps sales professionals move quickly and easily through the sales process during customer interaction and back in the office. Its main features are collaboration for sales participants, managers, and other departmental functions within the enterprise.
- Supply Chain Planning Interface—An interface that provides access to the supply chain components to third-party supply chain partners. The supply chain interface provides access to data for third-party planning and optimization tools, and it accepts forecasts and schedules from third-party supply chain systems.

Supply chain management has been the marketing cry of all the leading ERP vendors (Baan, Oracle, PeopleSoft, and SAP™), but they have been slow to produce special purpose products leaving the market to agile new companies such as i2, Numetrix, Yantra, and Manugistics. As companies commit to the ideas of business framework and the R/3™ infrastructure, they are seeking ways to bring many of the more strategic and company-specific activities together. In forecasting, for example, companies may use a variety of advanced statistical forecasting methods with real-time data from a variety of sources. Such integration enables businesses to capture changes in demand signals and patterns as early as possible, so that the supply side of the business can respond quickly and accordingly. Thus, the next generation of ERP products will no longer be limited to capturing individual transactions, but will be much more in tune with the strategic drivers of supply chain management.

Business blueprints play a prominent role in the supply chain management solutions that SAP™ plans to launch. The process models and their connections to business objects and organizations are maps for supply chain management and the basis for consistent, reliable integration at the business logic level. Without such meta data, companies would fail to make solutions the benefit from processes and subprocesses along the entire supply chain. For this reason, the business blueprint with its battery of business logic is the starting point for application integration.

17.5 ENTERPRISE APPLICATION INTEGRATION

No one application can solve all business problems. Not even SAP™ R/3™, with all of its complexity, can do everything that a company requires to run its business. Nor would it be prudent for most companies to bet their whole business on one vendor or business operating system. Enterprise Application Integration effectively allows companies to finally achieve a best of breed solution for their enterprise computing strategy.

SAP™'s Business Framework initiative is intended to provide to support the integration of ERP application components. SAP™'s Business Framework supports the integration between:

- SAP™ R/3™ and COM-based front ends, such as the Microsoft Office
- SAP™ R/3™ and a specialized ERP application (e.g., SAS, Aurum, Siebel)
- SAP™ R/3™ and another ERP application (e.g., Baan and SAP™ R/3™)
- SAP™ R/3™ and any custom application or legacy system that can interact with COM or CORBA objects (e.g., VB, VBA, C++, Java, mainframe applications wrapped with appropriate middleware)

SAP™'s Release 4.0 technology, developed in part by the Cambridge, Massachusetts-based Component Software, makes it possible for companies to select the best elements from various vendors, glue them together in useful and meaningful ways, and adapt them to make them suitable to their technical, cultural, and business environment. A number of vendors, such as CrossRoute, Vitria, Active Software, and CrossWorld have already initiated special products that augment the SAP™/Component Software solution. These vendors aim to create a new class of middleware, which they term "processware," indicating the prominent role of business process models in the application integration market. Processware combines the basics of business process blueprints with special purpose application servers called "enterprise integration servers."

These integration or integration platforms make it now possible for companies to employ a best-in-class software strategy. Figure 17-2 illustrates a typical

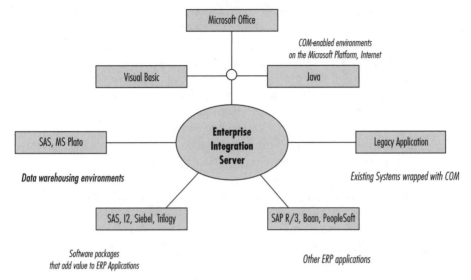

Microsoft Office

*COM-enabled environments
on the Microsoft Platform, Internet*

Visual Basic

Java

**Enterprise
Integration
Server**

SAS, MS Plato

Legacy Application

Data warehousing environments

Existing Systems wrapped with COM

SAS, I2, Siebel, Trilogy

SAP R/3, Baan, PeopleSoft

*Software packages
that add value to ERP Applications*

Other ERP applications

▶ **Figure 17–2**   Enterprise integration presents a new challenge for ERP vendors

integration scenario for the Next Generation Enterprise. In this example, a company with a variety of manufacturing plants might decide to combine SAP™ Procurement for the headquarters office, Baan Manufacturing for satellite plants, SAS Institute products for consolidation and analysis, and custom-built VBA programs running under Microsoft Office for departmental reporting. Even though it is reasonable for a company to wish to perform this sort of interpackage integration and customization, in practice it is very difficult to do. Each packaged application has its own business framework and application programming interface (API) or, in many cases, set of APIs; SAP™ offers RFCs, BAPIs, and ALE IDOCs, for instance, and each has different protocols and behaviors. To use a packaged software vendor's API requires in-depth understanding of the behavior of the package, and performing an integration may require an in-depth understanding of the behavior of all participating packages.

The primary goal of an enterprise integration platform is to greatly simplify the task of integrating software applications by making the interface mechanisms between them far easier to understand and use. Making them easier to understand is largely a matter of presenting the mechanisms in a homogeneous format, rich with business context and content, so that someone who understands a particular business requirement can easily determine how to do what they need to do. Most important, they can do it without an in-depth technical understanding of a specific ERP Application. Making them easier to use is a matter of hiding the complexities and idiosyncrasies of each proprietary API behind a consistent, standards-based, repository-enabled interface layer.

A secondary goal of the enterprise integration platform is to enable third-party vendors to create value-adding extensions to packaged ERP software applications without having a live connection to the package. A small vendor wishing to add a specialized financial tracking module to SAP™ R/3™, for example, might not have ready access to an R/3™ system. Hence it is important to provide features that enable the coding and rudimentary testing of such a module by substituting component "stubs" for actual R/3™ function calls. Eventually, of course, the vendor will have to test its creation against a real R/3™ system (at a "Component Software Integration Factory," perhaps). Sophisticated enterprise integration development tools, however, contain the R/3™ Reference Model as a blueprint for application coordination and minimize the amount of time required in bridging business applications.

In the next generation of ERP applications business objects, business processes and organizational objects will constitute the "nouns and verbs" of application integration. SAP™'s Business Framework and Business Engineer are well positioned for becoming the basis of application integration efforts. The evolution of the business blueprint will increase the prominence of both business objects and processes. New repository technology from Microsoft, Component Software, and SAP™ ushers in the new era of application integration by bringing the business logic, the technical programming implementation, and the run-time execution all into one repository. Figure 17-3 illustrates the convergence of business and technology within integration repositories.

Business Object Integration Model

Objects play an important role in both business engineering and application integration. Business object integration models can describe business objects in an ERP-vendor-independent representation. They are used to help developers and users locate specific functionality offered by an ERP application without requiring in-depth knowledge of the underlying ERP software or the proprietary APIs it might expose. In Microsoft Repository terms, each business object integration model contains meta-data about certain business concepts as they relate to application integration.

In addition, business object integration models include constructs necessary to effect translation between a business object method and a method call to an underlying ERP application. In some cases, implementing a business object-style interface may require introduction of a script, packaged as a component, which invokes several function calls to satisfy a method request. This component must be stored in the repository.

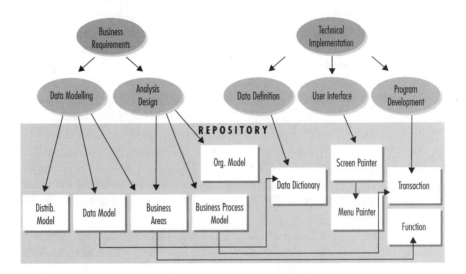

▶ **Figure 17–3** New repository technology integrates business requirements with technical implementation

Business Process Integration Models

Business process integration models describe business activities in an easy to understand, ERP-vendor-independent representation. They are used to help developers and users locate specific functionality offered by an ERP application without requiring in-depth knowledge of the underlying ERP software or the proprietary APIs it might expose. In Microsoft Repository terms, each business process integration model contains meta-data about certain business activities. The basis for business process integration models is the vendor-specific business blueprint, including:

- EPC diagrams that support R/3™'s Business Blueprint
- Petri Net descriptions of business processes built to support Baan's Dynamic Enterprise Modeling
- UML-based Activity Diagram built to support the Open Application Group conventions
- Any other materials for any other ERP application that might be of use

The business process integration model describes the business from the standpoint of what the business does (that is, the business processes) as opposed to the things with which the business deals (that is, business objects.) in a context that is both internal (company operations) and external (market competition, customers) to the organization. The need for a business process integration model that spans the conceptual models of each ERP system is based on the observation that the flow of business activities often involves multiple organizations such as in electronic commerce and supply chain management.

17.6 *ELECTRONIC COMMERCE*

Many experts feel the next wave of Internet use will be driven by business-to-business electronic commerce. From 1994 to 1995, sales over the Internet grew from $60 million to $200 million. Estimates for the year 2000 project sales to range anywhere between $70 billion and $200 billion worldwide.

Electronic commerce is a prime target for Internet economic growth. Electronic commerce essentially represents consumer-to-business and business-to-business communication. Using digital communications standards and technology, electronic commerce facilitates the buying and selling of goods and services and the transfer of funds. It also embraces such intercompany and intracompany processes as procurement, order handling, production, marketing, sales, and distribution. Electronic commerce has many offshoots in such areas as electronic data interchange, electronic funds transfer, bank card operations, digital cash, and so on.

Although at present the state of electronic commerce is still in its infancy, soon it will begin maturing when the complex logic of the Next Generation Enterprise begins to take shape. SAP™ plans to allow customers and third-party developers to use and develop the massive amount of business logic in R/3™ to make superior Internet applications for electronic commerce. On one hand, SAP™ will make it easier for third parties to work with BAPIs, and on the other, SAP™ may incorporate third-party modifications and improvements into the standard system as time goes on. The larger, more market-shaping activity, however, will take place in the field of Next Generation Enterprise application components. These software products will tap into information contained in the Business Blueprint to drive process-oriented electronic commerce between companies. The benefits for Next Generation participants will be more fluid information exchange and common process definition around which a business transaction can be based.

SAP™'s commitment to enhanced Internet-based business is evident in R/3™. The Internet application scenarios delivered with Release 4.5 support consumer-to-business, business-to-business, and intranet relationships.

Consumer-to-business: In a consumer-to-business relationship, the customer or potential customer uses a Web browser to access the vendor's business system to review a product catalog, place an order, or inquire about a product or service. Consumer-to-business applications using the Internet benefit from offering products and services to consumers worldwide. The Internet application scenarios in Release 4.5 include:

- Order entry for variant products (e.g., on-line ordering)

- Electronic correspondence (e.g., automated Internet reminder notices)

- Interactive requests (e.g., on-line customer information, giving customers access to information such as current bank information or account balances, billing status)

- Employment opportunities (e.g., direct recruiting through the Internet)

Business-to-Business: A "killer app" is the term used to describe a product that makes a particular software market or platform mainstream. Business-to-Business will undoubtedly be a killer app for the Internet and spawn a whole array of new commercial opportunities. In Business-to-Business relationships, integrated business systems can cooperate with each other by using emerging open standards for business transactions (i.e., BAPIs). Potential applications create an electronic marketplace that facilitates ad hoc Business-to-Business matching, including synchronization of purchase requisitions and sales orders from independent R/3 ™ systems through a common transaction. Release 4.5 scenarios include:

- Business-to-Business Procurement

- Kanban (e.g., checking and replenishing product inventories)

- Special stock inquiries (e.g., on-line stock inquiries for commission, contract and job processing, work-in-process inventory)

- Bank data transfer (e.g., on-line banking, allowing for the exchange of banking, accounting, and bookkeeping data through the Internet while supporting different country-dependent standards)

Business-to-Employee (Intranet): Using their own Intranets, businesses can employ Internet technology within their organization to enable their employees to take advantage of technological progress and better communications. Release 4.5 intranet scenarios cover:

- Service calls (e.g., customer service on-line logging, which allows customers to identify product problems by choosing from a catalog of preidentified potential problems)
- Who is who (e.g., communications between employees of large companies using the company's Intranet as an extension of SAPoffice)
- OLAP server (e.g., consolidated information for analytic and reporting purposes)
- Purchase requisitions (e.g., simplified internal purchase requisitions)
- Reporting actuals (e.g., ad hoc Web browser-style interface to post activity allocations remotely from one cost center to another)

As SAP™ and other software vendors continue to make such commitments to the communication infrastructure provided to their customers, Intranets will play a pivotal role in the Next Generation Enterprise.

17.7   DESKTOP ERP: AUTOMATING THE WAY PEOPLE WORK

With the enlarged footprint or system definition, ERP vendors have taken the cross-functional integration to the analytic and decision support aspects of companies. In the early days, ERP targeted functionality coverage. In other words, they tried to develop a software function in their product that would address the business function. In technical jargon, they focused on the transactions, which are essentially data input on blocks of screens.

In the Next Generation Enterprise, software will take a more prominent role in everyday work. With the emphasis on supply chain and business processes, software vendors are already introducing new technologies such as improved browsers, synchronous integration with desktop applications, role-centered application clients, and autonomous software agents.

Improved Browsers

As we discussed earlier, SAP™'s presentation server SAPGUI (SAP™ Graphical User Interface), affectionately called "the toaster" by many clients, is a multi-platform product that makes it possible to enter transactions into the R/3™ application server and later post them to the database system. Accustomed to more modern event-based interfaces, such as Microsoft Office and Netscape Navigator, users are often frustrated quickly by SAPGUI's lack of flexibility. In 1998, after an open declaration that he can no longer use his company's flagship R/3™ product, SAP™'s founder and CEO Hasso Plattner launched a marketing initiative called "EnjoySAP! Software that Works the Way I Do." The initiative is destined to revolutionize the way people interact with business software and is very much similar to the way the Macintosh changed personal computing. To help him recreate the interface to SAP™ R/3™, Plattner sought the advice of Hartmut Esslinger, founder of Federal Republic of Germany (FROG) Design (http://www.frogdesign.com), and Alan Cooper, author of a leading book on user interface design *ABOUT FACE: The Essentials of User Interface Design* and a pioneer in user interaction (http://www.cooper.com).

Desktop ERP

Usability and comprehensibility are the two significant barriers to information in R/3™. The problem of poor information delivery in SAP™ R/3™ continues to be a sore subject for SAP™ customers. In fact, SAP™'s SAPPHIRE '98 was focused squarely on the need for solving this problem for the R/3™ end user. The problem, in a nutshell, is that the R/3™ system is overly complex, especially for occasional users. Because of R/3™'s complexity, tasks such as reporting in R/3™ presents the nonexpert with several barriers to information, for examples: an unwieldy GUI, a confusing notation system, and an esoteric language in ABAP/4. Thus, the current R/3™ system prevents users from easily being able to access mission-critical data.

U.S. software manufacturers have promised simpler links to complex systems for years. Allowing common connections between software systems means that users require less training and need less expertise in fewer software packages. Currently 97% of the computer literate know and use Microsoft Office products. Many experts see these products as a plausible gateway to using technology that is more complex.

The new wave of Desktop ERP products are working to solve the usability problems of ERP applications by integrating them into the Microsoft Office desktop.

The first wave of these integrated desktop ERP applications has been engineered to solve the reporting problems in ERP applications, whose complexity and specialized language and functions make it difficult for nonexpert users to understand and use ERP data for reporting purposes. Indeed, end users often must rely on SAP™ consultants and ABAP/4 programmers just to create a report in R/3™.

The initial entry into the Desktop ERP Desktop market is a product called Activesheets. ActiveSheets effectively integrates Microsoft Excel and SAP™ R/3™. ActiveSheets allows the user to create live reports in R/3™ using Excel as its front end. It provides an Excel add-in that lets the user access R/3™ data from Excel. The application works differently than simply downloading SAP™ data into Excel (which R/3 ™ users already do regularly) because it gives the user live numbers to work with—hence, the crucial active data element to ActiveSheets. Once the report is created the user can send the report to whomever needs it. If they have ActiveSheets, they have live data as well. Every time they open the Excel workbook, the report is refreshed with the live data.

Products such as ActiveSheets greatly improve information delivery in R/3 ™. A good example of ActiveSheets use would be for sales. Typically only a few power users are competent R/3 ™ users. They are responsible for disseminating reports with R/3 ™ data to other sales people and, typically, sales management. The problem with this system is that, not only the range of reports is necessarily limited, but that the data is "old" by the time it gets into the hands of decision-makers. ActiveSheets can give the entire sales force the ability to create their own reports, and decision-makers have up-to-date data each and every time they open their Excel workbooks. The bottom line is, if the user knows how to use Excel, they can use ActiveSheets. There's little to learn about SAP ™ R/3 ™; thus, ActiveSheets greatly shortens the R/3 ™ learning curve.

Autonomous Software Agents

Autonomous software agents are programs that act independently and are the hands and eyes for software components. They are adaptive and can make decisions for the user rather than, as in the case of current software programs, depending on interface designs that require direct manipulation.

According to Pattie Maes, an associate professor of media arts and sciences at MIT, "Agent programs differ from regular software mainly by what can best be described as a sense of themselves as independent entities. An ideal agent knows what its goal is and will strive to achieve it. An agent should also be robust and adaptive, capable of learning from experience and responding to unforeseen situations with a repertoire of different methods. Finally it should be autonomous so that it can sense the current environment and act independently to make progress toward its goal."[1]

Researchers are currently developing software programs that understand how the user interacts with a software program. At MIT, researchers have built agents that continuously watch users' actions, monitor their habits, and auto.mate any patterns that the agent detects. This research has many possible applications. For example, an autonomous software agent can be used for searching for information on the Internet. These agents will learn the user's habits and then use search engines on the Internet. They learn what kind of information the user likes or consistently searches for and bring that information to him

---

1. Pattie Maes, "Intelligent Software," *Scientific American*, Vol. 273, No. 3 (Sept. 1995), p. 84.

or her automatically. Because the Internet has created too much information for any one person to handle, business agents will have a direct and immediate impact on the Internet.

Drawing on the information about business processes in the Business Blueprint, software agents will evolve as clever interpreters of how to harvest information related to any business process. They will do this by understanding the process model and the repository metamodel. An agent will look at the metamodel and interpret the relationships between business processes and business objects, thereby providing to the consumer or decision maker the wealth of information associated with the business process. For example, a company wants to provide its customers with a new capability to do "rush orders" over the Internet. From the enterprise software point of view, that of R/3™, for instance, providing this capability would mean changing or configuring the model for rush order handling. After the appropriate changes are made, the model would serve as a blueprint for an autonomous software agent. The agent would be able to query the process model and understand what information is relevant. This data would be contained in business objects such as "Customer" or "Customer-Order," and the agent would make proposals about what to look at and how to prepare the information.

Autonomous agents don't necessarily have to be designed around performing specific actions, however. The more radical possibilities lie in their ability to make decisions by themselves. Whereas today's software programs rarely go beyond a set of yes/no parameters, autonomous agents can make decisions when there are more than two options. In fact, they can base their decisions on sets of options learned from past experiences. Hence, with autonomous agents, there will be a renaissance for artificial intelligence in business technology.

There are two basic types of autonomous agents in the Next Generation arena: business agents and learning agents. Business agents perform specific functions based on particular business practices or habits, and learning agents bring users information they need to know by weeding out extraneous material and focusing on only what is absolutely necessary for the user to learn.

Autonomous agent technology can perform many organizational functions for a company. For example, an autonomous agent in an electronic commerce setting may be based on buying and selling agents on the Internet. In this way, a buyer can go to a buying agent and say, "I want X. Go out and find X for me." Or "Make a deal for me within these parameters" or "Buy only up to this amount." Thus, a dynamic business agent actually performs the negotiating function. The buying agent goes to the selling agent and negotiates terms and brings the information back to the buyer.

A research project at MIT called KASBAH is a kind of prototypical example of business agents working on the Internet. The KASBAH project is built around classified ads. Someone can say, for example, "I want an apartment and I want to pay this much." The agent goes out, finds the apartment for you, makes the deal, and brings a contract back to you to sign. Next Generation agents will perform even more complex business functions.

Certainly, SAP™ will benefit from business agents by using them to make certain decisions in the R/3™ business environment. For example, a possible business agent scenario might focus on commodities trading. Companies could use business agents to keep their competitors from knowing what they're buying or in what quantities. A manufacturer, for instance, might run into a shortage and would undoubtedly want to keep this information quiet. The manufacturer could make use of business agents, dedicated solely to its interests, that would conduct on-line searches for the necessary supplies without tipping off competitors.

The second area of autonomous agent research revolves around learning agents, which are essentially electronic teachers. Learning agents can teach the user according to the problems the user is having. They can teach about a particular software object, the software's new functionality, or the functionality the user should be interested in, based on his or her problems. For example, if the user encounters a repeated set of problems regarding the use of a certain function, the agent will point to the areas that the user should know. It will base its instruction not only on the specific problem but also on the level of skill of the user. Thus, the learning agents improve the user's skills needed to perform a specific function.

Like Internet agents, learning agents are especially adept at choosing the information that the user does or does not need to know. If the user is new to a certain functionality, the agent will recognize that and get the user up to speed. If the user is experienced, the agent will filter out the information that the user doesn't need.

Learning agents can, of course, be used as a teaching tool, which is especially relevant for companies that have to train large numbers of employees. Companies don't have to move employees to a training center and incur training costs but can train them on the job site. In this way, learning agents help to accomplish the goal of what companies call "learning while earning." Moreover, given that today's companies are leaner, the typical employee now requires a much broader set of skills than ever before. Learning agents can be very useful in this area because they can assess the employee's current skill level and broaden it where necessary. Furthermore, the agents will use the knowledge content in business blueprints to propose organizational changes and optimize informal communication channels.

Germane to organizational change is insight about how people collaborate. Enterprise software vendors have been slow to understand this phenomenon. Companies like IBM (http://www.ibm.com) and Microsoft understand the importance of collaboration and provide products, such as Lotus Notes and Microsoft Exchange, which enable enterprise collaboration. Radnet, a small Cambridge, Massachusetts, software startup, bet the whole company on the concept that enterprise collaboration via the Internet will be a "killer app" in the Next Generation. However, in a recent discussion with David Scult, Radnet's CEO, we were surprised to discover that the company reinvented itself as a consulting company and abandoned the idea of an Internet collaboration product. The problem, besides the immense marketing expenses required, was that Radnet failed to understand the connectivity into the bloodstream of the company, namely the ERP system. Potential Radnet customers, such as the Barvarian Hypothekenbank and the publishing company Burda, made integration with SAP™ R/3™ a knockout criteria for collaboration software. As this failure illustrates, companies wish to incorporate the Business Blueprint for automating their products and introducing software agents for enterprise collaboration.

How would learning agents work for SAP™? One vision would be to use SAP™'s R/3™ and its interfaces with learning agents, which would aid in accessing information better on the Internet. As teaching tools, learning agents will help solve various problems that occur during R/3™ installations. In the past, SAP™ has had difficulty informing business engineers about relevant products, functions, and relevant data. Even though the IMG does filter out a lot of the information that consultants don't need to know, there is still far too much information for consultants to digest. In the future, better information tools must be generated for better productivity. Ultimately, learning agents should serve as an extended information tool for SAP™ data. Their success could drive down the price of enterprise software implementation and radically change the way companies deploy enterprise software products.

Undoubtedly, SAP™ and other enterprise software vendors such as Baan, PeopleSoft, and Oracle will discover that autonomous agents are a logical next step in the future of open systems and information technology.

As intriguing as this new technology is, there are still some major obstacles to overcome. Any autonomous agent needs a stable infrastructure that's not proprietary. Today's market leaders have recognized that the Internet is such an infrastructure and are building their environments to work seamlessly with the Internet. In the near future, Microsoft should have numerous products that enable any Windows-based PC to communicate with any type of Web site, software, or scripting language (such as JavaScript) that runs on more than one platform. This should give autonomous agents the infrastructure they need to launch out and communicate with many different environments—not just Windows- or Windows NT-based environments, but systems like R/3™ as well.

17.8   CONCLUSION

On the horizon for enterprise computing is a new generation of standard software. The Next Generation Enterprise promises many changes for corporate computing. These changes will be ushered in with the Internet and the host of innovative technology that relates to this public domain infrastructure. As today's market leaders reposition their current applications to adopt these technologies, software users will witness a quantum leap in user friendliness and CIOs will feel relief from the proprietary enterprise computing infrastructures that dominated the '80s and '90s. Whether the software giants such as SAP™ are nimble enough to master these changes depends heavily on their ability to open their applications for new application components. These hybrid software parts will permit companies to go beyond the functionality that vendors offer and integrate specialized parts that fuel their productivity and satisfy their desire to have a company-specific enterprise computing platform. Advances in the area of open transaction management and business-process blueprints will spawn new types of intracompany collaboration and drive the market in the Next Generation Enterprise.

Given that SAP™ continues to invest roughly 25 percent of its profits in research and development, the future capabilities of SAP™ software should remain as one of the company's strongest selling points. Not surprisingly, the Internet is a high development priority for SAP™. The World Wide Web can serve as an alternative user interface for R/3™ business applications and can open up new access paths and new business processes to customers. Although many technical obstacles still remain to be overcome, the Next Generation Enterprise, along with its advances in electronic commerce, third-party software development, and autonomous software agents, shows great promise for doing business with R/3™ on the Internet. As we have shown in the many intriguing areas currently under development, the possibilities inherent in the Next Generation Enterprise are virtually limitless. At the very least, the Next Generation Enterprise promises that the most spectacular fruits of business engineering are yet to come.

Index

ActiveSheets

Component Software specializes in bringing SAP R/3 to the desktop. ActiveSheets and its suite of prepackaged workbook solutions put live SAP R/3 data at your fingertips in a familiar environment - Microsoft Office. Whether you are a sales, controlling, purchasing, or production professional, our solutions will solve your critical business problems. ActiveSheets uses the R/3 Business Blueprint to navigate through the SAP system and extract information about business processes.

With little R/3 expertise users can:

- **Evaluate sales performance**
- **Analyze purchasing trends**
- **Create better budgets**
- **Identify quality issues**

With ActiveSheets you can easily bring your live R/3 data into Microsoft Excel. Data is not downloaded from R/3 into Excel. ActiveSheets dynamically links your Excel workbooks and R/3.

If you're unfamiliar with the R/3 system and its many options, you can work within the confines of Microsoft Office. This shortens the learning curve, especially if you already have expertise in Excel and its easy-to-use interface.

ActiveSheets works with all R/3 application areas. It supports R/3 versions 3.1G and 4.0B and it is available in English, German, and Japanese.

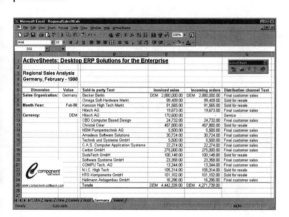

Contact Information:
Component Software
179 Sidney Street
Cambridge, MA 02139 USA

Phone: +1 888 218 0171
Fax: +1 617 218 0179

Email:
info@component-software.com

URL:
www.component-software.com

component
software

○ **Yes, I am interested in learning more about ActiveSheets and Component Software.**

Name

Company

Address

City

State   Zip

Country

Phone

Email